EX LIBRIS

THE
DOUGHTY STREET NOVELS

THE
DOUGHTY STREET NOVELS

PICKWICK PAPERS, OLIVER TWIST,
NICHOLAS NICKLEBY, BARNABY RUDGE

David Parker

AMS PRESS, INC.
NEW YORK

LIBRARY OF CONGRESS CATALOGING-IN-PUBLICATION DATA

Parker, David.
The Doughty Street Novels: Pickwick Papers, Oliver Twist, Nicholas Nickleby, Barnaby Rudge / by David Parker.
   p. cm. – (AMS Studies in the Nineteenth Century; no. 26)
   Includes bibliographical references (p.) and index.
   ISBN 0-404-64456-2 (alk. paper)
   1. Dickens, Charles, 1812-1870—Criticism and interpretation.   2. Dickens, Charles, 1812-1870—Homes and haunts—England—London.   3. Dickens, Charles, 1812-1870. Pickwick papers.   4. Dickens, Charles, 1812-1870. Oliver Twist.   5. Dickens, Charles, 1812-1870. Nicholas Nickleby.   6. Dickens, Charles, 1812-1870. Barnaby Rudge. I. Title.   II. Series.
PR4588.P37   2002
823' .8—dc21   2001022564
                                                              CIP

All AMS books are printed on acid-free paper that meets the guidelines for performance and durability of the Committee on Production Guidelines for Book Longevity of the Council on Library Resources.

AMS Press, Inc.
Brooklyn Navy Yard, Bldg. 292, Suite 417, 63 Flushing Ave.
Brooklyn, New York 11205
U.S.A.

Manufactured in the United States of America

CONTENTS

ILLUSTRATIONS

To Elinor, who made the writing of this book possible, and without whom I would not have cared to write it.

"Things aren't always what they
seem. But usually they are."

Old Saying

PREFACE

For many years, this book was writing itself without my knowing it. It began to take shape between 1978 and 1999, while I was curator of the Dickens House at 48 Doughty Street in London, Charles Dickens's home in the late 1830s. The curator's duties in a small museum, with no public funding and just a handful of staff, are many and arduous. Any research I wanted to do, unconnected with the operation of the museum, had to be crammed into evenings and weekends. Though I dreamed of more than one book on Dickens, scarcity of time and abundance of obligations made the short scholarly article a more realistic vehicle for such thoughts as I had.

During the working day, though, study of Dickens formed part of my duties. There was research to be done on the collections and for exhibitions. And there were scholars, collectors, and inquirers to be assisted, with information culled from the collections, the catalogues, and the library. It was work to stretch the repertoire of someone trained as a literary scholar. Middle-class interior decoration in the 1830s, the date of manufacture of a nineteenth-century desk, the provenance of a portrait of Mrs. Dickens, the illustrators of the Household Edition of Dickens's works, Dickens's connections with Padstow, his interest in the Polish question: these are just a tiny sample of topics I had to investigate. They gradually combined to give me what I like to think of as a distinctive and coherent perspective on Dickens, if an unusual one.

It was a perspective which increasingly informed my personal research, and I was able to maintain a modest output of this. To time made during evenings and weekends, I could rely on an additional week of paid leave per year, for attending conferences, which the Trustees of the Dickens House more often than not granted me. As my children became more independent, I more than matched this week by devoting holiday leave to the same end. Universities, other museums, branches of the Dickens Fellowship, and other societies provided an incentive by asking me to give lectures. Editors of journals encouraged me by publishing them as papers.

When I retired from the Dickens House in 1999, to spend more time writing and lecturing, this book emerged into the open and declared itself. I realized that, amid all the tasks I had been performing, a central one had shaped itself. I had been thinking and writing about the novels Dickens worked on at Doughty Street, and how they were affected by his life there. Selecting material, revising it, and augmenting it, were all that was needed to make a virtual into an actual book. That is what I have done.

It is a book unlike much recent writing on literature. Barthes declares that an author does not exist prior to or outside of language, that writing makes an author, not the other way around. It is easy to detect an intelligible meaning in this, and a bracing one too, but Barthes's polemics hurry readers past questions at which they should pause. How is it to be explained, for instance, that some authors are pretty consistently made by good books, some pretty consistently by bad?

All intellectual fashions give way or change under pressure of questions unasked, answers unprovided. It may be that we are witnessing the beginning of such a change now. It is not my purpose to hasten it here, however. I want only to assert what more than twenty years of working with things and with factual data have impressed upon me, what no theory of literature has dismantled. Whatever else might be said, in an inescapable sense, books are made by authors. Authors are like other people. Their lives can be profitably studied and at least provisionally understood, which is enough. I believe that books can often be better understood and appreciated when we think about what might have prompted the author to write them in the way he or she did. Someone, I submit, should be interested in such matters. I am. Hence this book. Let the proof of the pudding be in the eating. Read and judge.

I could not have assembled the book for publication, without the good will and cooperation of publishers and editors responsible for books and journals in which some of the material has already been published in forms more or less embryonic. I am particularly grateful to the Orion Publishing Group for permission to recycle, in chapter five, material I used in the introduction and critical apparatus I provided for my Everyman Paperback Edition of *Nicholas Nickleby* (London, 1994). In agreeing to publish *The Doughty Street Novels*, AMS Press accepted that I should be reworking some of its own copyright material, but I am nonetheless grateful for a decision reached so readily. Two sections of the book are based on papers which first appeared in AMS titles. In my first chapter I incorporate material from "Dickens at Home," published in *Homes and Homelessness in the Victorian Imagination*, edited by Murray Baumgarten and H. M. Daleski (New York, 1999). "*Oliver Twist* and the Fugitive Family," published in *Dickens Studies Annual* 29 (2000), forms the basis of chapter four.

The final section of my second chapter grew out of "Dickens and the Death of Mary Hogarth," published in *Dickens Quarterly* 13 (1996). I am indebted to the Dickens Society of America for permission to rework it here.

Three other items I have used, in chapters one and three, originally appeared in *The Dickensian*: "Dickens's Archness," in volume 67 (1971); "The Reconstruction of Dickens's Drawing-Room," in volume seventy-seven (1982); and "Mr. Pickwick and the Horses," in volume 85 (1989). I am happy to acknowledge the appearance of these prototypes in a journal which I have long enjoyed both reading and contributing to.

All the illustrations for the book are from the Dickens House collections, and I am grateful to the Trustees for permission to use them.

Indeed, I am grateful to the Trustees for encouraging my research activities over the years, and to individual members of the Board for advice. Nor did the House and its collections cease to be useful to me on my retirement. Since then, Andrew Xavier, my successor as curator and my colleague for many years, has been unfailingly helpful in making the collections available to me, as has his assistant Martha Hawting.

Under the directorship first of Murray Baumgarten, then of John Jordan, the University of California Dickens Project has provided me with invaluable stimulation, year after year, which profoundly influenced the shaping of this book. Much of it began as lectures delivered during the Project's annual summer school in Santa Cruz, the Dickens Universe. Ideas developed for this purpose were refined in faculty discussions. I should not have been able regularly to involve myself with the Dickens Project had it not been for generous funding from the Friends of the Dickens Project. I am grateful both to the Project and to its Friends.

Having read the book in draft for AMS Press, Duane DeVries supplied me with useful advice and heartening encouragement, in equal and generous measure. He gave me what I needed, and I am indebted to him.

My special thanks are offered to Alan Watts, secretary to the Trustees of the Dickens House for many years, Honorary General Secretary of the Dickens Fellowship for as many, now one of its Vice-Presidents, and a man with unrivalled knowledge of Dickens and his books. He read every chapter in draft as I finished it, corrected errors, made suggestions, disentangled obscurities of style, offered encouragement when confidence faltered, and calming counsel when confidence was too great. He has a special way with the words, "Don't be flowery, Jacob! Pray!" Perhaps unwisely, Jacob did not always heed the advice. If this book is still flowery here and there, it is not Alan Watts's fault.

1

BIOGRAPHICAL : 48 DOUGHTY STREET

Charles Dickens rented 48 Doughty Street from the spring of 1837 until the end of 1839.[1] It was his first "dwelling-house," but it was more than that. It was the home where he took control of his life and settled down, as a householder, a husband, a father, and a writer [fig. 1]. For the first time, he found himself making most of the decisions shaping his future. Other people's began to matter less.

He had married just a year before moving there, but to begin with had lived with his wife Catherine [fig. 2] in chambers which, although remembered fondly in later years, were cramped and inconvenient. They may have been adequate for newlyweds but were plainly unsuitable for raising children. It must have been clear to the young couple that, sooner or later, they would have to move. The new house, in contrast, was a substantial family home, where Dickens was able to lay down the pattern of his domestic, personal, and social life for years to come.[2]

Until he met Catherine, Dickens's search for a marriage partner had left him too little in control of his life for his liking. Even afterwards, for much of their courtship, he had been anxious lest control slip away. Now he was securely and happily married to a young woman, beautiful by any standards, and evidently sympathetic, whom he loved, who loved him, and who was, moreover, a daughter of the cultivated professional classes among which he sought acceptance. They must have seen 48 Doughty Street as a fitting establishment for her to preside over. Eventually, sad to say, they would part, but the marriage was to last twenty-two years, most of them apparently happy.

At Doughty Street, certainly, they worked confidently to build a future together in the plainest possible way, by raising a family. In January 1837, three months before they moved there, Catherine had given birth to a son, Charles, usually called Charley within the family. Two daughters were born at Doughty Street – Mary, or Mamie, in March 1838, and Kate, or Katey, in October 1839. There were to be ten children in all.

Before Doughty Street, Dickens's career had been too much at the mercy of other people and of chance, for his liking. Now he was escaping from subordination, and turning away from short-term projects, towards something more demanding and fulfilling – towards the writing of novels. He was free from the authority of the newspaper editors who had so recently employed him. He was giving up short fiction written on speculation for magazines, or at the order of editors. He was no longer on the margin, looking for openings, eagerly seizing projects proposed by others. Now he was at the center of things, making openings, and doing the proposing himself. He was assuming the role and dignity of a successful author, who could initiate his own books, and negotiate with publishers, knowing his work to be marketable.

And he was finding his identity as an author. As a writer of fiction, needless to say, he was finding many voices, but the many voices joined in a distinctive harmony. Dickens was emerging as a brilliant but unsparing observer of contemporary manners, as a master of a unique kind of irony, at once incisive and sublimely comic, and as a champion of the ill-used and dispossessed, victims of the economic and social upheavals of the Industrial Revolution.

He worked on four of his novels at Doughty Street: *Pickwick Papers*, *Oliver Twist*, *Nicholas Nickleby* and *Barnaby Rudge*. Three of these are coherent works of art – much more so than they are often given credit for. Less successful than the others, *Barnaby Rudge* was nevertheless a valuable test bed for Dickens, and a key text in the development of his art. *Pickwick Papers*, *Oliver Twist*, and *Nicholas Nickleby* are themselves less than perfect, and sometimes bear the mark of improvisation, but each has a distinct identity, each addresses a sharply defined subject, and each is infused with an extraordinary dynamism. Questions can be asked, certainly, about how consciously Dickens shaped them into what they are. It seems evident to me that

Figure 1   Charles Dickens in 1838, by Samuel Laurence. (By permission of the Dickens House Museum, London.)

Figure 2   Catherine Dickens in 1847, by Daniel Maclise. (By permission of the Dickens House Museum, London.)

Nicholas Nickleby was carefully planned and consciously crafted. *Pickwick Papers* and *Oliver Twist* seem to have been more driven from within. Good reason, then, to look at what was happening to the man, for insight into what we find in the books. That is one of the chief purposes of this study.

I am not suggesting that the phase in Dickens's life to which I am calling attention had a clean beginning, or a clean end. Such a phase rarely does. Even if it were possible to demarcate it precisely, it would not be possible exactly to match it with his occupation of 48 Doughty Street. Nor can the writing and publication of the novels I propose to study be exactly matched with his time there. Dickens did work on all of them at Doughty Street, but *Nicholas Nickleby* is the only one he began, ended, and published in its entirety while there. He wrote and published most of *Pickwick Papers* and part of *Oliver Twist* before moving to Doughty Street. He wrote most of *Barnaby Rudge*, and published all of it, after leaving – indeed, after writing and publishing *The Old Curiosity Shop*. Yet, however inexact the chronology, the artistic stability and sense of direction that yielded Dickens's earliest novels can be related to the domestic stability and sense of direction he so clearly sought and so clearly found at Doughty Street.

The first anniversary of Dickens's marriage was Sunday 2 April 1837. It must have struck him as a satisfyingly neat measure of progress if that, as it seems to have been, was the weekend he moved with his family into 48 Doughty Street. They were moving only from one part of the London parish of Holborn to another, but Dickens, and more particularly Catherine, must have been relieved. They had been living in Furnival's Inn, an apartment block where he had leased just three small rooms on the third floor (fourth floor American style), with a kitchen and a cellar in the basement, and a lumber room in the attic. Inconvenient at the best of times, such an arrangement would have been especially trying after the birth of the baby in January.

48 Doughty Street was more convenient and comfortable. The house was of a kind and in a quarter of which a young professional man had no need to be ashamed. And it was much more commodious. There was room not only for Dickens, his wife and the baby, but also for a growing squad of servants, and for Dickens's younger brother Fred, who was working for John Macrone, Dickens's first publisher. There was room,

Figure 3   Mary Hogarth. Copy by F. G. Kitton of lost posthumous portrait by Hablot Knight Browne.   (By permission of the Dickens House Museum, London.)

too, for Catherine's younger sister, Mary [fig. 3], a frequent guest during their first few weeks in Doughty Street, until her sudden death on 7 May 1837, deeply mourned by Dickens and Catherine.

Thanks chiefly to the Dickens Fellowship, 48 Doughty Street has been preserved. Since 1925 it has been the Dickens House Museum [fig. 4]. It is a typical late Georgian three-bay terraced house, of three principal stories, plus basement and attic. It was built some time between 1799 and 1801, as part of a development of land once owned by the Coram Foundling Hospital, still there two blocks away in the 1830s. The centrepiece of the development was Mecklenburgh Square, originally a square of first-rate houses (as defined in the 1774 London Building Act), designed by S. P. Cockerell and Joseph Kay. The plan provided for streets of third-rate houses to the south (Olsen 26). Doughty Street was the principal street running south from the square, and still is. Beyond the Guilford Street intersection, the houses, of which number 48 is one, are in no sense third-rate, but even so are clearly inferior to the imposing architect-designed houses of the square, some of which, on the eastern side, survive in their splendor today.

For all that, Doughty Street is wide, and the houses handsome. The entrance hall of number 48, like that of all the others, is a narrow passage to one side of the ground floor, but it flanks an elegant dining room, with curved rear wall and curved doors. In the basement there is an ample kitchen and other domestic offices, lit by windows looking onto sunken yards back and front, known as "areas." Through three tall sash windows, a spacious drawing room [fig. 5] looks onto the street from the first floor (second American style). Above that are two floors of bedrooms and nursery quarters. At the back there is a small garden – larger in Dickens's day, if not by much.

Dickens's study probably overlooked it. A dedicated study was a new luxury for him, made possible by the spaciousness of 48 Doughty Street. It was almost certainly the high-ceilinged, elegantly proportioned room behind the drawing room. Habits formed by more cramped accommodation persisted, however. Too much should not be made of it, doubtless, but in spatial terms alone his writing and his domestic life were closely integrated at Doughty Street. Later, his family was firmly given to understand he was not to be disturbed when at work. Evidence suggests an extra door was fitted at his next home, to insulate the library against noise (Ackroyd 562), and a gate was installed on the stairs, to stop children playing on the same floor (Sladen 274). But now things were more relaxed. Dickens clearly enjoyed combining the roles of householder and writer. Study notwithstanding, he could and did work in company, as his brother-in-law, Henry Burnett, reports:

> One night in Doughty Street, Mrs. Charles Dickens, my wife and myself, were sitting round the fire, cosily enjoying a chat, when Dickens, for some purpose, came suddenly from his study into the room. "What, you here!" he exclaimed, "I'll bring down my work." It was his monthly portion of *Oliver Twist* for Bentley's. In a few minutes he returned, manuscript in hand, and while he was pleasantly discoursing he employed himself in carrying to a corner of the room a little table, at which he seated himself and recommenced his writing. We, at his bidding, went on talking "our little nothings"; he, every now and then (the feather of his pen still moving rapidly from side to side), put in a cheerful interlude. It was interesting to watch, upon the sly, the mind and the muscles working (or if you please, playing) in company as new thoughts were being dropped upon the paper. And to note the working brow, the set of the mouth, with the tongue tightly pressed against the closed lips, as was his habit. (Kitton 1: 138–139)

But whatever the circumstances under which he chose to write, for Dickens domestic life and the life he described in his novels were closely related. The classic statement of the writer's capacity for synthesizing experience of life, and making it into literature, is T. S. Eliot's. Eliot admired the metaphysical poets' mastery of this capacity:

> When a poet's mind is perfectly equipped for its work, it is constantly amalgamating disparate experience; the ordinary man's experience is chaotic, irregular, fragmentary. The latter falls in love, or reads Spinoza, and these two experiences have nothing to do with each other, or with the noise of the typewriter or the smell of cooking; in the mind of the poet these experiences are always forming new wholes. (287)

For all that his medium was prose fiction, Dickens's imagination was no

Figure 4   48 Doughty Street, London. Now the Dickens House Museum. (By permission of the Dickens House Museum, London.)

Figure 5   Dickens's drawing room at 48 Doughty Street, reconstructed. The armchair in which Cruikshank sketched Dickens (see figure 6) is on the right of the picture. The pedestal table believed to have been bought with the help of Mary Hogarth is behind it. (By permission of the Dickens House Museum, London.)

less capable of synthesis. Indeed, with him it was a two-way process. His domestic life helped to shape his fiction, his instinct for fiction helped to shape his domestic life.

Home for him could never be an inert pile of bricks and mortar. He wanted his house to speak to him and to others of wider matters, of past, present and future. He wanted it to provoke laughter, to provide a backdrop for dramas of his making – to act a part, even, in such dramas. He was an inveterate story-maker, and he looked for narrative significance in his home, just as he gave it to the homes of characters in the novels:

> It was one of those delightfully irregular houses where you go up and down steps out of one room into another, and where you come upon more rooms when you think you have seen all there are, and where there is a bountiful provision of little halls and passages, and where you find still older cottage-rooms in unexpected places, with lattice windows and green growth pressing through them. Mine, which we entered first, was of this kind, with an up-and-down roof, that had more corners in it than I ever counted afterwards, and a chimney (there was a wood-fire on the hearth) paved all around with pure white tiles, in every one of which a bright miniature of the fire was blazing. (*Bleak House* ch. 6)

Bleak House, in Esther Summerson's description, is as full of twists, turns, surprises and revelations as the novel to which it gives its name. And just as eloquently as any other part of the novel, it speaks of its owner, John Jarndyce, welcoming, bountiful, surprising, eager to make the best of detail, hostile to the grand design.

The eloquence of Bleak House was something Dickens strove to contrive in his own home. He devoted time and energy to the houses he lived in. He compulsively organized and reorganized his surroundings and those of his family – those of others, too, when he got the chance. At Doughty Street he had less money to spend on his home than later in his career. He was there for less than three years, moreover, and had no long-term lease on the property, only a rental agreement. He could afford attention, however, and that he lavished upon it. Often he took upon himself tasks others might have been expected to perform.

Catherine evidently stood aside from some of the duties early Victorian wives undertook. The cash book recording domestic expenditure at Doughty Street, for instance, is in his hand, not hers.[3]

Evidence indicates he set his own mark on the house through interior decoration. He had the drawing room [fig. 5] completely redecorated, for instance (Parker, "The Reconstruction of Dickens's Drawing Room"). The hand rail, or chair rail, was removed, and paper hung from cornice to skirting board. What kind of paper it is not possible to say, but it has proved possible to determine the color he chose for the woodwork – a shade of lilac, surprisingly lurid to twenty-first century eyes. Instructions he gave in 1844, for the redecoration of his next drawing room at 1 Devonshire Terrace, indicate he liked a jazzy mixture of strident colors and patterns. He would doubtless have chosen such a combination for Doughty Street. His friend Thomas Mitton supervised the Devonshire Terrace redecoration for him, because Dickens and his family were abroad in Italy at the time. Mitton was told:

> I should like to new-paper the drawing-room; taking away the ugly hand rail, and bringing the paper down to the skirting board. I should like the skirting board to be painted in imitation of Satin-Wood – the ceiling to have a faint pink blush in it – and a little wreath of flowers to be painted round the lamp. The paper must be blue and gold or purple and gold – to agree with the furniture and curtains, and I should wish it to be cheerful and gay. I can safely trust to your taste, if you will choose it. I have sd. nothing about this to Mrs. D: wishing it to be a surprise, if I do it at all. – Gold moulding round the paper. (Pilgrim *Letters* 4: 297–98)

Catherine, was to have no say in the matter. She was just to be astonished. It was emphatically a case of Dickens stamping his own identity on the room, his own overstated sense of style. Such a hectic mixture of colors and decorative details was the fashion of the era, and often works much better in practice than verbal prescription can lead us to suppose. Even so, it is clear that serenity was not what Dickens aimed for. He wanted his home to speak, to family and to visitors, in a loud and distinct voice.

He liked the contents of his home, his furniture, to be just as

Figure 6   Dickens at Doughty Street. Engraving after a sketch by George Cruikshank. Dickens is seated in an armchair now on display in the Doughty Street drawing room (see figure 5). (By permission of the Dickens House Museum, London.)

eloquent. Despite featuring them to good effect in the novels, he
declined to have antiques (as we should call them) in his own home.
There, he believed in newness when he could afford it, in French polish,
in having things sparkling about him. But he also believed in keeping
what he had, and letting it accumulate narrative significance. To discard
furniture was, for him, to discard part of a story, to sacrifice narrative
coherence.   Consciousness of accumulated meaning in furniture
probably accounts for his dislike of newness for newness' sake – the
newness that, with their name, tells us so much about the Veneering
family: "what was observable in the furniture, was observable in the
Veneerings – the surface smelt a little too much of the workshop and
was a trifle sticky" (*Our Mutual Friend* bk. 1, ch. 2).

At Doughty Street, thanks to Dickens's modest means, much of the
furniture was second-hand, or cheap (Parker, "The Reconstruction of
Dickens's Drawing Room"). But for the rest of his life he kept the not
very well-made armchair, in which George Cruikshank had sketched
him at Doughty Street [figs. 5 and 6]. He had bought it first for the
bachelor chambers he occupied in Furnival's Inn, before moving to
larger ones for the accommodation of his bride. There are reasons for
believing that the Biedermeier occasional pedestal table [fig. 5], now in
the drawing room at 48 Doughty Street, was the one he bought with the
help of Catherine's sister, Mary, for Catherine's bedside, the day Charley
was born in 1837. Its workmanship, its date, its foreign provenance,
would all have made it the rather grand second–hand piece Dickens's
diary entry, a year after the purchase, suggests (Pilgrim *Letters* 1: 630).
Though he moved house often, this piece remained with him throughout
his life. Thrift was doubtless a consideration but, as he grew more and
more prosperous, it could scarcely have been a compelling one. It is as
if, for him, the chair and the table were their stories, however
melancholy, however consoling. The Spanish mahogany sideboard [fig.
7] he bought while still at Doughty Street, and probably other dining
room furniture too, remained in use in the Gad's Hill dining room until
the day he died, doubtless supporting memories as well as dinner and
diners.

In his fiction, Dickens exploits the sense of identity and change
furniture can provide. Chairs are particularly potent. "One little seat
may be empty . . . ," says the narrator of "A Christmas Dinner," to

Figure 7   Dickens's sideboard, bought in 1839. On display in the Doughty
Street dining room. (By permission of the Dickens House Museum, London.)

evoke grief at the loss of a child (*Sketches by Boz*). "Let him sit in his old chair," says Chuffey of old Jonas Chuzzlewit, "and he'll be well again" (*Martin Chuzzlewit* ch. 18). He hopes in vain. Old Jonas is dead. Scrooge's anxious question about Tiny Tim, in *A Christmas Carol*, is met obliquely at first, and heartbreakingly. "'I see a vacant seat,' replied the Ghost, 'in the poor chimney-corner, and a crutch without an owner, carefully preserved. If these shadows remain unaltered by the Future, the child will die'" (Stave 3). In *Bleak House*, Esther finds it hard to leave her benefactor, Mr. Jarndyce, and goes home "to occupy the old chair by his side; for I did not like to think of its being empty so soon" (ch. 64). And at the end of *Great Expectations*, Pip returns after eleven years to Joe Gargery's forge, where he was raised:

> There, smoking his pipe in the old place by the kitchen firelight, as hale and as strong as ever, though a little grey, sat Joe; and there, fenced into the corner with Joe's leg, and sitting on my own little stool looking at the fire, was – I again! (ch. 59)

"My own little stool" is powerful because of the cyclical implications. With other details of the text, it rounds off Pip's story, the story of those he loves, the story of the home from which he had yearned to depart, and to which he is now glad to return. And it is a sign of what home could mean to Dickens.

Dickens was able to afford 48 Doughty Street, thanks to his first novel. His debut as a novelist, though, was little better than accidental. The first years of his writing career had been devoted to different kinds of publication. Between 1831 when he was nineteen, and the move to Doughty Street in 1837, he had worked as a journalist for three newspapers, *The Mirror of Parliament*, *The True Sun*, and *The Morning Chronicle* – four newspapers if we count the latter's sister paper, *The Evening Chronicle*. From 1833, beginning with "A Dinner at Poplar Walk" in *The Monthly Magazine*,[4] he had contributed pieces of short fiction and impressionistic essays to various periodicals. John Macrone had published collections of these in 1836, under the title *Sketches by Boz*, first series and second series. Dickens had written two farces, *The Strange Gentleman* and *Is She his Wife?* plus the libretto of a comic operetta, *The Village Coquettes*. And he had produced an anti-sabbatarian pamphlet, *Sunday Under Three Heads*. At the end of 1836 he had resigned his staff position on *The Morning Chronicle*, to take up the editorship of a new monthly periodical, *Bentley's Miscellany*. Among the contents of the first issue, of 1 January 1837, was the first of a short series of comic papers by Dickens, later to be entitled *The Mudfog Papers*.

The miscellaneous, short, and ad hoc pieces of Dickens's apprentice years are worth reading, most of them for their intrinsic value, all of them for the insight they provide into how he learned his art (De Vries passim), but they did not earn him enough to support the kind of establishment and way of life he hoped for. It was not until his imagination was let loose within the ampler space of a novel that the reading public began to recognize the magnitude of his talent, and publishers vie to employ it. The enormous success of *Pickwick Papers* (1836–37) was what enabled him to afford the £80 annual rent of Doughty Street, the other expenses of a large and growing household, and the generous entertaining he enjoyed. The novel had been appearing in monthly parts for a year when he moved to Doughty Street. Within a week of his doing so, its publishers, Chapman and Hall, hosted a dinner to celebrate the anniversary. It was the rotund figure of Mr. Pickwick, we might say, that ushered Dickens into Doughty Street.

And Mr. Pickwick established him in the mind of the public as a novelist – perhaps in his own mind too. It was on the strength of his talent as such that the publisher Richard Bentley had offered him the remunerative editorship of the *Miscellany*. Dickens had also agreed to write two novels for publication by Bentley. The opening part of the first of these, *Oliver Twist*, had appeared in the second issue of the *Miscellany* in February. The rest appeared in subsequent issues, the final part in April 1839. Dickens extricated himself from his commitment to a second novel for Bentley, and *Nicholas Nickleby* (1838–39) was published by Chapman and Hall. *Barnaby Rudge*, which had been intended for Bentley, and which Dickens worked on fitfully at Doughty Street, was eventually published in 1841 in *Master Humphrey's Clock* (1840–41), a weekly periodical he edited and wrote – again for Chapman and Hall.

Not that Dickens devoted himself entirely to long fiction at Doughty Street, or even wanted to. He wrote *Sketches of Young Gentlemen* there, published by itself in 1838, but now normally appended to editions of *Sketches by Boz*. He wrote a play called *The Lamplighter*, never staged during his lifetime, but reworked as "The Lamplighter's Story" – his contribution to *The Pic-Nic Papers* (1841), a project to raise money for the widow of Macrone, who had died in 1837. He accepted a surprisingly plodding commission, to edit *The Memoirs of Joseph Grimaldi*, the pantomime clown (1838). He wrote various pieces for *Bentley's Miscellany* in addition to *Oliver Twist* and *The Mudfog Papers*. Perhaps he worked too on *Sketches of Young Couples*, published in February 1840, now also usually appended to *Sketches by Boz*. He even collaborated with George Cruikshank, illustrator of *Oliver Twist*, in the publication of a comic poem, *The Loving Ballad of Lord Bateman* (1839).[5]

Yet it is clear that imagination and ambition were driving Dickens away from short ad hoc pieces towards larger projects, of which the full-length novel is the paradigm. He never lost his love of journalism – of the journalist's life, the journalist's opportunity concisely to make his point, the journalist's power to sway opinion. Nor did he abandon the short story. But we can detect the first signs, at Doughty Street, of a determination that grew in him over the years, to place such short pieces as he chose to write, whenever possible, in a framework created and controlled by himself. He resigned his editorship of *Bentley's Miscellany* in January 1839, frustrated not least by challenges from Bentley to his editorial authority. There were to be no such challenges over *Master Humphrey's Clock*. In 1846, very briefly, he was to undertake the editorship of a new national newspaper, *The Daily News*. From 1850 he was to edit the weekly periodical *Household Words*, superseded in 1859 by *All the Year Round*, which he edited until his death in 1870. In all of these he sought to establish a voice and an outlook hospitable to his short journalistic and literary pieces. If he did not always choose to work on novels, he liked most of the time to feel he was contributing to something of comparable magnitude and scope, and of his own devising.

It is not too much to say that the same drive towards magnitude and scope can be observed in Dickens's domestic and recreational activities at Doughty Street. Whether he was working, or devoting himself to his family and friends, or just diverting himself, his imagination was voracious and synthezising, consistent with T. S. Eliot's specification. He was a compulsive creator of complex imaginative structures, more often than not with a strong fictional element. Sometimes these were in the service of his art, sometimes they were frivolous, but they were rarely just for fun. Even the most passing fantasy was likely to be pressed for textual service later.

One such fantasy, frivolous and extra-textual, was the comic myth – or series of comic myths – he constructed about his home, and the life he lived in it. With great gusto, he began to develop themes and roles, deliciously distorting and exaggerating actuality. He repeatedly presented himself, for instance, as the kind of lower-middle-class scapegrace we encounter so often in the novels, and would tell friends how he "arrived home at one o'Clock this morning dead drunk, and was put to bed by my loving missis" (Pilgrim *Letters* 1: 217).

For the most part, while living there, he spoke of 48 Doughty Street without irony. He was in awe of his own achievement in procuring such a home. But in retrospect he laughed at it, just as he laughed at all of his subsequent homes. As he grew more successful and confident, he liked to portray himself as presiding majestically – and agonizing – over a prodigious establishment. His evident enjoyment of homemaking was as often as not expressed through a mischievous insistence that the house he lived in was bigger and more imposing than it really was. It was a kind of inspired silliness, but it was more than that. It enabled him, all at the same time, demonstrably to enjoy the rewards of success, to acknowledge the danger of enjoying them too much, and to take pleasure in an extravagant pose.[6]

And there are signs of this attitude beginning to take shape even at Doughty Street. The houses around Mecklenburgh Square – still an impressive address in the 1830s – were too grand for Dickens to afford in his Doughty Street days, but he could bask in their glory. Early nineteenth-century Londoners sometimes included the name of the nearest notable square in their London address. This may have been designed to help the postman, but it is difficult not to detect an element of pretension in it. That Dickens should have chosen to head letters "48 Doughty Street, Mecklenburgh Square," especially early in his stay there, suggests just such an element.[7]

Yet close students of his imagination will not be surprised to find him deriding such borrowed glory, even while living in Doughty Street. In *Nicholas Nickleby* we are told how dwellers in Cadogan Place look upon their street:

> Cadogan Place is the one slight bond that joins two great extremes; it is the connecting link between the aristocratic pavements of Belgrave Square, and the barbarism of Chelsea. It is in Sloane Street, but not of it. The people in Cadogan Place look down upon Sloane Street, and think Brompton low. They affect fashion too, and wonder where the New Road is. Not that they claim to be on precisely the same footing as the high folks of Belgrave Square and Grosvenor Place, but that they stand, with reference to them, rather in the light of those illegitimate children of the great who are content to boast of their connexions, although their connexions disavow them. Wearing as much as they can of the airs and semblances of loftiest rank, the people of Cadogan Place have the realities of middle station. (ch. 21)

It is not difficult to see in this a kind of admission about Dickens's own attitude to Doughty Street.

The street, to be sure, did have a style of its own in the 1830s. It was a private road, with porters in mulberry-coloured livery and gold-laced hats on duty at gates at each end, admitting only those with proper business there. Impressive though this must have been, it was expedient too. Doughty Street was only one of many private roads. Fashion was moving westward. Furthest east of all the west-end housing estates, the Foundling Hospital Estate was remote from the perceived center, and close to less desirable quarters. Its eastern flank, marked by Mecklenburgh Square and Doughty Street, was adjacent and parallel to Gray's Inn Lane (now Gray's Inn Road). In the early nineteenth century this was a busy thoroughfare with an unsavory reputation, a route, moreover, along which cattle were driven to Smithfield on market days. Gates and porters protected Mecklenburgh Square, too, from "the low and noisy traffic" of Gray's Inn Lane (Olsen 92). They were needed to keep Doughty Street quiet, secure, and clean.

It was in fact a good address, but not a grand one – certainly not an exclusive one. Sydney Smith had lived there, at the beginning of the century, when the street was brand-new. And just as Dickens was to do, after three years, as soon as he could afford it, he had moved westwards to Marylebone. Now, many houses in the street were occupied by members of the professional classes, but some were occupied by successful tradesmen. Comic novelist R. S. Surtees evidently thought it appropriate to quarter his hero, Jorrocks, in Doughty Street, at exactly the time Dickens was living there. Jorrocks is a prosperous Cockney grocer, devoted to fox hunting, but careless about aspirates (*Jorrocks's Jaunts and Jollities*).

Dickens contrived to accommodate both the Mecklenburgh Square connection and the Jorrocks element: to look on Doughty Street both as the people in Cadogan Place look on their street, in *Nicholas Nickleby*, and as the narrator does. Doughty Street, he would hint, belonged to Mecklenburgh Square, not to Gray's Inn Lane, but at the same time he was aware of the pretentiousness of that hint. A primary characteristic of his imagination was affection for what it contemplated, undiminished by ironic judgment. He could love a thing, laugh at it at the same time, and laugh at himself for loving it.

This readiness to borrow glory from Mecklenburgh Square was characteristic. Many years later, in "Some Recollections of Mortality" (1863), he still seems eager to inflate the grandeur of Doughty Street, though by now he is more interested in the inflation than in the grandeur. The Uncommercial Traveller, whose voice we hear in the essay, recalls having taken, twenty-five years previously, "a house which then appeared to me to be a frightfully first-class Family Mansion, involving awful responsibilities" (*The Uncommercial Traveller*). Arithmetic, not to mention the naivety so fondly recalled, suggests it was Doughty Street Dickens was remembering. But as so often, he was weaving disparate facts into fiction in this text. The Uncommercial Traveller's house boasted a "desirable stable-yard," which 48 Doughty Street never could. His next home, 1 Devonshire Terrace, could though, and was indisputably a first-rate house under the terms of the Building Act (the terms "first-class" and "first-rate," for houses, seem to have been interchangeable). In 1863 Dickens conflated the two houses to make a better story, just as in the late 1830s he had conflated respectable Doughty Street with superior Mecklenburgh Square, to make a better address.

He cannot be entirely cleared of snobbish posturing in this, but for much of his life posturing, snobbish or otherwise, was central to Dickens's personality, and to his art. He committed himself to key values, there can be no doubt about that, but, as a young man at any rate, he did not seek or construct an essential or continuous self. Rather, he elaborated an intricate and variable self, moving for the sheer delight of it through a series of gorgeous postures, often contradictory. Constructing imaginary characters for his books came easily to him, because he was constantly constructing and reconstructing himself.

His way of doing it has something in common with Gatsby's. Scott Fitzgerald has this to say about his fictional creation:

> The truth was that Jay Gatsby of West Egg, Long Island, sprang from his Platonic conception of himself. He was a son of God – a phrase which, if it means anything, means just that – and he must be about His Father's business, the service of a vast, vulgar and meretricious beauty. (*The Great Gatsby* ch. 6)

Like Gatsby, as I shall show in the next chapter, Dickens had been propelled by early adversity into seeking escape from a selfhood of which he was ashamed. His friend John Forster – writer of the first indispensable biography of Dickens – draws attention to his "passionate resolve, even while he was yielding to circumstances, *not to be* what circumstances were conspiring to make him" (John Forster bk.1, ch. 3). A more fundamental meaning can be seen in this than Forster perhaps intended.

We turn to it, surely, when confronted by evidence like the letter Dickens wrote in July 1838, to Johann Heinrich Kuenzel, giving an account of his childhood and youth. It is as carefully edited and calculated as any of Gatsby's recollections:

> I had begun an irregular rambling education under a clergyman at Chatham, and I finished it at a good school in London – tolerably early, for my father was not a rich man, and I had to begin the world. So I began it in a lawyer's office – which is a very little world, and a very dull one – and leaving it at the expiration of two years, devoted myself for some time to

the acquirement of such general literature as I could pick up in
the Library of the British Museum .... (Pilgrim *Letters* 1: 423)

No word here of Warren's Blacking Warehouse, where Dickens toiled
unwillingly, or of the Marshalsea Prison, in which his father was
imprisoned for debt, but many a delusive word.

Dickens intended to deceive in this letter, to protect himself, but he
was in love with fiction anyway. He was a super-Gatsby, more protean,
more self-conscious, more ironic, more intoxicated by the sheer thrill of
performance. Gatsby constructed for himself a single identity, of
unfathomable complexity. Dickens constructed for himself serial
identities in profusion, enjoying not least the difficulty of reconciling
them. He subscribed to exacting moral values in a way Gatsby never
did, but consistency was not enough for Dickens – not enough for his
enjoyment, not enough for his restless imagination.

Like Gatsby, too, but self-consciously and to deliberately comic
effect, Dickens devoted himself to the service of a vast beauty, in his life
and in his work. It is not a vulgar or a meretricious beauty, but it
incorporates elements of both. The overstated, the dissonant, the showy
are indispensable to it. And yet it is incontestably authentic, thanks to
the amalgamating intelligence controlling it.

In later life, to his dismay, Dickens became in some respects a
mystery to himself and, in his life at any rate, recoiled from this
posturing. He changed into a very private man, guarding secrets. But
during the Doughty Street years, and for many afterwards, he was
gleefully protean. It was a strategy which enabled him to balance and
contain contradictions within himself and within his art, which would
have made most people unstable, most literary works messy, but which
he made into assets.

Critics have repeatedly found contradictions in Dickens's works. His
art is epitomized, Edmund Wilson suggested in 1939, by the two
personalities of Scrooge in *A Christmas Carol*, before and after
transformation – at first misanthropic, then philanthropic, but always
intensely vital (Edmund Wilson 88–89). Other critics have given us a
Dickens at once conformist and rebellious (Hillis Miller ch. 2), a
Dickens whose love of life is inseparable from his fascination with death
(Angus Wilson 294–96), a Dickens divided between fanatical

orderliness and the appeal of violence (Carey passim), a Dickens who
hated and needed metropolitan life (Schwarzbach passim), a Dickens
driven to express a despairing vision in comic language (Scott passim), a
Dickens in whose works every coherence is threatened with dissolution
(Connor part 2). "It is a leading characteristic of Dickens's mind," one
critic has noted, "that he is able to see almost everything from two
opposed points of view" (Carey 15).

Far from diminishing his art, most critics agree, this responsiveness
to inner contradictions yields solidity and vitality in Dickens's works. It
is not too pat a metaphor, I hope, to observe that two points of view are
essential to binocular vision, to the perception of depth. Dickens's
fiction never seems one man's two-dimensional projection, because
readers are constantly persuaded that things, people, events and
dialogues in it can be seen, heard and judged in more than one way,
from more than one perspective.

Dickens's irony, inevitably, is one of the most powerful persuaders.
Whatever else it does, as a mode of discourse for conveying widely
divergent meanings simultaneously, it underpins fictional illusion.
During the Doughty Street period, his irony is particularly apparent in a
stylistic device I have called "archness" (Parker, "Dickens's Archness").
It is a device Dickens used before the Doughty Street period, and was to
use afterwards, although his reliance upon it dwindled from the mid-
1840s. Like all verbal irony, it works through the narrative voice
contriving to suggest one thing is true, while pretending to believe quite
another is. It differs from most irony, though, in its effect. It is gleeful.
Whatever the indignation or reproof conveyed, there is delight in
illusion. The reader characteristically responds by feeling the narrator is
teasing him about a reality both have perceived independently.

The device evolved out of a blending of two stylistic sources. One
was the mock-heroic of the eighteenth century. Sterne declared that the
"Cervantic humour," as he called it, stemmed from "describing silly and
trifling events with the circumstantial pomp of great ones" (*Letters* 77).
Dickens, however, saw there was no graceful "circumstantial pomp" for
him to exploit in the early nineteenth century, comparable to the
Augustan prose style. He needed to find a new circumstantial pomp,
and he found it principally in the journalism of his day, of which he had
so much experience. But it was a degraded pomp. To achieve

superficial smoothness and dignity, even the best newspapers of the 1830s tended to rely on the sententiousness, the Latinate verbosity and the ponderous periphrasis of the Augustan style in its decline. Dickens, however, perceived the vast potential for comedy in this.

It enabled him, most characteristically, to spread ironic dignity over a squalid or melancholy subject. One such is the workhouse authorities' response to Oliver Twist's request for more gruel:

> For a week after the commission of the impious and profane offence of asking for more, Oliver remained a close prisoner in the dark and solitary room to which he had been consigned by the wisdom and mercy of the board. It appears, at first sight, not unreasonable to suppose that, if he had entertained a becoming feeling of respect for the prediction of the gentleman in the white waistcoat, he would have established that sage individual's prophetic character, once and for ever, by tying one end of his pocket-handkerchief to a hook in the wall, and attaching himself to the other. To the performance of this feat, however, there was one obstacle: namely, that pocket-handkerchiefs, being decided articles of luxury, had been, for all future times and ages, removed from the noses of paupers by the express order of the board in council assembled, solemnly given and pronounced under their hands and seals. . . .

The gentleman in the white waistcoat, needless to say, had predicted, "That boy will be hung" (*Oliver Twist* ch. 2).

> . . . Let it not be supposed by the enemies of "the system" that, during the period of his solitary incarceration, Oliver was denied the benefit of exercise, the pleasure of society, or the advantages of religious consolation. As for exercise, it was nice cold weather, and he was allowed to perform his ablutions every morning under the pump, in a stone yard, in the presence of Mr. Bumble, who prevented his catching cold, and caused a tingling sensation to pervade his frame, by repeated applications of the cane. As for society, he was carried every other day into the hall where the boys dined, and there sociably flogged as a public warning and example. And so far from being denied the advantages of religious consolation, he was kicked into the same

> apartment every evening at prayer time, and there permitted to
> listen to, and console his mind with, a general supplication of the
> boys, containing a special clause, therein inserted by authority of
> the board, in which they entreated to be made good, virtuous,
> contented, and obedient, and to be guarded from the sins and
> vices of Oliver Twist, whom the supplication distinctly set forth
> to be under the exclusive patronage and protection of the powers
> of wickedness, and an article direct from the manufactory of the
> very Devil himself. (ch. 3)

The comedy of this passage derives from a conflation of incompatible
moral attitudes. Bureaucratic harshness and indifference are joined to
journalistic sententiousness in comic osmosis. By using a degraded
circumstantial pomp, Dickens was able to diminish the lack of fit
between style and content characteristic of pure mock-heroic, so that
there is very little feeling of strain. Readers discover indignation
beneath surface blandness, chiefly in the way they find themselves
required to provide more than one interpretation for phrases like "the
wisdom and mercy of the board" or "permitted to . . . console his mind."
    Archness in his books parallels the posturing Dickens was given to in
his life, and may be supposed to grow out of it. Inevitably, he saw that
the way it worked made it useful for more than stylistic effects, and he
developed it into one of his principal methods of characterization. Many
of his characters betray in their behavior and language a yearning after
dignity their lives lack. That was something Dickens knew a lot about.
His dreamers, hypocrites, and self-deceivers are especially given to this,
and the narrator often apparently connives with them, yielding an effect
not of firm authorial irony, but of shared delight in illusion, which the
reader is made to feel he has to penetrate. The editor of the *Eatanswill
Gazette* attends Mrs. Leo Hunter's *fête champêtre*

> accoutred as a Russian officer of justice with a tremendous
> knout in his hand – tastefully typical of the stern and mighty
> power of the Eatanswill Gazette and the fearful lashings it
> bestowed on public offenders.
>   "Bravo!" shouted Mr. Tupman and Mr. Snodgrass from the
> passage when they beheld the walking allegory.
>   "Bravo!" Mr. Pickwick was heard to exclaim from the

passage.

"Hoo – roar, Pott!" shouted the populace. Amid these salutations, Mr. Pott, smiling with that kind of bland dignity which sufficiently testified that he felt his power and knew how to exert it, got into the chariot. (*Pickwick Papers* ch. 15)

This is more inward than the description of the board's response to Oliver's asking for more. The irony is located as much in character as in language. The passage represents Mr. Pott's own sentiments, apparently sympathetically. Its effect is to make us feel we need to circumvent a mischievous conspiracy between the narrator and Mr. Pott, to reinterpret assertions, for instance, about Mr. Pott's "bland dignity which sufficiently testified that he felt his power and knew how to exert it." It tempts us to suppose we achieve insight into Pott's personality, despite rather than because of the narrator.

Dickens's irony exposed his readers to divergent meanings. His posturing exposed his family and friends to divergent personae. At Doughty Street, he indulged weaknesses and vanities with gusto, dramatizing them in order to amuse. At the end of his stay in Doughty Street, prompted by a growing family and growing prosperity, he leased a much larger, much grander house, at 1 Devonshire Terrace, in the fashionable Regent's Park district. This he declared to be "a house of great promise (and great premium) 'undeniable' situation, and excessive splendour" (Pilgrim *Letters* 1: 598). Neither great premium nor grand posture, however, stopped him fulfilling promise and matching splendor. He bought whole new suites of furniture for the house, new curtains and blinds, new mirrors, and deep–pile carpets. He replaced deal doors with mahogany, wooden chimney pieces with marble. He fitted bookshelves in the study, and expanded his library to fill them. Circumstantial pomp was something he sought both in literary style and domestic environment. And he sought to subvert it in both.

Dickens's life at Doughty Street, then, mirrored his art. The same habits of imagination shaped the life he lived and the way he wrote. Unsurprisingly, he dazzled friends, family, and others with whom he mixed, as well as readers. In this chapter I have shown how those habits of imagination can be traced in his everyday behavior. But those habits and that behavior had themselves undergone shaping. In the next chapter I turn to what were great issues for him, precipitated by crises that lodged in his imagination, and enduringly modified it.

2

BIOGRAPHICAL : THREE CRISES

Dickens's imagination was nourished by long-term memory as well as by immediate circumstances. Crises in his life that had enduring effects on the man unsurprisingly had enduring effects on what he put into his books. The order and stability he cultivated at Doughty Street were intended as a defence against such crises. Nevertheless, the Doughty Street establishment was sustained by them. His writing paid for the order and stability, among other ways by recycling the crises.

That is not to say Dickens allowed himself to be a victim of his past – or a victim of his past and no more than that. Only an impoverished understanding of his imagination is reached by supposing every re-enactment of remembered events in his writings to have been involuntary, or at best therapeutic. Though he sometimes clearly relived old pain – and other feelings – he did not always revisit the past driven by them. Sometimes it was in order to recover the feelings. Sometimes it was to reassess the feelings. Simple hunger for material was often the spur. Past crises appear in different and contradictory guises, some laden with old emotion, some not. He was capable of using memory professionally, to provide purchase for imagination. Pursued by demons he might have been, but he had an uncanny aptitude for caging them and teaching them tricks. What is certain is that Dickens was able to find stirring incidents and strong emotions for his books, including those worked on at Doughty Street, by remembering what had stimulated him powerfully in the past.

Memories of past crises seem to have remained with Dickens, if not longer, then perhaps more distinctly than with most of us. The way he responded to them and accommodated them evolved, but they influenced him throughout his life. A memory of events before or during the Doughty Street period, still affecting him ten, twenty, thirty years later, was affecting him, we can safely assume, at Doughty Street too. We can look for its influence on the Doughty Street novels.

Three crises stand out. Two happened before the Doughty Street period, one during his first weeks in Doughty Street. The first, chronologically, was his employment as a child in Warren's Blacking Warehouse, and his father's imprisonment for debt in the Marshalsea Prison. The second was his failure to win the love of Maria Beadnell, an episode only apparently closed by his success in winning both the love and the hand of Catherine Hogarth. And the third was the death of Catherine's sister, Mary Hogarth.

2.1 WARREN'S BLACKING AND THE MARSHALSEA

This story will be familiar to many readers.[1] At one time, indeed, it was told as a kind of homily for children, along with exemplary episodes from the childhoods of other notable men and women.[2] It is told in his own words in a fragment of autobiography incorporated into the first indispensable life of Dickens, published after the novelist's death by his friend John Forster (bk. 1, ch. 2). And it is retold, with minimal changes, in the account of David Copperfield's childhood (*David Copperfield* ch. 11). The immediate access to Dickens's own feelings that these last two narratives seem to offer helps to account for the potency and currency of the story.

Because of his father's mounting debts and the need to augment the family income, early in 1824, perhaps at around the time of his twelfth birthday on 7 February, Dickens started work at a job profoundly uncongenial to him, sealing bottles of shoe blacking in Warren's Blacking Warehouse, at 30 Hungerford Stairs, the Strand, in London. His parents had been offered this opening for him by the manager, James Lamert, stepson of Mrs. Dickens's sister, and cousin of the owner, George Lamert. James Lamert at first arranged some modest privileges for his young relative – an hour's lessons a day, and a work-table in the counting-house instead of the workshop. Dickens's distress was redoubled when these were gradually forgotten, and he found himself laboring without interruption, alongside lads from much humbler backgrounds, lacking the aspirations of the Dickens family. His shame was intensified still further after the business moved to Chandos Street, Covent Garden, and he was required to work at a window in public view.

The six or seven shillings a week he earned by this work was no bad wage. Some farm-laborers kept a family on as little, if with difficulty. But it was only a means of easing the Dickens family's problems, never a way of solving them. Creditors grew refractory, and on 20 February, after a short interval in a sponging-house, John Dickens, the father, was gaoled for debt in the Marshalsea Prison, in the Borough of Southwark. Within a week or two, Mrs. Dickens and the younger children had joined him in lodgings within the prison precinct. Money was somehow found to keep Dickens's elder sister Fanny as a boarder at the Royal Academy of Music. Charles was lodged with a friend of the family in Camden Town. He walked to and from work six days a week, and fed himself out of his wages. Because of the demands of work, and the distance between Camden Town and the Borough, he was able to see his parents on Sundays only. This told on his spirits and, after about four weeks it is conjectured, John Dickens found lodgings for his son in Lant Street, three minutes' walk from the Marshalsea, where he could join the family for breakfast each morning, supper each evening (Allen 87–88).

On 28 May John Dickens was released from prison under the provisions of the Insolvent Debtors Act, and at about the same time family prospects were brightened by a legacy of £450 from his mother, Dickens's grandmother, who had died on 26 April. By the end of the year all the family were living together in Somers Town, and the crisis seemed to be receding. John Dickens, to be sure, was negotiating retirement from his position at the Navy Pay Office. He had perfectly genuine health grounds, but perhaps anxiety about official attitudes to insolvency prompted him too, not to mention the prospect of enjoying both a Pay Office pension and a salary from some other occupation. For Charles Dickens, however, there was no sign of liberation or fresh prospects. He seems not to have been released from Warren's until March or April 1825, when he was sent to school, at Wellington House

Academy (Allen 101–12). Even then, by his own account, his release was opposed by his mother.

This year or more in Dickens's life – a long time for a distressed twelve- or thirteen-year-old – affected his sensibility permanently. It played a formative role, I submit, in his habitually ironic perception of things (see pp. 24–27 above), but memories more conscious than those which underpin habit persisted too, often troubling Dickens, often providing him with models for fiction. To understand how this episode affected him so profoundly, we need to see it in the context of the age, and against other experiences of Dickens's childhood.

It was an age of high social mobility relative to preceding ages, predominantly but not invariably upward. There were many new recruits to the middle classes at the end of the eighteenth century and beginning of the nineteenth, thanks to the expansion of industry, trade, and government. As always, class distinction and snobbery were signs of such mobility. They intensified during the century, along with the mobility.

Whatever distinctions people made, however, the classes were undeniably distinct. To move from one class to another was to change identity as much as status. Broadly speaking, differences of income, expenditure, and culture, between the working classes and even the lowest fringe of the middle classes, were very much greater than they are today in Europe or North America. Laborers might earn as little as £20 a year. Average lower-middle-class incomes have been estimated at £60 to £200 a year. £300 a year was sometimes held up as the amount a professional man needed before marrying ("Money Values," *Oxford Reader's Companion to Dickens*). Nor should we forget that the early nineteenth-century middle classes, for all that they were expanding, were still a smaller proportion of the population than today's and, relative to their working-class contemporaries, much more privileged. Even as late as 1889, it was estimated that only about 17 percent of Londoners might be deemed middle-class, or of higher status (*Times London History Atlas* 102). Forster evidently found it unsurprising that John Dickens maintained the middle-class privilege of keeping a servant, even while in prison (bk. 1, ch. 2). More to the point perhaps, despite improving education, a significant proportion of the working classes was illiterate, or barely literate, and accordingly ignorant. Reliable figures are hard to come by but, as late as 1845, 33 percent of the male population of the United Kingdom were calculated to be illiterate, 49 percent of the female population (Newsome 146). Plainly, illiteracy would have been concentrated among the lowest classes. "I don't know nothink," Jo's refrain in *Bleak House* (1852–53), articulated a widespread condition even in the 1850s, and for Dickens embodied a remembered thrill of horror. Boys like Charley Hexam, in *Our Mutual Friend* (1864–65), had to struggle out of an abyss onto the lowest rung of the middle-class ladder. That was the most difficult ascent of them all – out of the working classes into the middle classes. *Oliver Twist* (1837–38) registers the dismay aroused at the prospect of a boy with a middle-class birthright trapped in a working-class milieu, or worse.

Dickens's earlier childhood experiences, until he reached the age of ten at any rate, had encouraged him to suppose that his father had achieved middle-class status for the family, that they were secure in that status, and that they could look forward to rising within it. John Dickens had evidently felt his was an upward trajectory. As a young man, before his marriage and the birth of his children, he had become a clerk in the Navy Pay Office. He was attached to Portsmouth dockyard when his second child, Charles, was born in 1812. The Royal Navy had expanded during the Napoleonic Wars. Annual expenditure on it, during the period 1793 to 1815, was more than seven times what it had been during the peace of 1784 to 1792 (Baugh 121). Thanks to this, there were opportunities in naval administration for bright young men to better themselves.

And better himself John Dickens did. The clerkship was a position to which he could feel he had risen. His parents had been domestic servants – superior domestic servants to be sure, butler and housekeeper to Lord Crewe, probably each earning as much as many a clerk – but domestic servants for all that, without middle-class status. Their son John was confident of his, and is likely to have felt it confirmed by his marriage, although this confirmation was soon snatched away.

His bride was Elizabeth Barrow. When they married, in 1809, John Dickens became the son-in-law of a senior official in the Pay Office, another new recruit to the middle classes, who had risen even higher. Charles Barrow, evidence suggests, had once been a musical-instrument maker – a skilled artisan, that is to say, but scarcely middle-class. Not long after the marriage, however, he was discovered to have embezzled Pay Office funds, and forced to flee beyond the reach of the law (Staples 11–24).

His fate highlights the insecurity of the new middle classes. His son-in-law would have done well to heed Charles Barrow's undoing. A sense of proportion is necessary, though, if John Dickens's behavior is fairly to be judged. Expenditure beyond present means, and debt, are arguably defining characteristics of middle-class status. Today they take the form of mortgages, bank loans, and purchase agreements, rather than the informal credit and bills of exchange of the early nineteenth century. Today, however, there are safety nets in place against emergencies, which were not there for new members of the middle classes in the early nineteenth century, and the penalties for defaulting are less severe. Caution and luck were needed to preserve liquidity for those without capital or security to carry them through financial crises. Otherwise, they could face destitution and degradation. The historical records of the era, as well as the fiction, abound with references to the pawnshop, the broker's man, the sponging-house, and the debtors' prison.

Before 1822, these institutions evidently caused John Dickens no more anxiety than his father-in-law's misfortunes. The Pay Office job required him, every so often, to move with his family from naval establishment to naval establishment. They moved from house to house even more often. Debt and the need to economize, it would seem, was often the spur. But early in his career at any rate, he was evidently no deeper in debt than many of his Pay Office colleagues (Allen 59–60), or indeed than many of the new recruits to the middle classes, with incomes and expectations encouraging new consumption. John Dickens, however, was incautious or unlucky or both.

The reckoning, though, was postponed. In 1817 his prevailing optimism seemed vindicated. That year, he was ordered to Chatham dockyard. The move promised well for family liquidity, and the five years in Chatham seem indeed to have been happy ones for them. John Dickens was not free of financial problems at this time, but his income was augmented considerably (Allen 59). Dickens remembered the period with yearning nostalgia. His lifelong love of Kent began during the Chatham years. The most profitable phase of his formal education was at William Giles's school in Chatham, and he undertook some of his most formative reading at this time. Above all, perhaps, he was able to observe his father, an official of some standing in a small dockyard town, play a part in society suited to his ambition.[3]

But in 1822, John Dickens was transferred to the headquarters of the Navy Pay Office, then at Somerset House in the Strand, London, a move which brought diminished income, higher expenses, and his absorption into the vast anonymous army of London clerks (Allen 71–79). The family took a house at 16 Bayham Street, in a part of Camden Town Dickens later remembered as a poor one. His memory may have exaggerated the seediness of it, but it is clear that his own circumstances had deteriorated. Money was no longer found to send him to school, he felt himself to be neglected, and he had little but the spectacle of London to distract him from the process that, in less than eighteen months from his arrival there, culminated in Warren's and the Marshalsea.

Dickens was born, then, into a class delighting in new affluence, status, and opportunity. Members of it like John Dickens modelled themselves on the professional classes and the gentry, but were all too easily reminded of how flimsy their new privileges were. Unforeseen misfortune could reduce unlucky families to shabby gentility or unqualified poverty or worse. Of this the Dickenses could be in no doubt. Charles seems never to have met his maternal grandfather, but would doubtless have been told how the musical-instrument maker rose to become a senior civil servant, only to fall into disgrace and exile. His father's misfortunes needed no telling. Dickens knew only too well the story of a son of the servant classes who, with talent, industry, luck – and probably some help – had entered a middle-class profession and grown to insist upon his status as a gentleman (Allen 11–20), but was not to be saved from the taint of gaol, nor was able to save his son from the taint of plebeian labor.

This reversal was utterly demoralizing for the boy. In Chatham Dickens had been encouraged to think of himself as the son of a gentleman, as a young person of consequence, talent and promise. His schoolmaster, William Giles, had thought highly of him, as well he might of a boy who, at the age of nine, wrote a tragedy, "Misnar, the Sultan of India" (lost to posterity, perhaps mercifully). Long before he thought of buying Gad's Hill Place, not far from Rochester, long before he settled there as squire of Higham in all but name, Dickens told Forster how, during his boyhood, his father had declared he might one day come to own the house, if only he worked hard enough (bk. 8, ch. 3).

It would be a remarkable twelve-year-old, faced with the withdrawal of such prospects, whose first thought was of his parents' predicament. Dickens, doubtless, was a remarkable twelve-year-old, but not that remarkable.   His unsurprising response was self-pity.   Like most children not yet in their teens, Dickens understood society, his own position in it, and his prospects, as his parents had coached him to. He shared his father's optimism and sense of opportunity, not easily overturned.   But now degradation and disgrace more than threatened. Shabby gentility was the best that could be hoped for.   The worst was scarcely to be thought of.

Inevitably, the son was distraught at his father's imprisonment. Forster's account of the episode (bk. 1, ch. 2) tells us that "the last words said to him by his father before he was finally carried to the Marshalsea, were to the effect that the sun was set upon him for ever. 'I really believed at the time,' said Dickens to me, 'that they had broken my heart.'"   But, as the consequences for him of his father's misfortunes persisted month after month, so the autobiographical fragment reveals, grief turned to a sense of betrayal:

> no one had compassion enough on me – a child of singular abilities, quick, eager, delicate, and soon hurt, bodily or mentally – to suggest that something might have been spared, as certainly it might have been, to place me at any common school. Our friends, I take it, were tired out. No one made any sign. My father and mother were quite satisfied. They could hardly have been more so, if I had been twenty years of age, distinguished at a grammar-school, and going to Cambridge.

Above all, he feared what he might be turning into – an undifferentiated member of the group of shabby ignorant working-class boys, devoid of aspirations or prospects, who were his workmates. David Copperfield's account of one of his workmates at Murdstone and Grinby's plainly echoes Dickens's disquiet. Mealy Potatoes' father, we are told, was "a waterman, who had the additional distinction of being a fireman, and was engaged as such at one of the large theaters; where some young relation of Mealy's – I think his little sister – did Imps in the Pantomimes" (*David Copperfield* ch. 11). Dickens feared contamination at Warren's:

> No words can express the secret agony of my soul as I sunk into this companionship; compared these every day associates with those of my happier childhood; and felt my early hopes of growing up to be a learned and distinguished man, crushed in my breast. The deep remembrance of the sense I had of being utterly neglected and hopeless; of the shame I felt in my position; of the misery it was to my young heart to believe that, day by day, what I had learned, and thought, and delighted in, and raised my fancy and my emulation up by, was passing away from me, never to be brought back any more; cannot be written. My whole nature was so penetrated with the grief and humiliation of such considerations, that even now, famous and caressed and happy, I often forget in my dreams that I have a dear wife and children; even that I am a man; and wander desolately back to that time of my life.

Nor was that necessarily the worst. For three months, his father was in prison. He himself was degraded. What was to stop him sinking even lower? "I know," he commented, " that, but for the mercy of God, I might easily have been, for any care that was taken of me, a little robber or a little vagabond." It must have occasioned as much bitter irony as relief, when his fellow workers referred to him, probably not always unmaliciously, as "the young gentleman."

The final betrayal, in Dickens's eyes, was his mother's opposition to his being removed from Warren's. Perhaps she was more practical than her husband, less beguiled by ambition, or more hopeful about what their Lamert relations might do for her son, but she sought to accommodate the quarrel between James Lamert and her husband that led to Dickens's dismissal. Whatever her motives, her representations left him, after twenty-odd years, still able to say, "I never afterwards forgot, I never shall forget, I never can forget, that my mother was warm for my being sent back."

It was probably not until 1847 that Dickens wrote for Forster the account of the Warren's episode from which I have been quoting.[4] By then he was a thirty-five-year-old family man and a world-famous novelist. From this perspective he might have seen that, however distressing the Warren's experience had been for him, something like it, save the isolation, was the normal experience of boys the age he had then been, in the greater part of the population. It was doubtless a dismal experience. Few adults today, let alone twelve-year-olds, would be happy working long hours, six days a week, in unappealing conditions, on a repetitive manual task. But it was a common experience. Yet Dickens recollects the sufferings of his twelve-year-old self without reflecting on this – indeed without any of the kind of distancing an adult perspective might afford. If anything, he seems proud of seeing from the child's point of view, and chooses to emphasize it: "I often forget in my dreams . . . that I am a man," he says. If we look in autobiography for evidence that the writer has changed and learned from experience, the autobiographical fragment must be deemed deficient.

Its hold on the imagination of readers, however, cannot be disputed. In it, Dickens articulated the anxieties of an entire class. The reading public eagerly greeted the revelations in Forster's *Life* (1872–74). An edition of it published with the Household Edition of Dickens's works, only seven years after the first part of the *Life* was first issued, endorses Dickens's self-pity graphically – literally so. Fred Barnard's title-page vignette [fig. 8] is no portrait of Dickens, but an icon of the abandoned child victim, of the suffering little mophead. Homiletic versions of the story grow naturally out of the attitude encapsulated in this image. Today's biographers and critics are more often than not fastidious about such endorsement of Dickens's self-pity, but continue, like me, to be fascinated by the Warren's episode and its effect upon him.

The power of the fragment is not difficult to explain, though. In writing it, Dickens was doing what he did well. It is no more than a fragment because he abandoned the attempt to write a more complete story of his life, and recast what he had written as fiction – as part of *David Copperfield* (Forster bk. 1, ch. 2). The decision is scarcely surprising. What qualified Dickens as a novelist, disqualified him as an autobiographer. George Orwell speaks of reading *David Copperfield* when he was about nine, and of imagining the author was a child of his own age (36). Dickens's gift, in writing about childhood, was the ability

AT THE BLACKING WAREHOUSE.

(Drawn by FRED. BARNARD.)

Figure 8   The boy Dickens at Warren's Blacking Warehouse. Fred Barnard's title-page vignette for the Household Edition of John Forster's *Life of Charles Dickens* (1879). (By permission of the Dickens House Museum, London.)

so thoroughly to evoke its experiences and sensations, that child readers find themselves in an utterly familiar world, and adults are transported back into such a world. It was a gift scarcely likely to be diminished, when the child he was writing about was his own younger self. *Great Expectations* (1860–61), to be sure, shows he did eventually learn to balance vivid apprehension of childhood experience with adult judgment, but the means he learned were those of the fabulist – reversal, recognition, irony. It is fashionable to argue that the autobiographer is no less a fabulist than the novelist but, in practice, it is hard not to be aware of a different distribution of techniques between them. The autobiographer tends to reconstruct his past more discursively, less dramatically. The fragment is vividly dramatic. That is to say, it is an artful literary construct, a good story, something akin to fiction, not a judicious attempt to present a balanced account of the Warren's episode.

It is important to understand this, because such an understanding authorizes a readiness to recognize quite different versions of the Warren's episode in Dickens's works. The fragment, the related section of *David Copperfield*, and some sections of other books featuring the suffering of children, are the rawest and among the most powerful renderings of the Warren's experience, but they are not the only ones. Different versions, usually less extended and more disguised, are to be found, in the Doughty Street novels and elsewhere. In these, inventive exuberance often overrides or effaces distress.

Even while working at Warren's, and spending time with his parents in the Marshalsea, Dickens was using his imagination inventively to explore alternative ways of seeing dismal circumstances. He loved to hear his mother's stories about other prisoners, but was not content with unadorned fact. At his father's instigation, the debtors signed a petition for funds with which to drink the king's health on his birthday. "I made my own little character and story," Dickens relates, "for every man who put his name to the sheet of paper." He used fiction for a more practical end when he was taken ill one day, at Warren's, and imagination carried him further than the situation strictly demanded. Another boy employed there insisted on taking him home. This was Bob Fagin (whose name Dickens was to remember), an orphan living with his brother-in-law, a waterman. "I was too proud to let him know about the prison," Dickens says,

> and after making several efforts to get rid of him, to all of which
> Bob Fagin in his goodness was deaf, shook hands with him on
> the steps of a house near Southwark-bridge on the Surrey side,
> making believe that I lived there. As a finishing piece of reality
> in case of his looking back, I knocked at the door, I recollect,
> and asked, when the woman opened it, if that was Mr. Robert
> Fagin's house.   (Forster bk. 1, ch. 2)

The economy and stylishness of this finishing touch were not called for,
but Dickens evidently enjoyed the flourish of it.

Despite his desolation, he even became ready, surprisingly swiftly,
imaginatively to enter the world of the utterly dispossessed and to find
comedy in it – perhaps not while he was still at Warren's, but certainly
very soon afterwards. School friends at Wellington House Academy
remembered some laddish antics instigated by Dickens. Dr. Henry
Danson, for instance:

> I quite remember Dickens on one occasion heading us in
> Drummond-street in pretending to be poor boys, and asking the
> passers-by for charity – especially old ladies; one of whom told
> us she "had no money for beggar boys." On these adventures,
> when the old ladies were quite staggered by the impudence of
> the demand, Dickens would explode with laughter and take to
> his heels. (Forster bk. 1, ch. 3)

This is not easily reconciled with the notion of Dickens forever
mournfully nursing the secret wound of Warren's. It admits the
possibility of alternative imaginative constructions of the episode,
alternative responses to it. There is no reason to doubt that Dickens had
genuinely been filled with horror at the abyss of poverty and worse
Warren's opened up before him, that he had genuinely been humiliated
by having to perform menial tasks in public view, that well into adult
life he was genuinely unable to pass the scene of his humiliation and
remain composed (Forster bk. 1, ch. 2). Nor should we be surprised at
such reactions in a sensitive twelve-year-old boy. Nor, least of all,
should we blame these reactions. But although he refrained from
showing it in the story he made of the episode for Forster, he knew there
were different ways of building upon it imaginatively, and he knew it

early on. Within months of all that humiliation and suffering, once the danger had gone and his old status was restored, he was able gleefully to play in public the part of someone sunk to the very bottom of the abyss, play it for laughs, and lead others in doing the same. Teenage boys, with characteristic bad taste, do things like that, to take revenge on predicaments which have hurt them, or threaten to. It is as well to remember that, sensitive as he was, Dickens could do what other teenage boys do. He was not locked into just one version of this crisis in his life.

Biographical evidence indicates Dickens was able in later years to think about Warren's without self-pity. Sometimes, indeed, it is possible to detect a secret mischievous enjoyment. Late in his life, fellow players of a word game at Gad's Hill noted a twinkle in his eye and a curious tone of voice, when some contribution of his consisted of the words, "Warren's Blacking, 30, Strand" (Johnson 2: 1058). Evidence suggests he divulged the plain facts of Warren's only to Forster and to his wife during his lifetime, but he hinted at it to others. He was, not least, capable of taking pride in the experience. When his sixteen-year-old son Edward (the beloved "Plorn") was leaving for a new life in Australia, Dickens wrote majestically to him, "I was not so old as you are now when I first had to win my food" (Nonesuch *Letters* 3: 668).

Scattered throughout Dickens's books, surprisingly frequent references to Warren's, or to anonymous blacking warehouses, or to blacking, or to shoe-cleaning, betray no distress, and hint at the mischievous enjoyment I speak of. Sam Weller, bringer of street-wisdom to the Corresponding Society of the Pickwick Club, is introduced to the reader in the yard of the White Hart Inn, in the Borough, cleaning boots and shoes (*Pickwick Papers*, ch. 10). His labors yield "a polish which would have struck envy to the soul of the amiable Mr. Warren (for they used Day and Martin at the White Hart)." Sam's experience as a boots, I suggest, is a token of his valuable street-life experiences. He certainly finds opportunity for shrewd observation, thanks to it. "There's a pair of Wellingtons a good deal worn, and a pair of lady's shoes, in number five," is the way he chooses to inform on the eloping Mr. Jingle and Miss Wardle. The boots is, in fact, a recurrent figure in Dickens's works, from "The Great Winglebury Duel" (1836, *Sketches by Boz*), through "The Holly Tree" (1855, *Christmas Stories*), to *Great Expectations* (1860-61). The one thing these figures have in common is supreme self-confidence, and they tend to be sources of robust decision-making or wise reflection.

Blacking advertisements are part of the secret joke. Advising his son on the composition of valentines (and alluding to verse advertisements), Tony Weller remarks, "Poetry's unnat'ral; no man ever talked poetry 'cept a beadle on boxin' day, or Warren's blackin', or Rowland's oil, or some of them low fellows . . . " (*Pickwick Papers*, ch. 33). Derogatory this may be, but scarcely anxious. Joe Gargery, too, is mindful of advertisements. As soon as he arrives in London for the first time, he discloses, "'me and Wopsle went off straight to look at the Blacking Ware'us. But we didn't find that it come up to its likeness in the red bills at the shop doors: which I meantersay,' added Joe, in an explanatory manner, 'as it is there drawd too architectooralooral'" (*Great Expectations* ch. 27). For Dickens, blacking and comedy were by no means alien.

With Mr. Micawber, shoe-shining is a sign of mental elasticity. Dunned by his creditors, he would be "transported with grief and mortification, even to the length . . . of making motions at himself with a razor, but within half-an-hour afterwards, he would polish up his shoes with extraordinary pains, and go out, humming a tune with a greater air of gentility than ever" (*David Copperfield* ch 11). Preparatory grooming is an appropriate activity for Mr. Micawber at this point, but it did not have to be shoe-shining.

The authority of the autobiographical fragment, though, is perhaps most directly challenged by an obscure manifestation of the Warren's experience, almost entirely unrecognized as such, so heavily is it disguised. Blacking is unmentioned, but once the parallels are perceived the source is scarcely to be denied. It is to be found in a minor Christmas story Dickens wrote for the 1852 Christmas number of *Household Words*, one of a set of stories by several hands. "The Poor Relation's Story" is a gimmicky piece comprising a poor man's fantasy (only revealed as such at the end), in which the misfortunes of his life are reversed. Among other details of a rich and fulfilled life he never had, the poor relation imagines, for himself and for his imaginary loyal business partner, a "room of business, on our little wharf, overlooking the river," a counting-house, the windows of which, "shaped like the stern windows of a ship," open on a view of ships. One of the quickly discontinued privileges granted Dickens when first he started work at Warren's, remember, was the right to work, not in the workshop with the other boys, but in the counting-house. From the perspective of the workshop, it must have seemed yet another lost Eden. "The counting-house," he told Forster, "was on the first floor, looking over coal-barges and the river" (bk. 1, ch. 2). The accumulation of contingent detail makes it difficult not to suppose Dickens was drawing on memories of Warren's when he composed this idyll. And when we look at figure 9, it becomes even more difficult. Warren's warehouse is to the right of the steps. The first-floor window overlooking the river, presumably, is the middle one in the vertical row next to the corner. The bottom one looks as if it lights a floor only a little above street level. The floor below, without a window, must be a cellar. So the middle one is the first-floor window, and the print does indeed suggest it was more elaborate than others we see – pilastered, and arched or bowed or both – easily transmuted into "the stern windows of a ship" by the imagination of a bored and unhappy child, remembering from happier times the great stern windows of warships in Chatham docks.

Two years after the completion of *David Copperfield*, then, in which the self-pitying version of the Warren's episode is most powerfully expressed, we find Dickens using memories of it to construct an image of an ideally safe and cosy world. Perhaps the entrepreneurial experience of running *Household Words*, which had commenced publication in March 1850, inspired him to think through another conceivable issue of the Warren's experience, an issue which may well have been in the minds of John and Elizabeth Dickens, when they found their son a position in a business run by their Lamert relatives. If events had unfolded differently, Dickens at forty might have been a partner, prosperous and contented, in a celebrated blacking business.

One of the last distinctive manifestations of the Warren's and Marshalsea episode, and one of the oddest, in contrast, thoroughly endorses the autobiographical fragment. But it adds a new sentiment to it. In *A Tale of Two Cities*, Dr. Manette, rescued from the Bastille, at times of stress reverts half-unconsciously to his prison occupation of shoe-making. His friends solve the problem in a way that cannot be accounted for naturalistically. With the most elaborate circumlocution,

Figure 9   Hungerford Stairs by G. Harvey, with figures added by D. Digton, c. 1823.   Warren's Blacking Warehouse is to the right of the steps.   (By permission of the Dickens House Museum, London.)

Mr. Lorry taxes Dr. Manette over the wisdom of keeping the bench, tools, and materials. Reluctantly, Dr. Manette agrees it to be unwise. Taking this as permission, Mr. Lorry and Miss Pross, in the dead of night, while Dr. Manette is away from home, chop up and burn the bench, and bury tools, leather, and shoes in the garden (bk. 2, ch. 19). It seems no serious impertinence to ask why Dickens did not have them go out in broad daylight, and give everything to a deserving cobbler's apprentice, a street or two away. But to ask this is to neglect the volatile combination, for Dickens, of memories of jail and of humble manual labor connected with boots and shoes. The ritualistic burning and burying have little to do with the occasion or characters in the novel, everything to do with Dickens's past.

For all that, this manifestation of Warren's declares the wisdom of burying at least something of the past. Perhaps it reflects a recognition by Dickens that it was time to put a stop to the revival of distress that so often accompanied memories of Warren's and the Marshalsea. *A Tale of Two Cities* was written, it is worth remembering, during 1859, when great changes were taking place in Dickens's life. He had separated from his wife. His relationship with the young actress Ellen Ternan, who was to become so important to him, was evolving. Circumstances were calling upon him to rethink his past. It was also the year before he began work on *Great Expectations*, the masterpiece which George Bernard Shaw called Dickens's "apology to Mealy Potatoes" (Shaw vi), and in which the self-pitying myth of the Warren's episode is arguably repudiated. The protagonist of *Great Expectations*, Pip, has no natural claim to gentlemanly status, and is disappointed by it. This is compensation, Shaw felt, for the hero's disdain, in *David Copperfield*, towards Mealy Potatoes (ch. 11). Few critics today would disagree, although Sam Weller alone might be deemed an apology in advance, and a sufficient one.

The Warren's experience, then, did not give birth to a private self-pitying myth so dominant in Dickens's imagination that it crowded out others. There was such a myth, and it would break out, seemingly unbidden, from time to time, or could at any rate be summoned. But his imagination was powerful enough radically to reshape the experience, when he wanted to, and free it from distress. Perhaps the intensity of the Warren's experience contributed to the power of his imagination. If it did, it was ultimately liberating rather than imprisoning. Nor was liberation delayed – until, for instance, a falling of scales from eyes enabled Dickens to write *Great Expectations*. He was able to use the Warren's experience inventively, and in contrasting ways, early in his career, even during the Doughty Street period.

2.2 MARIA AND CATHERINE

One evening in 1843, Dickens was dining with the American philanthropist Samuel Gridley Howe and his new wife, when she addressed her husband as "darling." "Instantly Dickens was on his back on the floor, partly under the table, waving his legs in the air, and crying, 'Did she call him darling?'" (*Dickensian* 31: 192). Make what allowance you will, this was extraordinary behavior on Dickens's part. The use of "darling" as an affectionate epithet was established long before 1843. It may well have seemed too informal and intimate for the occasion, at a time when it was not unusual, in public at least, for husband and wife to address each other by surname, prefixed by Mr. or Mrs. Even so, that is no excuse. Perhaps English and American manners had diverged on such niceties. Nor is that an excuse. Dickens's behavior was a graver breach of manners than the occasion of it. The trigger was a category error committed by Mrs. Howe in Dickens's estimation, not just a social gaffe. She was a wife in public, but had used the language of a lover in private.

This pantomime signifies a distinction rooted deep in Dickens's imagination. He had sharply differentiated and discontinuous imaginative models for courtship and for marriage. The mirth of the 1843 dinner table is prefigured in *Sketches of Young Couples*, which Dickens published anonymously in 1840. The Plausible Couple are disparaged for calling each other "darling" and "dearest" in public, the Loving Couple for caressing each other. These are married couples acting like lovers. For most people today such behavior seems, if not endearing, at least forgivable, but for Dickens it was a conflation of categories which yielded comedy or bathos.

The origins of this sharp distinction, I suggest, can be found in his own experience of erotic love in early manhood. There were two young women he loved profoundly. The first he courted ardently but lost. Any man rejected by the first woman he loves suffers, but Dickens seems to have been permanently marked by the experience.   He preserved it in his memory, as a model for stories of sexual attraction, and the transactions of lovers.   He did not use it as a model, however, for stories of successful marriage, narrated in any detail beyond the wedding.

He married the second of the two young women. Clearly reacting to the earlier episode, this time he tried to restrain his ardor and, if not dispense with the rituals of courtship, at least simplify and rationalize them.   From their engagement, if not sooner, he strove to shape the young woman into an ideal wife.   This time, that is to say, he constructed a model in advance, and in reaction to the loss of the young woman he did not marry.   The model preceded both his perception of the real relationship, and his shaping of fictional relationships based upon it.

In 1830 at the age of eighteen, Dickens fell helplessly in love with Maria Beadnell [fig. 10].[5]   She seems to have tolerated his advances, but not his only. For three years, Dickens pursued her ardently, and endured her caprices. The relationship, such as it was, finally foundered in 1833.   Throughout it, Dickens seems to have been a subordinate partner, but an active one too, eagerly responding, adjusting, contriving, pleading.

Maria, it seems, was the first young woman he loved deeply. She was at any rate the first clearly indicated in surviving documentary evidence, and the one he often remembered in later life, wistfully, sometimes painfully. She was thirteen months his senior, the youngest daughter of a banker, living with her parents in bank premises on Lombard Street, in the City of London. Dickens may first have met her in 1830, or perhaps in 1829. By 1831, it is clear, he was an established member of the circle in which she and her sisters moved, under the watchful eyes of their parents.

Maria's well-documented prettiness and vivacity doubtless attracted Dickens, but to these was probably added the erotic charge of social superiority, always powerful, especially so for Dickens, afflicted by distressing memories.   Maria, he said, inspired him "with a determination to overcome all the difficulties" (Forster bk. 1, ch. 3).

Figure 10   Maria Beadnell in 1831, by Henry Austin. (By permission of the
Dickens House Museum, London.)

Specifically, she inspired him to succeed as a journalist, in an effort to become the social equal of her family.

Mr. Beadnell was a clerk with the Smith, Payne and Smith Bank, when that meant something. Maria's uncle was the manager of the bank. Her education was completed at a finishing school in Paris. While Dickens was courting her, a high standard in suitors was set: one of her sisters married a prosperous tea and coffee merchant. If her family could scarcely be called upper-middle-class, they would certainly have resented being called lower-middle-class, a designation the Dickens family would have found hard to repudiate. For all their acceptance of Dickens as a member of Maria's circle, it seems unlikely her parents saw him as a prospective son-in-law. Dickens, clearly, was anxious about their perception of him. Early in the relationship, he told his friend Henry Kolle how unsure he was of "coming off well" with the Beadnells (Pilgrim *Letters* 1: 14).

That is understandable. Although he was an established young journalist by the time he and Maria went their separate ways, to begin with he was still struggling to break into the profession, with no guarantee of success. There was no sign, certainly, of his ever matching the tea merchant in prosperity. In 1831, moreover, John Dickens was again sued in the Insolvent Debtors' Court, with unwelcome attendant publicity (Slater, *Dickens and Women* 51). Relations between Dickens and the elder Beadnells were apparently never less than friendly. After Maria's rejection of him, after Dickens had become famous, they continued to correspond. In the early 1830s, however, the banker could scarcely have rejoiced at his daughter being wooed by the son of a bankrupt.

Dickens sought to overcome his disadvantages, however, punctiliously doing what was expected of a suitor, undeterred by difficulties, hiding his anxieties behind a screen of self-confidence and stylishness. He sought on the one hand to dazzle Maria and her parents, on the other materially to improve his prospects. He was very much on his mettle with Maria. The earliest surviving letter he wrote to her asks her to accept an annual (as yearbooks were known): "Surely, surely you will not refuse so trivial a present: a mere commonplace trifle; a common present even among the merest 'friends'" (Pilgrim *Letters* 7: 777). The nineteen-year-old packs a lot into this: a demonstration of his mastery of etiquette; an argument that she may accept the gift as a friend; and an invitation to agree they are more than friends. Yet, for all its cleverness, it is an uneasy letter. Even at this early stage Dickens is clearly apprehensive about her response. He was probably more successful at social gatherings where, characteristically, he sparkled, where others would applaud, and where he could show off his talent for frothier kinds of composition, into which more earnest sentiment could be smuggled. At a dinner party to which the Beadnells invited him in 1831, he presented a "Bill of Fare" – clever light verse, complimenting his hosts, but also, however light-heartedly, declaring his love. He characterized himself as "a young Summer Cabbage, without any heart":

> Not that he's *heartless*, but because, as folks say,
> He lost his a twelve month ago, from last May.
> (*Collected Papers* 2: 285)

He wrote poems for an album Maria kept, too, and he organized ambitious private theatricals, something he would probably have done anyway, and indeed continued to do for much of his life, but at the time perhaps especially motivated by a desire to shine before Maria. In 1833, he even wrote a musical parody of Shakespeare, *O'Thello*, for a private performance, though that may well have been too late usefully to impress Maria.

Meanwhile he strove to establish himself in a career, with success. A bad cold foiled his attempt to audition for an acting job. This made him concentrate on the journalistic ambitions he had first conceived as a clerk in the office of solicitors Ellis and Blackmore, after he had left Wellington House Academy. By 1832 he was working in the press gallery of the House of Commons, reporting for the *True Sun* and the *Mirror of Parliament*. And his prospects were even better. His uncle John Barrow, editor and proprietor of the *Mirror of Parliament*, recommended him to John Payne Collier, staff member of the much more prestigious *Morning Chronicle*. This intervention probably counted for less, though, than Dickens's mastery of shorthand and reputation for exactness, when finally he was appointed to a permanent position on the *Chronicle* in 1834.

None of this was enough to win Maria, however, whose indifference to Dickens's passion seems to have put an end to matters between them, more distinctly than any misgivings her parents might have had. Michael Slater's convincing suggestion is that, while Dickens sought Maria's love, she sought only excitement from the game of love (Slater 55–57). For a period during 1832 at least, his letters to her were evidently clandestine, smuggled via Kolle, by then fiancé of her elder sister. It is unlikely restrictions imposed by Maria's parents made this necessary. Dickens was still plainly at liberty to see her. In a letter to Kolle of this period, he apologizes for enclosing yet another surreptitious note, explaining that he had been unable the previous evening to say what he wanted to Maria because of his efforts, doubtless appreciated, to keep Mr. Beadnell out of the engaged couple's way (Pilgrim *Letters* 1: 8). This makes the secrecy look more like a romantic game than anything forced upon Dickens and Maria.

It was a game, though, that he seems to have played as eagerly as she did. He was evidently energized by difficulties, real or imagined, and the need to devise expedients against them. Maria may have taken the initiative, but Dickens responded to it eagerly and enterprisingly. In the letter about the annual, written the previous year, he carefully reassures Maria she may reply to him at home: "You need not fear the fact of your writing being known to anyone here for I shall be very busy at home and alone all day tomorrow as my mother and sister will be in town." John and Elizabeth Dickens may have been making difficulties, may have seen Maria's behavior for what it was, or declared their disapproval of her, wounded by the Beadnells' attitude to them, but it is difficult not to feel Dickens was enjoying the plotting, and the sense of intimacy it generated. The difference between them was that, however much he enjoyed the game, he was deeply in love. She was not.

Evidence suggests she behaved coquettishly throughout their relationship (Slater 52–55). In the letter that marks the end of things between them, Dickens speaks bitterly of his constancy being met with "kindness and encouragement one day and a total change of conduct the next" (Pilgrim *Letters* 1: 17). The album to which he contributed survives, in the Dickens House. He was not the only young male contributor, nor indeed the only one to contribute sentimental verses to a capricious enchantress. She herself inscribed verses in it, including the lines:

Truth, darling of a heart sincere,
In women never can reside.   (Slater 54)

What plainer declaration can there be, of a young woman's resolve to enjoy to the full, while she can, the pleasures of uncommitted flirtation? In "Birthday Celebrations," which Dickens wrote thirty years later, the essayist recalls his coming-of-age party, during which he was cast off by a young woman, older than himself, who had "pervaded every chink and crevice of my mind for three or four years" (*The Uncommercial Traveller*). She had used "a short and dreadful word of three letters, beginning with a B." Given the circumstances, there could scarcely have been an easier way out of the relationship for Maria, once she had tired of it, than putting down Dickens as a mere boy. The voice of the essayist, of course, cannot with any precision be identified with Dickens's own, but perhaps this detail of "Birthday Celebrations" is only lightly fictionalized. At any rate, it is clear that the final breach between Dickens and Maria came within weeks of his reaching the age of twenty-one. The meddling of a mutual acquaintance, Mary Anne Leigh, and a disagreeable scene at a performance of the popular play *Clari*, which Dickens organized that spring, seem to have brought matters to a head. He wrote to Maria complaining, "Our meetings of late have been little more than so many displays of heartless indifference on the one hand, while on the other they have never failed to prove a fertile source of wretchedness and misery" (Pilgrim *Letters* 1: 16–17).

Emotionally, Dickens had invested deeply in his courtship of Maria. Now, all had come to nothing, and his confidence in his courtship skills was damaged. Most of his surviving letters to Maria show how she repeatedly wrong-footed him. They quiver with self-justification, misery, and reproach, and make painful reading, the fruitless self-exposure of an infatuated young man, made a plaything but failing to see it, for all his cleverness. In the aftermath of indignation, betrayed confidences, and returned letters, which followed the breach between them, Dickens wrote thus to Maria:

> Wretched aye almost broken hearted I wrote to you – (I have the note for you returned it, and even now I do think it was written "more in sorrow than in anger", and to my mind – I had almost said to your better judgment – it must appear to breathe anything

but an unkind or bitter feeling) – You replied to the note. I
wrote another and that at least was expressive of the same
sentiments as I ever had felt and ever should feel towards you to
my dying day. *That note you sent me back by hand wrapped in
a small loose piece of paper without even the formality of an
envelope and that note I wrote after receiving yours.* It is poor
sport to trifle on a subject like this: I know what your feelings
must have been and by them I regulate my conduct. (Pilgrim
Letters 1: 25)

The very incoherence of this, the anguished analysis of courtship
protocol, the embarrassing lapses into melodramatic phraseology, reveal
the intensity of Dickens's pain, and hint at the remedy. This was not the
way it would be in the future. He would see to that. The sudden dignity
of the last sentence betokens a removal of blinkers, and shows Dickens
to be taking control. From now on, his conduct in such matters would
be regulated with a vengeance.

Memories of Maria, nevertheless, remained important to Dickens for
the rest of his life. Not only were they easily triggered: he needed them.
As a writer, for the best part of his career he had no more serviceable
personal recollection of anxious and resourceful courtship, against the
odds. When he wanted to depict intense desire in fiction, hope against
hope, all the sensations, stratagems, and deceits of courtship, his
experience with Maria was the readiest model.

Doubtless he remembered it with special clarity when writing, for
instance, about the kind of artful coquetry that seems to have been
Maria's speciality. It is reasonable to suppose that the actress, Miss
Snevellicci (whom he quarters in Lombard Street, Portsmouth),
replicates this on her first meeting with Nicholas Nickleby:

"I beg your pardon," said Miss Snevellicci, sidling towards
Nicholas, "but did you ever play at Canterbury?"
"I never did," replied Nicholas.
"I recollect meeting a gentleman at Canterbury," said Miss
Snevellicci, "only for a few moments, for I was leaving the
company as he joined it, so like you that I felt almost certain it
was the same."
"I see you now, for the first time," rejoined Nicholas with all
due gallantry. "I am sure I never saw you before; I couldn't have

forgotten it."

"Oh, I'm sure – it's very flattering of you to say so," retorted Miss Snevellicci with a graceful bend. "Now I look at you again, I see that the gentleman at Canterbury hadn't the same eyes as you – you'll think me very foolish for taking notice of such things, won't you?"

"Not at all," said Nicholas. "How can I feel otherwise than flattered by your notice in any way?"

"Oh! you men are such vain creatures!" cried Miss Snevellicci. (*Nicholas Nickleby* ch. 23)

Memories of Maria must have been useful to Dickens, though, whenever he was writing about courtship, about the excitements, anxieties, and confusions of sexual attraction – even when he was writing about artless dissembling such as Ruth Pinch's, when she encounters someone other than the brother she is looking for, in the precincts of the Temple:

Either she was a little too soon, or Tom was a little too late – she was so precise in general, that she timed it to half a minute – but no Tom was there. Well! But was anybody else there, that she blushed so deeply, after looking round, and tripped off down the steps with such unusual expedition? Why, the fact is, that Mr. Westlock was passing at that moment. The Temple is a public thoroughfare; they may write up on the gates that it is not, but so long as the gates are left open it is, and will be; and Mr. Westlock had as good a right to be there as anybody else. But why did she run away, then? Not being ill dressed, for she was much too neat for that, why did she run away? The brown hair that had fallen down beneath her bonnet, and had one impertinent imp of a false flower clinging to it, boastful of its license before all men, *that* could not have been the cause, for it looked charming. Oh! foolish, panting, frightened little heart, why did she run away! . . .

Oh, foolish, panting, timid little heart, why did she feign to be unconscious of his coming! Why wish herself so far away, yet be so flutteringly happy there!

"I felt sure it was you," said John, when he overtook her, in the sanctuary of Garden Court. "I knew I couldn't be mistaken." She was *so* surprised. (*Martin Chuzzlewit* ch. 45)

"Oh, foolish, panting, timid, little heart . . . !": this scarcely sounds like Maria. *Mutatis mutandis*, it sounds more like the Dickens who had courted Maria, though it is doubtful whether his heart was ever timid. However, if we turn from the characters to the class of experience represented, the debt becomes clearer. Unresolved, apprehensive, intoxicating sexual attraction is what Dickens learned about from his relationship with Maria, and is what his professional memory could not dispense with.

Maria's role in supplying such recollections can be the more readily proposed, because Dickens's relationship with the young woman he married seems to have been short on the unresolved, the apprehensive, and the intoxicating. It is hard to believe it was free of these qualities, but Dickens was clearly intent on not recognizing anything of the kind. He seems so single-mindedly to have inscribed their marriage as something destined to be, that little room was left for open-ended feelings.

In 1834, the year after he abandoned his courtship of Maria, he began regularly to visit the Fulham home of George Hogarth, a senior colleague on the *Morning Chronicle*, and editor of the *Evening Chronicle* in which some of the *Sketches by Boz* were originally published. He became engaged to Hogarth's eldest daughter Catherine [fig. 2] in the spring of 1835, and married her on 2 April 1836.[6] Evidence points to his distrust, this time, of the raptures of courtship. He seems to have looked forward to the calm he hoped would follow marriage, more than to immediate gratification. In *Sketches of Young Couples*, Dickens reserves his warmest commendation for the Old Couple, who exhibit the serenity that comes with looking back at joy rather than forward to it. His decision to include an old couple in a book declared to be about young couples seems a significant error. It is hard not to find in their serenity something Dickens's sought.

It is a different Dickens we see writing to Catherine, from the one we saw writing to Maria. He is no longer the dazzled adorer, utterly absorbed by the object of his love, eager to prove himself, but essentially reacting. Now he acts, and looks to Catherine for reaction. If he is still hiding self-doubt, he is doing it much more successfully. He plays the role of busy self-confident man of the world, sure not only of himself but also of his beloved, perfectly in control, determined to remain so, and scornful of what he sees as feminine wiles. He is prepared to tolerate behavior reminiscent of Maria's, only because not too much of it is forthcoming from Catherine, and because he is confident he can correct it. "I would have you do justice to yourself," he lectures her, "and shew me that your love for me, like mine for you, is above the ordinary trickery, and frivolous absurdity which debases the name, and renders it ludicrous" (Pilgrim *Letters* 1: 62).

From his engagement to Catherine, possibly earlier, Dickens strove to construct her as a wife. "Construction" is a useful concept here. Whatever the merits of the theories that gave rise to it (few, in my view), it allows us to see perception, imagination, and personal influence as continuous, not discrete. It privileges or prioritizes neither life nor literature. And, protest though theorists may at this view, it hints at solipsistic hubris. Dickens's understanding of Catherine was essentially creative – too much so, I believe, for his good and for hers. He fashioned her, in his mind and hers, as an immaculate wife. He wanted her to do justice to herself, he told her. And he told her how to do it. Meanwhile, he created immaculate wives in fiction. Neither preceded the other. The construction of the real wife and of the fictional wives were divisions of the same project.

Dickens and Catherine knew each other for several months before deciding to marry, but the presumption must be that, once they had begun to take an interest in each other, the passage to engagement had been short and smooth. Otherwise, how could Dickens have denounced the "ordinary trickery" and "frivolous absurdity" that debase the name of love? What we know of how Dickens and Catherine came to love each other is based almost entirely on letters he wrote to her after she had accepted his offer of marriage. No surviving document provides testimony of what they were to each other previously – no letter that passed between them, no mention of the one by the other in a letter to someone else, no observation by a third party. It is striking, though, how, in all of the letters, Catherine is seen as the wife-to-be rather than the sweetheart once pursued. Reminiscence about the past, indeed, is singularly lacking from all of Dickens's letters to Catherine, both before and after the marriage. Recriminations are rare, nostalgia even rarer. The focus is always upon the present and the future: what is to be endured or laughed at, what is to be done, how it is to be done. If there had been turbulence in their relationship before their engagement, Dickens quickly put it behind them, as he put behind them the occasional emotional eddies during it, the better to get on with preserving stability.

It would be a mistake, however, to suppose this was coldly done. If Dickens sometimes sounds cool, it was because he was lowering the temperature with an effort. His deepest emotions were engaged. There are unmistakably intimate and tender avowals in his letters. But much of the time emotion can be sensed in its exclusion, much of the time Dickens was clearly restraining himself, avoiding effusiveness. He often declares his love for Catherine by indicating what he is not going to say, what she will not believe, what she cannot know. On one occasion, rather than expose feelings afresh, he reminds her of previous exposure – "of my repeated and solemn assurances of entertaining for you a love which nothing can lessen – an affection which no alteration of time or circumstance can ever abate. I have the vanity to believe that these professions must be gratifying to you, knowing the sincerity with which they come from me" (Pilgrim *Letters* 1: 62–63). This is curiously adjectival, as if part of Dickens had to stand aloof, observing coolly the risky professions of another part. Jane Austen's Mr. Collins might have approved. "And now nothing remains for me," Dickens never quite said, "but to assure you in the most animated language of the violence of my affection" (*Pride and Prejudice* ch. 19). He might almost have done so, though. No wonder Catherine made at least one complaint about the stiff and formal way he had of writing to her (Pilgrim *Letters* 1: 109).

Yet it is clear that he loved her – that she deserved to be loved, indeed, much more than Maria had. For all their reticence, the letters reveal Dickens's deep affection for Catherine, their like-minded way of looking at the world, and his determination that their relationship should prosper. The affection is shown not least in Dickens's characteristically tender conclusions:

> ... without any disparagement to your letters my own dear Girl I would much rather have one kiss from you than half a dozen letters each on as many quires of paper.
> Love to all
> Believe me
> My ever dearest Katie

Most sincerely and affecy. Yours
Charles   Dickens
(Pilgrim *Letters* 1: 101)

Catherine seems to have been touchingly hungry for news of what her fiancé had been doing, seeing and hearing, he to supply it. The letters are full of stories, thoughtful and amusing, designed to satisfy this hunger, and they promise more: "I have been to-day over Newgate, and the House of Correction," one declares, "and have lots of anecdotes to tell you of both places when I see you tomorrow" (Pilgrim *Letters* 1: 88). Several letters touch on preparations for their life together. Dickens clearly kept Catherine informed of his initiatives, and consulted closely with her. "As your Mama has not seen the sideboard," he says in a letter about the chambers he was preparing for his bride, "and as there are a great number of new purchases even *you* have not seen (!) I think the best way will be for you, and she, and Mary,[7] to spend the day here, on Saturday" (Pilgrim *Letters* 1: 138).

Nor was Dickens concerned with domestic preparation alone. He wanted Catherine to think, as he did, about how they would relate to each other once married. From time to time she evidently became what they called "coss," at the way work kept him from her. That was as close as she got to Maria, in unkind behavior. Responding, clearly, to one such episode, Dickens writes:

If you knew how eagerly I long for your society this evening, or how much delight it would afford me to be able to turn round to you at our own fireside when my work is done, and seek in your kind looks and gentle manner the recreation and happiness which the moping solitude of chambers can never afford, you would believe me sincere in saying that necessity and necessity alone, induces me to forego the pleasure of your companionship for one evening in the week even. You will never do me the justice of believing it however, and all I can do until my book is finished will be to reflect that I shall have (God willing) many opportunities of shewing you for years to come how unjust you used to be, and of convincing you then of what I would fain convince you now – that my pursuits and labours such as they are are not more selfish than my pleasures, and that your future

advancement and happiness in the main-spring of them all.
(Pilgrim *Letters* 1: 95)

It is a wonderfully warm and tactful letter, beautifully calculated to ease
the distress of a young woman starved of the company of her husband-
to-be. Little wonder Catherine cherished it, with all the others, even
when she and Dickens separated after twenty-two years of marriage.

For all that, it is still a reticent letter. Dickens declines to become
effusive: Catherine does not know, will not believe, will find out only
later. In this case we could ascribe the reticence to literary technique.
Emotion named is less powerful than emotion shown. The novelist-in-
the-making was discovering the power of indirectness. This cannot be
more generally argued, though, as we have seen. None of the letters, in
fact, could be described as ardent. Intense erotic passion, longing, and
frustration are nowhere to be found: only longing for companionship,
contentment, tranquillity. Courtship as it is generally understood was
ruled out. Catherine was Dickens's wife-to-be. He was not going to
forget that, or let her do so. There is a kind of imperiousness in the way
he calls upon her to see their relationship, their impending marriage.

It seems to have worked, though, and not just in the short term.
Letters Dickens wrote in the aftermath of their marriage, to Catherine
and to others, show that the companionship, contentment, and
tranquillity he had hoped for were realized by it. In their first home at
Furnival's Inn, at Doughty Street, and in subsequent homes, the work of
construction went on, and entered a new phase. Dickens was a loving
and conscientious husband but, as always, an inveterate story-maker.
He could behave seriously and soberly when the occasion called for it,
and did, but he began immediately to elaborate a personal domestic
comedy, dramatized in his letters, in which Catherine plays an
appropriately comic part. It was probably one of the pleasures of her
marriage, to play along with Dickens's fabulizing, although it would
have taken a stronger woman than Catherine to do so without erosion of
the self.

Dickens was one of those young men who quickly fall into the arch
habit of speaking of their marriages, as if both they and their wives were
middle-aged, long married, and long settled into the humdrum. "My
missis" was the term he favored for Catherine (Pilgrim *Letters* 1: 134).

Edgar Johnson's biography of Dickens surely misinterprets some of the stories he told about Catherine. Johnson postulates suppressed anger in what Dickens has to say of mishaps that befell her, errors she committed (Johnson 905). Michael Slater's rebuttal enables us to see such stories as scenes in the carefully constructed domestic comedy (Slater 126-28). A letter to the Hon. Richard Watson, of October 1851 is typical. In it, Dickens bewails the activities of builders and decorators in Tavistock House:

> Catherine is here with me and sends her kind love. She is all over paint, and seems to think that it is somehow being immensely useful to get into that condition. We sit in our new house all day, trying to touch the hearts of the workmen by our melancholy look and are patched with oil and lime and haggard with white lead. (Pilgrim *Letters* 6: 533)

If there is a joke against Catherine here, there is equally one against Dickens himself, evidently just as spattered, just as ineffectual. Catherine's thoughts, truly represented or not, are announced not for the sake of ridicule, but to make the story funnier. And they do.

Dickens's talent for improvising comedy doubtless helped make the marriage the happy one it was, throughout the Doughty Street period and for many years afterwards. It is one thing to be constructed as an immaculate wife, another to be so constructed and to be laughing almost all the time. He and Catherine were content, at least until the early 1850s, enjoying good fortune together, enduring bad. Dickens's feelings for Catherine were deeper, if less intense, than his feelings for Maria had been. And for all its apparent repression during the engagement, desire plainly had a place in the marriage. She did bear him ten children, and Dickens could speak mischievously of one of her pregnancies as "that uninteresting condition" (Pilgrim *Letters* 5: 383). But companionable affection, tenderness, and laughter were what sustained the relationship, more important in the long run than extremes of passion. In the early days of their marriage, her sister Mary declared Dickens to be "kindness itself" to Catherine (*Dickensian* 63: 77). After seeing them both off to America in 1842, when they left their children behind, and faced the rigors of a January Atlantic crossing, Forster wrote to Daniel Maclise praising "Mrs. D's cheerfulness." "She deserves to be what you know she is so emphatically called – the Beloved" (Pilgrim *Letters* 3: 9n). This plainly reveals Dickens's attitude to Catherine for many years. In one respect only does it foreshadow the crisis that was to come.

Their happiness was achieved at a cost, I submit, paid by Catherine in the surrender of her will to his. She paid more still, in later years. Unlike "the Inimitable," which licenses almost any kind of behavior, "the Beloved" is a constraining sobriquet, prescribing a narrow range of behavior, and revocable at Dickens's will. We can glimpse here and there in the fiction the narrowing of personality Dickens's vision of the ideal marriage demanded. One of the *Sketches of Young Couples* shows what Catherine was called upon to become. The perfect marriage of the Nice Little Couple is sustained by the perfections of the wife:

> Mrs. Chirrup is the prettiest of all little women, and has the prettiest little figure conceivable. She has the neatest little foot, and the softest little voice, and the pleasantest little smile, and the tidiest little curls, and the brightest little eyes, and the quietest little manner, and is, in short, altogether one of the most engaging of all little women, dead or alive. She is a condensation of all the domestic virtues, – a pocket edition of the young man's best companion, – a little woman at a very high pressure, with an amazing quantity of goodness and usefulness in an exceedingly small space. Little as she is, Mrs. Chirrup might furnish forth matter for the moral equipment of a score of housewives, six feet high in their stockings – if, in the presence of ladies, we may be allowed the expression – and of corresponding robustness.

The cloying nature of this is offset by the humor, but none of it comes from Mrs. Chirrup, or gets back to her. The joke is shared only between narrator and reader. Mrs. Chirrup's business is to be little, and the littleness, surely, is a displaced acknowledgement of the constraining nature of the exercise. It is a physical manifestation of the narrow prescription needed to sustain Dickens's ideal.

It is hard to let Mrs. Chirrup pass without protest. We can see, though, how the imposition of such an identity might be made palatable by a context of good humor, high spirits, and abundant jokes. The wife of Scrooge's nephew, Fred, in *A Christmas Carol*, is from the same mould as Mrs. Chirrup, but is allowed the freedom of repartee, and of appeal to her friends:

"He said that Christmas was a humbug, as I live!" cried Scrooge's nephew. "He believed it too!"

"More shame for him, Fred!" said Scrooge's niece, indignantly. Bless those women; they never do anything by halves. They are always in earnest.

She was very pretty: exceedingly pretty. With a dimpled, surprised-looking, capital face; a ripe little mouth, that seemed made to be kissed – as no doubt it was; all kinds of good little dots about her chin, that melted into one another when she laughed; and the sunniest pair of eyes you ever saw in any little creature's head. Altogether she was what you would have called provoking, you know; but satisfactory too. Oh, perfectly satisfactory!

"He's a comical old fellow," said Scrooge's nephew, "that's the truth: and not so pleasant as he might be. However, his offences carry their own punishment, and I have nothing to say against him."

"I'm sure he is very rich, Fred," hinted Scrooge's niece. "At least you always tell *me* so."

"What of that, my dear!" said Scrooge's nephew. "His wealth is of no use to him. He don't do any good with it. He don't make himself comfortable with it. He hasn't the satisfaction of thinking – ha, ha, ha! – that he is ever going to benefit Us with it."

"I have no patience with him," observed Scrooge's niece. Scrooge's niece's sisters, and all the other ladies, expressed the same opinion.

"Oh, I have!" said Scrooge's nephew. "I am sorry for him; I couldn't be angry with him if I tried. Who suffers by his ill whims! Himself, always. Here, he takes it into his head to dislike us, and he won't come and dine with us. What's the consequence? He don't lose much of a dinner."

"Indeed, I think he loses a very good dinner," interrupted Scrooge's niece. Everybody else said the same, and they must be allowed to have been competent judges, because they had just had dinner; and, with the dessert upon the table, were clustered

round the fire, by lamplight.
"Well! I'm very glad to hear it," said Scrooge's nephew,
"because I haven't great faith in these young housekeepers. . . ."
(*Christmas Carol* Stave 3)

The coaxing narrative voice of *A Christmas Carol* contributes much here, of course, in counterpoint with the dialogue.

Neither of the above examples is from the novels, where readers rarely encounter unridiculed representations of contented married life in middle-class households. The exceptions that are found tend to be middle-aged or elderly couples, long set in their ways. Marriage itself, indeed, is relatively rare in the novels, except as a blissful coda to courtship, briefly narrated. Whenever Dickens relates at length both a courtship and the marriage that follows it, either the marriage is a failure, or his presentation of it is. Marriage is strongly featured in the Christmas books, to be sure, but the novels abound with bachelors, spinsters, widows, widowers, and irregular arrangements of one kind or another. Married life is featured chiefly to provoke laughter or despair, or both.

This is an observation that needs to be got into proportion. Good stories, for the most part, are about problems and solutions. The commonest class of problem in novels is that of finding the right partner in marriage. Novels, therefore, frequently end with weddings, and treat what follows only briefly or sketchily. They also offer warnings, grim or absurd, about the results of choosing a partner badly. Even so, it is hard to avoid the conclusion that successful middle-class marriage is rarer in Dickens's novels than even such reflection warrants. Needless to say, courtship is heavily featured throughout the novels. It is what they are for the most part about.

Perhaps Dickens had an uneasy sense of how forced and flimsy his vision of ideal marriage was. In one novel in particular, he strives imaginatively to encompass both courtship and marriage. Yet *David Copperfield* (1849-50) is arguably about their discongruity. It is noteworthy, too, for a vision of ideal marriage grounded, surely, much more in fiction than in experience of life. Courtship and marriage in fiction differ from courtship and marriage in life. In novels of courtship with male protagonists, it is usual for what we might call the wife-in-waiting to be foreshadowed as such before being acknowledged as such. The literary technique of foreshadowing merges imperceptibly into the literary construction of destiny. Very often, novelists contrive to make readers see the foreshadowed wife as the destined wife. Dickens clearly did this in writing *David Copperfield*. He had done something comparable in constructing his and Catherine's understanding of their life together, during their engagement. A few years after writing *David Copperfield*, he would do something comparable again, but negatively, rewriting his marriage, writing Catherine out of his life. But that is to look ahead.

The structure of *David Copperfield* reflects precisely what I have been saying about the discontinuity in Dickens's imagination between his conception of courtship and his conception of marriage. David courts Dora Spenlow and marries her. The marriage is a failure. He does not court Agnes Wickfield, but marries her all the same. The marriage is a success.

Both as a fictional character within the world of the novel, and as a product of Dickens's imagination shaped from disparate sources, Dora is complex, but the passion David feels for her is the passion Dickens had felt for Maria. Maria re-entered his life, briefly and absurdly, in 1855. Dickens told her the effect on him of seeing her handwriting on the envelope of the letter she sent him: "Three or four and twenty years vanished like a dream, and I opened it with the touch of my young friend David Copperfield when he was in love" (Pilgrim *Letters* 7: 532–33). Dora captivates David utterly. He courts her ardently, and overcomes obstacles. Once married, however, she finds it difficult to develop beyond girlish charm, and proves an incompetent wife. Fate intervenes. She dies. Having made the mistake of marrying a young woman not destined to be his wife, David must now discover his destiny.

He must in fact understand words his aunt, Betsey Trotwood, had uttered during their first conversation about Dora: "blind, blind, blind." "And so you think you were formed for one another . . . ?" she had asked sadly (ch 35). She knows Agnes Wickfield is David's destined wife, Agnes whom David had first met as her father's "little housekeeper," who had an air of tranquillity about her – "a quiet, good, calm spirit" – and who, pausing on a staircase above David, had seemed a figure from a stained-glass window (ch 15). Clearly Agnes offers David what Dickens sought in a wife, and more. David at last recognizes his love for her, but his aunt spares him the indignities and distresses of courtship, by telling him she suspects Agnes "has an attachment" (ch 60). The attachment is to David. Short of irresponsible playfulness, it is difficult to know what impels Aunt Betsey to say what she does, but the end justifies her means. David blunders into telling Agnes his love, while denying he could be jealous of anyone else. Readers attentive to foreshadowing, however, are not surprised to hear Agnes tell David, "I have loved you all my life!" (ch 62).

Uncertainty, delay, ambiguities of expression, ambiguities of love of different kinds, paradoxically charge the last few chapters of *David Copperfield* with an intense eroticism, and make them absorbing reading. Perhaps this offers a clue to how Dickens was sustained in what can seem his all too didactic construction of Catherine as a wife (Kucich 229–35). It is clear, at any rate, that *David Copperfield* is underpinned by his imaginative rereading of his wooing of Maria and wedding of Catherine. Reading the novel as a biographical source, against the lucidity implicit in his making David's marriage to Dora a failure, we must set the self-delusion implicit in the vapidity of Agnes. She is not much like Catherine. She is not much like anyone. Loyal whenever he could be, even Forster was wearied by "the too unfailing wisdom and self-sacrificing goodness of the angel-wife" (bk. 6, ch. 7). For Dickens, though, that was the point of her. Agnes was not modelled on Catherine. She was the ideal to which Dickens tried to make Catherine conform. The failure of Agnes as a fictional construction foretold the failure of the real Catherine perfectly to match the wife Dickens constructed in his imagination – foretold indeed the failure of Dickens's marriage.

Events in Dickens's life after the Doughty Street period are no concern of this book, except in so far as they illuminate the period, but the failure of his marriage does that, not least by revealing the interpenetration in his mind of raw fact and fictional construction. From the early 1850s, Dickens showed signs of becoming dissatisfied with his marriage. Catherine's loss of her beauty would not have helped. One observer in 1853 described her as "a great fat lady – florid with arms thick as the leg of a Life Guard's man and as red as a beef sausage" (*Oxford Reader's Companion* 155). The pretty little woman was gone from the ideal marriage which Dickens had constructed with so much imaginative effort, and this eroded his identity as much as hers. When he looked into the mirror, he told Wilkie Collins, "my blankness is inconceivable – indescribable – my misery, amazing" (Pilgrim *Letters* 8: 423).

In 1857 he became acquainted with an attractive seventeen-year-old actress, Ellen Ternan.[8] A month later, he was telling Forster, "Poor Catherine and I are not made for each other." She was not his destiny after all, that is to say. Irresistibly attracted to someone else, he found he could write Catherine out of it. Their parting was foreshadowed during the early days of their marriage, he discovered: "What is now befalling me I have seen steadily coming, ever since the days you remember when Mary was born" (Pilgrim *Letters* 8: 430).

Incident followed incident. Dickens grew closer to Ellen, more distant from Catherine, until they agreed the following year to separate. Meticulous as ever about the arrangements being made, Dickens was nevertheless consumed by rage and despair. If he displayed little self-knowledge, he clearly felt more than a touch of self-contempt. Katey, his daughter, remembered his being "like a madman" at the time (Storey 26). But after the separation, it is clear, despite scanty evidence, that he became devoted to Ellen. During the years that followed, she acquired homes in London, then Slough, then Peckham, probably with assistance from Dickens. There is evidence that he set up a trust fund for her (Ackroyd 994). They probably became lovers. That is certainly the most convincing hypothesis.

It is hard not to conclude that Dickens's exacting construction of Catherine, and of their marriage together, had always denied him satisfaction of impulses not easily suppressed. I am speaking not just of sexual impulses, which seem to have been pretty well satisfied by the marriage, for many years at any rate. Dickens's personality was nothing if not active, striving, exploratory. Everything in his marriage was too carefully composed and stabilized. It was a marriage deficient in dynamics. Maria had inspired him "with a determination to overcome all the difficulties." While his marriage to Catherine lasted, he had from time to time allowed himself to become chastely infatuated with other women. This was usually quietly tolerated by Catherine. There was usually at least a touch of the burlesque in Dickens's avowals of passion. These episodes seem to have met his need, in his imagination at any rate, to struggle against difficulties. In 1844, for instance, he was troubled, rather more seriously than usual, by his feelings for an eighteen-year-old pianist, Christiana Weller. On discovering she was being legitimately courted by his friend T. J. Thompson, he wrote her a magnanimous letter in support of Thompson's suit, not scrupling to remark, however, that had he been free, it would have been "the greatest happiness and pleasure of my life to have run him through the body. In no poetical or tender sense, I assure you, but with good sharp Steel. . . ." (Pilgrim *Letters* 4: 99).

A revival of the "determination to overcome all the difficulties" promised to repair Dickens's sense of identity, threatened by the collapse of his ideal marriage. Ellen restimulated this determination, together with the hyperbolic language of his earlier infatuations. He wished an ogre had taken Ellen "to his stronghold on the top of a high series of mountains, and there tied her up by the hair," Dickens declared. "Nothing would suit me half so well this day, as climbing after her, sword in hand, and either winning her or being killed" (Pilgrim *Letters* 8: 488).

One reason, perhaps, why Dickens's relationship with Ellen endured for the rest of his life was that, however much he might possess her, it preserved the need to overcome difficulties, which he found so energizing. Divorce from Catherine was no option under the law as it stood. Dickens's financial responsibilities to his family – not to mention to Ellen herself – were too great for him to risk alienating his public by following the example of G. H. Lewes and George Eliot. He had to contrive a concealed intimacy. He had perpetually to struggle against discovery, prejudice, and public opinion. It was the delicious anguish he had experienced with Maria all over again, but this time without the pain of rejection.

Dickens wrote *Great Expectations* during 1860 and 1861, two years after he had parted from Catherine, three years after he had met Ellen. In this novel, discontinuity between courtship and marriage is maintained, but with a surprising and vitalizing touch of verisimilitude. Pip courts Estella ardently, but she marries Bentley Drummle. After Drummle's death, she is free to marry again, but the novel ends teasingly. Bulwer-Lytton persuaded Dickens not to part Pip and Estella for ever in the last chapter, but Dickens still avoided precision. "I saw no shadow of another parting from her," Pip concludes (ch. 59). He could have been made to say, "Reader, I married her," or words to that effect, but Dickens's imagination refused to allow a transition from courtship into marriage. The complexity of their situation was doing the same for Dickens and Ellen. He at any rate seems to have been content. Perhaps that is why he ended *Great Expectations* as he did.

2.3 THE DEATH OF MARY HOGARTH

On 6 May 1837, Dickens spent the evening at the theater with his wife and her seventeen-year-old sister, Mary. Afterwards, they all returned to 48 Doughty Street, intending that Mary, as so often, should spend the night under her sister's roof. In Dickens's own words, Mary

> went up stairs to bed at about one o'Clock in perfect health and her usual delightful spirits; was taken ill before she undressed; and died in my arms next afternoon at 3 o'Clock. Everything that could possibly be done *was* done but nothing could save her. The medical men imagine it was a disease of the heart. (Pilgrim *Letters* 1: 263)

The intensity of Dickens's response to Mary Hogarth's death, and the significance of the way he remembered her, are things biographers and critics have striven to explain. Speculation about their relationship can be plotted on a scale between two extremes, too much of it clustering towards one end or the other. At one end are interpretations, often cloyingly sentimental, insisting that the relationship was chaste in every sense of the word, that her death, and his memories of it, were chastely inspiring. At the other end are interpretations, often debunking, insisting that the relationship and the memories were charged with erotic passion. Michael Slater's careful study of the evidence, therefore, has been widely welcomed (Slater 77–102). Yet the very sobriety of his account, I feel, minimizes some features that are irreducibly strange, all the more so for not being seen as such by Dickens's contemporaries.

As time passed, Dickens insisted more and more on the closeness of their mutual understanding. Twenty-one years later, for instance, as his marriage was crumbling, his memory told him Mary had intuitively seen, in its first months, that it was "as miserable a one as ever was made" (Pilgrim *Letters* 8: 558–60). But Slater is surely right to point out that, far from suggesting a league of understanding against Catherine, the evidence we have from the few years during which Dickens actually knew Mary, indicates nothing between the two of them that was not normal, correct, scarcely more than commonplace. He certainly took notice of her during those years, but nothing survives of what he said or wrote then, to indicate more than respect, cheerful affection, and gratitude.

Gratitude stands out. Mary's behavior deserved it. She was useful to the young couple: before their marriage as a chaperone; after the birth of their first child as an attentive aunt; between, as companion and helpmate to the bride of a busy journalist, often absent.

The letters Dickens wrote to Catherine before their marriage often contain polite inquiries after Mary's health, and send love – but usually to Mrs. Hogarth as well (Pilgrim *Letters* 1: 81, 85, 90). Only one singles out Mary. In it, Dickens invites his fiancée and her sister to breakfast in his chambers. Catherine is instructed to tell Mary, "I rely on her characteristic kind-heartedness and good nature to accompany you" (Pilgrim *Letters* 1: 65). Dickens intended a compliment, to be sure, but he wanted a practical result as well. Without Mary's presence the breakfast party would have been deemed improper.

In a letter written from Ipswich on 27 May 1836, after their marriage, Dickens tells his bride, "Give my *best love* to Mary" (Pilgrim *Letters* 1: 152). Catherine, it should not be forgotten, became pregnant almost immediately after the marriage on 2 April 1836 and, until her child was nearly three months old, lived in three small rooms, on an upper floor of Furnival's Inn, five miles by foot or horse-drawn vehicle from her parents' home in Fulham. This letter singles Mary out, but love is sent via Catherine, after all, and is surely an indication Mary was staying with her sister during Dickens's absence, as we know she often did. By this time, Catherine is likely to have guessed she was pregnant, and to have asked for a companion. The young couple were indebted to Mary.

Nothing we know of Mary's own views suggests the adulation of her brother-in-law some commentators have postulated, abetted not a little by Dickens himself in later life. To her, he was "such a nice creature and so clever he is courted and made up to by all the literary Gentlemen" (Pilgrim *Letters* 1: 689). This scarcely indicates infatuation. In a letter written after the birth of Charley, Mary praises Dickens for his attentions to Catherine, and remarks chirpily on the way "his time is so completely taken up that it is quite a favour for the Literary Gentlemen to get him to write for them" (*Dickensian* 63: 77). This contrasts with the serious tone in which she describes Catherine's suffering at not being able to nurse the baby. We can see that Mary loved her sister and was very fond of her brother-in-law, but there is evidence of nothing more intense than that. It is worth remembering, moreover, that there were advantages for her in the relationship, just as there were for Dickens and Catherine. From the age of fourteen, she was offered by it what was probably her first extended promotion to an adult role, with all the privileges that brings, and one played out, moreover, in the company of someone the world was beginning to take notice of.

That is not to say all was calculation on both sides. Dickens and Mary would have found much to admire in each other, and were evidently, in some sense, compatible. Nor should we discount erotic interest, I submit. He was personable, brilliant, and charming. By all accounts she was sympathetic, intelligent, and beautiful. The well-known engraving, after Phiz's lost posthumous portrait, gives her a rabbit-faced appearance absent from F. G. Kitton's appealing water-color copy of the original, on display in the Dickens House [fig. 3].

Whatever passed through Mary's mind, it seems unlikely that a man of Dickens's experience, instincts, and imagination would never have fantasized about a sexual relationship between them. More to the point, though, there is no indication whatsoever, before her death, that he was troubled by such fantasies. There is no trace even of wistfulness. The customs, manners, assumptions, and values of the day, and Dickens's own rectitude, seem to have enabled him to fence off any such fantasies, and prevent their disturbing him. We can assume, in other words, that any erotic interest on Dickens's part was no more than might be expected in the circumstances.

Nor should it be forgotten that, when he married Catherine, Dickens submitted himself to injunctions, both legal and liturgical, forbidding all hope of sexual intimacy with any of her sisters, forever. Psychologists declare fantasies about the death of one's spouse all but universal, yet had Dickens allowed himself such fantasies, he would still have seen his way to Mary blocked. Marriage to a deceased wife's sister remained illegal till 1908. The first attempt to legalize it was not until 1841. The Book of Common Prayer condemned as incest any sexual congress with the sister of a wife, before or after the wife's death. While Mary lived, there was ample incentive for Dickens deeply to suppress any such thoughts.

Dickens's relationship with Mary, then, while she lived, was unremarkable. Unless we suppose a loss of data, or uncharacteristic reticence on the part of Dickens, not given to concealing flirtations, that is what the evidence requires us to think. Extravagant things he said about her after her death, far from revealing feelings previously concealed, indicate a change and intensification of feeling, not merely permitted by her death, but caused by it. We can witness the process of change in the days and weeks following her death. The eventual intensity of Dickens's feelings for Mary, surprising to us, was evidently readily accepted by his family and friends. They would scarcely have been easy in their minds about such intensity while Mary lived, and must be supposed to have seen it as something permitted by bereavement.

On the day following Mary's death, Dickens wrote four letters (or four that have survived), to George Thomson, Harrison Ainsworth, Richard Bentley, and George Cox (Pilgrim *Letters* 1: 256–58). These tell of grief shared equally, by Dickens and Catherine. In each, key pronouns are predominantly in the first-person plural. Dickens speaks of what Mary had meant to "*us*," of her having been "*our* constant companion since *our* marriage." Several times he uses the phrase, "the grace and ornament of *our* home" (my italics). Catherine's own surviving words on the subject paint precisely the same picture of grief shared by husband and wife, mindful of each other's sorrow. "My dear husband loved her as much as I did," she says. "We have often said we had too much happiness to last, for she was included in all our little schemes and pleasures" (*Dickensian* 63: 79).

After the four letters of 8 May, the next relevant letter to survive is one written by Dickens to Edward Chapman on 12 May. This begins to register a change of emphasis that will quickly dominate. He broods on the funeral of the following day: "I hope that for one day at all events I may be able to bear *my* part in it with fortitude, and to encourage and console those about me – it will be no harder time to *anyone* than *myself*" (Pilgrim *Letters* 1: 259. My italics). This does no more than place him in the front rank of grievers. Others are still thought of. But the first-person singular begins to prevail, and his own sufferings to become the theme. And in a letter to Ainsworth of 17 May, Dickens speaks of "the dear girl whom I loved, after my wife, more deeply and fervently than anyone on earth" (Pilgrim *Letters* 1: 260). His love for Catherine is still declared the greater, but the love for Mary now spoken of is only his own, not Catherine's. One is left wondering, too, what kind of place Dickens was leaving in his affections for his own blood relations.

Before long, he became heedlessly eager to proclaim his grief and loss to be greater than anyone's: greater than the mother's who bore Mary, than his wife's, whose grief was held to have brought on a miscarriage. It was Dickens who bought the plot for the grave, a double plot in Kensal Green Cemetery, the second space in which he intended for himself. "I have lost the dearest friend I ever had," he famously declared (Pilgrim *Letters* 1: 263). He found himself unable to produce parts of *Pickwick Papers* and *Oliver Twist* that June, and an announcement inserted in that month's issue of *Bentley's Miscellany* told readers their author had lost "the chief solace of his labours." Later in the year, he told Mary's mother, "I have never had her ring off my finger by day or by night" (Pilgrim *Letters* 1: 323). At the beginning of the following year, he remembered Mary as "sympathizing with all my thoughts and feelings more than any one I knew ever did or will" (Pilgrim *Letters* 1: 629).

And if the sense of acute bereavement diminished, thoughts of Mary remained with Dickens for the rest of his life. On 7 May 1848, for instance, he wrote to Forster, remarking that "this day eleven years, poor dear Mary died" (Pilgrim *Letters* 5: 299). As late as 1869 he was saying,

> She is so much in my thoughts at all times, especially when I am successful, and have greatly prospered in anything, that the recollection of her is an essential part of my being, and is as inseparable from my existence as the beating of my heart is. (Forster bk. 11, ch. 3)

Lionized in America in 1842, he felt "something of the presence and influence of that spirit which directs my life, and through a heavy sorrow has pointed upwards with unchanging finger for more than four years past" (Pilgrim *Letters* 3: 35). Niagara Falls, especially, brought Mary to mind (Pilgrim *Letters* 3: 211).

More mysterious were the visions and thoughts of her that came to him unbidden. For months after her death, he dreamed of her every night (Pilgrim *Letters* 3: 483-84). When he told Catherine of this, the dreams stopped until one night in Genoa in 1844. A Madonna-like figure appeared in his sleep to Dickens, which he knew to be "poor Mary's spirit." Remarkably, given Dickens's prejudices, the spirit suggested in the dialogue between them that, for him, Roman Catholicism, among all the creeds, "is the best" (Pilgrim *Letters* 4: 196-97).

There is even a possibility that Dickens regularly commemorated the anniversary of his loss by devoting it to reflection upon all kinds of past suffering. He chose the twentieth anniversary of Mary's seizure (not of her death) as the day for making the 1857 visit, described in the preface to *Little Dorrit*, to what remained of the Marshalsea Prison (Pilgrim *Letters* 8: 321).

The perceptible intensification of Dickens's feeling for Mary, after her death, is surprising, and so is the apparent lack of concern this intensification provoked in others. One correspondent, not in the know, supposed it was his own sister Dickens was mourning (*Dickensian* 17: 152), but neither Catherine nor Mrs. Hogarth registered any kind of protest we are aware of, at what it is easy for us to see as a remarkable up-staging display of grief, not merely unconcealed, but positively publicized. Dickens delayed telling Catherine of his dreams, to be sure, but his eventual disclosure suggests the delay was designed more to spare her than to conceal anything. With Mrs. Hogarth, if we can judge from the tone of letters to her, Dickens had a kind of pact, jointly to cultivate grief. Six months after the event, he could speak to her of his having possessed "the affection of the gentlest and purest creature that ever shed light on earth." Far from worrying lest she start asking questions about her eldest daughter's place in his affections, Dickens looks forward with dismal relish to their time together during Catherine's forthcoming confinement, when "our words may be where are thoughts are, and . . . we may call up these old memories" (Pilgrim *Letters* 1: 323).

We might be tempted to suppose that Dickens's grief, when new, provoked criticism which has simply been lost, were it not for the fact that, twenty-one years later at the time of his separation from Catherine, none of the accusations brought against him, apparently, in any way recalls this episode or reproaches him for his part in it. There was gossip about others, precisely or vaguely identified: about Ellen Ternan, and about Georgina Hogarth, the sister-in-law who kept house for Dickens after Catherine's departure. But no one other than Dickens himself seems to have thought of Mary Hogarth, or to have recalled the episode as the focus of an old grievance or suspicion (Slater 135–62).

Mary's death, and Dickens's response to it, were real-life events which are generally agreed to have yielded effects in literature. But a more complex understanding of the way life and literature influence each other can be used to explain how Dickens's feelings for Mary, unremarkable during her lifetime, intensified after her death in a way unsurprising to his contemporaries, however surprising to us. Mary's death was an event shaped in Dickens's imagination, and as a result in the imaginations of family, friends, and contemporaries, by narrative – by literature, fantasy, a myth-making habit of mind. After her death,

Dickens's reconstructed his relationship with Mary, in a series of swift steps. He reconstructed aspects of her life and death. He constructed an after-life for her, because he believed in an after-life, to be sure, but also in order to meet his own emotional needs, and (what amounts almost to the same thing) in order to assimilate her into narratives he would make, about himself and about the creatures of his imagination. For Dickens, death released Mary from context into text: context over which he had no control; text subject to his imagination. What before her death had been unthinkable, and therefore not thought, became thinkable after her death, and therefore thought.

Dickens was of a literary generation fascinated by dangerous ambiguities of love. Great works it yielded, within a dozen years of Mary's death, include not only Dickens's own *David Copperfield*, but also Emily Brontë's *Wuthering Heights*, sailing even closer to the wind. Both novels tell of love which incorporates but transcends the erotic, love which blurs distinctions between the consanguineous and the erotic, love unaffected by marriage to other partners, love which persists even in the face of death.

Such texts were made possible by the eighteenth-century cult of sentiment, encouraging risk-taking analysis of feeling between the sexes, within which, however delicately, every possibility might be explored. Behind such texts stood Sterne with his Jenny and Eliza, Wordsworth with his Lucy. Sterne conducted sentimental correspondences with Catherine de Fourmantelle and Mrs. Draper. Lucy never existed. The poems probably record some of Wordsworth's feelings for his sister. But in each case, textual exploration of the complexities of love masks whatever real-life object of the writer's affection there might have been. Openness to possibility prohibits sharpness of focus, and invites the reader's indulgence.

Mary Hogarth, then, was by no means the first young woman, out of temptation's way, to be seen by a writer, at once or serially, as a child to be protected, a friend like no other, an object of sexual desire, and an object of religious veneration. Dickens was by no means the first writer to see a young woman in this way, and to meet with tolerance in doing so.

Writing to Forster as he was finishing *The Old Curiosity Shop*,

Dickens declared, "When I think of this sad story . . . dear Mary died yesterday . . . . Old wounds bleed afresh . . . " (Pilgrim *Letters* 2: 181-82). Michael Slater argues that this shows only how the experience of imagining Little Nell's death restimulated Dickens's grief at Mary's, not that Little Nell is shaped out of Dickens's feelings towards Mary. He draws attention to the lack of point-to-point correspondence between Mary and Nell, between what evidence shows Dickens felt for Mary during her lifetime and what the reader is invited to feel for Nell. But Mary became Dickens's Eliza or Lucy: a test bed for emotional experiment, a compensation for real-life emotional disappointments. Once she was released by death from the constraints of context, she became for him, within text, the object of every ardent and tender emotion it is possible for a man to feel for a young female.

Nell, who dies at the age Mary was when Dickens first met her, is placed at the center of an extraordinary complex of emotion. We are called upon to respond to her in ways, not easy to reconcile, but which, being reconciled, bring peculiar emotional rewards. "Child she certainly was," Master Humphrey tells us, "although I thought it probable from what I could make out, that her very small and delicate frame imparted a particular youthfulness to her appearance" (ch. 1). She experiences a child's terrors and anxieties. The text demands our protective instincts. Yet she is also the staunchest of friends: to her grandfather of course, to Kit, to virtually the whole population of the village where she ends her days. We are persuaded to admire her, as well as to yearn for her protection. Allowing what we will for difference of emphasis, motivation, and self-knowledge, we also have to admit that she is repeatedly an object of sexual interest: for Dick Swiveller, for Quilp, and for Kit. We are invited to sense the possibility of this interest, too, if only to deplore it in two out of the three cases.

And finally, of course, we are called upon to see Nell as an object of religious veneration, angelic, no less. The narrator contemplates her dead body:

> And still her former self lay there, unaltered in this change.
> Yes. The old fireside had smiled upon that same sweet face; it
> had passed like a dream through haunts of misery and care; at
> the door of the poor schoolmaster on the summer evening,

before the furnace fire upon the cold wet night, at the still
bedside of the dying boy, there had been the same mild lovely
look. So shall we know the angels in their majesty, after death.
(ch. 71)

Little Nell is placed at the heart of *The Old Curiosity Shop* to call up
in us a complex of emotions, initially painful and bewildering but
ultimately rich and satisfying, such as Mary's death, but not her life, had
permitted Dickens to feel towards her. His imaginative reshaping of
Mary after her death, and of their relationship, was not so much a
preliminary to the imagining of Little Nell, as part of the same process.

An extension of the process can be seen at work in Dickens's strange
dream in Genoa, three years later. From Moses to Freud, before and
since, attempts have been made to find deep significance and hidden
truth in dreams. Doubts, though, about the magical prescientific nature
of such interpretations have been reinforced in recent years by rival
neurologically-based theories, explaining dreaming as a process,
meaningless in itself, for sorting the contents of memory or dumping
mental trash. Old-fashioned Freudians have never been able to
construct an entirely satisfactory interpretation of the Italian dream, nor I
suspect ever will, seeking as they do profound significance, preferably
shocking. It does yield, however, to a more commonsense, less creaky
approach. Sometimes dreams contain accessible meaning, it seems
reasonable to assume, sometimes they do not. Often a dream can be
profitably interpreted by recognizing it as a mixture of sense and
nonsense. This, I feel, is the case with Dickens's Italian dream.

It does have to do with the big issues of Dickens's life, but not very
much. The iconographic pun made by his sleeping mind is revealing.
That *his* virgin Mary should become *the* Virgin Mary confirms and
augments what I have been saying about the way Dickens came to look
upon Mary after her death, and is suggestive about ways he had of
looking upon young girls and women in his fiction. Everything that
follows, however, has more to do with Dickens's art than his life – with
an artistic sense still vigilant even in his sleeping mind. Unsurprisingly,
in a dreamer in Italy striving to accommodate the tokens of Catholicism
by which he was surrounded, the iconography of the dream is utterly

Catholic. Mary appeared to Dickens like a Raphael Madonna. The rest follows from that. Dickens's veneration of Mary's spirit prompted his question about religion. In the dream Mary had to stand up for Roman Catholicism. Given the dream plot, she could scarcely have told him to reject papist flummery and stick to his Protestant guns.

When he contemplated Catholicism, especially as it was practiced in Italy in the 1840s during the reactionary aftermath of the Napoleonic Wars, sympathy and empathy were at war in Dickens. He was a man of his age, nation, and class, but his hostility to Catholicism grew out of more than that. It could not easily be accommodated with his demands for reform, his suspicion of obfuscating tradition, his dislike of reactionary and hierarchical authority. For all that, he had a genius for empathy, and a practical need to get inside the skins of Catholic men and women, for compositional purposes alone.   He had already attempted this, with only moderate success, in *Barnaby Rudge* (1841). In letters he was writing home to Forster, during his year in Italy, he was creating a prototype text for *Pictures from Italy* (1846).   There is no denying the anti-Catholic bias of the book, but Dickens could not have painted some of his cameo portraits of Italians without imagining what it was to be Catholic: the cowherd of the Villa Bagnerello, for instance, who tries to convert Dickens by repeating the story of St. Peter, "chiefly, I believe, from the unspeakable delight he has in his imitation of the cock"; or the Capuchin friar on the boat in Nice harbor, who "fasted, and talked, fasting, to everybody, with the most charming good humour; answering jokes at the expense of friars, with other jokes at the expense of laymen, and saying that, friar as he was, he would engage to take up the two strongest men on board, one after the other, with his teeth, and carry them along the deck" ("Genoa and its Neighbourhood").   These benignly depicted Catholics prefigure others Dickens was to imagine: the French peasant women who succor Mr. Peggotty, for instance (*David Copperfield* ch. 40), or Giovanni Baptista Cavaletto (*Little Dorrit* passim).

The dream refashioned Mary arbitrarily.   Perhaps it was appropriate that she should have been the one to give Dickens permission to enter minds counter to his own.   She became for Dickens, on this occasion, a mediator of reconstruction, gate-keeper, so to speak, to the transformational part of his imagination. The dream is a lesson about how, in Dickens, the imperatives of textual integrity could prevail over the imperatives of memory.

3

PICKWICK PAPERS: HORSES AND IGNOMINY

Pickwick Papers is about social mobility.[1] The possibility of such an uncluttered reading of the novel has been challenged in recent years. The book features too great an abundance, we are told, of "elements in excess of those required for the work's inner aims" (Smith 179). Social mobility, however, leaves little untouched for the individual experiencing it. *Pickwick Papers* is about many things, but very few of them cannot be related within the framework of such experience. Dickens had risen swiftly through the class system in the year or two preceding his move to Doughty Street, and he was continuing to do so. It is a subject with which he was understandably preoccupied, and out of which, in *Pickwick Papers*, he made an extraordinary book.

The central figure of the novel, Mr. Pickwick, is wealthy, but his background brings him few social advantages, and his behavior often betrays this. He seeks recognition as "a learned and distinguished man," and this is granted by his friends, members of the Pickwick Club. Others grant it too, persuaded by kindness of heart or reciprocal self-delusion. But knavery, especially of status seekers in competition with the Pickwickians, and folly, especially their own, repeatedly expose them to ridicule.

Mr. Pickwick does not achieve precisely what he seeks: he achieves something akin to it – but better. In an unemphatic way, the novel is a bildungsroman. Mr. Pickwick's redemption comes, thanks chiefly to a new manservant, the streetwise Sam Weller. Sam's guidance and assistance enable the goodness of Mr. Pickwick's heart to prevail. As a result, he acquires wisdom and the wider respect he craves. At the end of the book, he is able to abandon his pretensions to learning and intellectual eminence. He is content to be the man he is.

He jostles his way towards wisdom through a throng of other status seekers: the curmudgeonly Mr. Blotton (ch. 1), the officers of Rochester and Chatham (ch. 2), the Leo Hunters (ch. 15), Mr. Wardle's bad-tempered neighbor Captain Boldwig (ch. 19), Mr. Nupkins, the mayor of Ipswich (ch. 25), the company at the Bath assembly rooms (ch. 35), the rival editors of Eatanswill (ch. 51), and many others. The name alone of one such status seeker says it all. Its owner, Peter Magnus, complacently observes, "It's rather a good name, I think, sir?" (ch. 22).

And amid this throng, Mr. Pickwick is dogged by a subversive jester, Mr. Jingle, actor and fraud, who repeatedly, through mastery of style alone, dishonestly snatches the respect Mr. Pickwick struggles honestly to attain.

The phrase "learned and distinguished man" perfectly encapsulates the recognition Mr. Pickwick seeks, but it is not from *Pickwick Papers*. It is from the autobiographical fragment incorporated into Forster's biography. At Warren's, Dickens had despaired of ever becoming "a learned and distinguished man," but by the time he came to write *Pickwick* he was discovering what it was to be admired and rewarded for carefully cultivated skills and rare talent. The despair and the triumph are both recycled in the novel, ironically distanced. Dickens's longing for recognition and respect, still undiminished, emerges as Mr. Pickwick's. But we are invited to laugh at such longing, to recognize where it can lead when uninformed by experience of the world and judgment.

These come with the help of Sam Weller. Dickens acknowledges what he learned from the Marshalsea and Warren's in the figure of Sam – off the streets and streetwise. In the figure of Mr. Jingle he explores his own bewitching fluency of address, and the temptation it exposed him to.

The project of *Pickwick Papers* was launched by its original illustrator, Robert Seymour. In his preface to the 1847 Cheap Edition of the novel, Dickens tells how William Hall, of Chapman and Hall, visited his chambers in February 1836, to put to him proposals for contributions to a "monthly something":

> The idea propounded to me was that the monthly something
> should be a vehicle for certain plates to be executed by Mr.

Seymour, and there was a notion, either on the part of that admirable humorous artist, or of my visitor (I forget which), that a "Nimrod Club," the members of which were to go out shooting, fishing, and so forth, and getting themselves into difficulties through their want of dexterity, would be the best means of introducing these. I objected, on consideration, that although born and partly bred in the country, I was no great sportsman, except in regards of all kinds of locomotion; that the idea was not novel, and had already been much used, that it would be infinitely better for the plates to arise naturally out of the text; and that I should like to take my own way, with a freer range of English scenes and people, and was afraid I should ultimately do so in any case, whatever course I might prescribe to myself in starting. My views being deferred to, I thought of Mr. Pickwick, and wrote the first number.

Written more than ten years after the event, these words are disingenuous. Dickens was probably right to doubt the marketability of a "Nimrod Club" (Seymour's idea, not Hall's). For years, writers and print-makers, Seymour among them, had been poking fun at the sporting misadventures of "Cockneys" – not of working-class Londoners, that is to say, but of middle-class town folk, newly prosperous, keen to rise in society, keen to emulate the gentry, but handicapped by ignorance of country pursuits. Dickens did, of course, make his own way, with a freer range of English scenes and people. His thinking of Mr. Pickwick was clearly a momentous event in the history of English literature, not a lot affected by Seymour's plans. But despite his suicide after he had prepared the illustrations for the second number, Seymour left more of a mark on the project than Dickens chose later to recognize (Dexter and Ley passim; Kinsley xxii–xxix).

The very wrapper Seymour designed for the monthly parts [fig. 11] is made up of sporting motifs (Grego 1: 27–29). We see Mr. Winkle (or someone very like him) shooting at a bird and missing, Mr. Pickwick falling asleep over his fishing, clusters of whips, guns, nets, rods, bows and arrows. The "Sporting Transactions" of the Pickwick Club are advertised in a larger more elaborate font than its "Perambulations, Perils, Travels" and "Adventures." In the first chapter of the book, Dickens shows members' interests to be predominantly scientific, geographical, and antiquarian. Only Mr. Winkle is a sportsman. But in Seymour's first illustration, "Mr. Pickwick Addresses the Club" [fig. 12], we see a cluster of fishing tackle and a gun in the foreground and, to their left, what looks like a pool or snooker triangle (their predecessor in the early nineteenth-century was a game called "pyramids"). A bulldog at one member's feet suggests he is Mr. Blotton. A pelmet is decorated with a stag's skull and antlers. Pictures display horses, stags, and hunters. Significantly, such details are more numerous in the etching than in Seymour's preliminary sketch (Grego 1: 57, 59). Far from diminishing them, he was evidently intensifying sporting allusions.

Evidence that Dickens too was still mindful of the original plan is to be found in his agreeing with Chapman and Hall that Hablot Knight Browne should be appointed as Seymour's successor (Pilgrim *Letters* 1: 603). "Phiz," as Browne soon chose to be known, had already been commissioned to illustrate *Sunday Under Three Heads*, and *The Library of Fiction* (1836–37), a monthly magazine to which Dickens contributed. He etched two plates for later issues of the third number of *Pickwick*, to replace ones made during an unsuccessful trial by R. W. Buss, and went on to provide all the rest of the illustrations for the book.

Phiz was eminently qualified to provide sporting illustrations and, in agreeing to his appointment, Dickens kept his options open. Another applicant for the commission, whatever else he had to offer, clearly lacked this qualification. The young William Makepeace Thackeray, still seeking work as an illustrator in 1836, was rejected. As he admitted (a dozen years later in different circumstances): "I have not the slightest idea how to draw a horse, a dog, or a sporting scene of any sort" (Welcome 135).

It may have been John Jackson who recommended Phiz for *Pickwick* (Kinsley xxxvi). Jackson and his brother were engravers who worked for Chapman and Hall. Mason Jackson engraved the wrapper for the parts of *Pickwick* [see fig. 11], and probably thought of the book as sporting in emphasis: "I had seen sporting etchings by Seymour in Chapman and Hall's window in the Strand, and I suppose, if I thought about it at all, I must have looked upon this cover or title page of the 'Pickwick Club' as being intended for something of the same kind" (Hatton and Cleaver 23). Or it may have been J. G. Fennell who recommended the young artist (Kinsley xxxvi). Fennell, whom Phiz

Figure 11   Wrapper for the monthly parts of *Pickwick Papers*, designed by Robert Seymour, engraved by Mason Jackson. (By permission of the Dickens House Museum, London.)

Figure 12   "Mr Pickwick addresses the Club."   Illustration for *Pickwick Papers* by Robert Seymour. (By permission of the Dickens House Museum, London.)

would doubtless have met during his apprenticeship with William Finden, had made his reputation with artwork for *The Field*, still a country sports journal today.

Both Jackson and Fennell would have known what was probably, in 1836, Phiz's most celebrated achievement. Three years previously, at the age of eighteen, he had won the Society of Arts Isis Medal for an etching illustrating William Cowper's poem "John Gilpin" [fig. 13]. It shows the unfortunate linen-draper clinging desperately to the hired horse which, instead of conveying him docilely on a family excursion to Edmonton, runs away with him to Ware, and all the way back to London again. Readers of Dickens will spot some familiar details. We are shown a short, fat, bald, London businessman, who likes to cut a figure ("A train-band captain eke was he"), but who is not doing so, thanks to a horse. The poem is one of the earliest manifestations of the Cockney sportsman genre ("John Gilpin" was first published in 1782), and the illustration offers us a prototype Mr. Pickwick, characteristically afflicted.

Strictly speaking, of course, it is not a sporting illustration at all. Nor, with one debatable and trifling exception, were any of Phiz's illustrations for *Pickwick*. Two only feature horses, "The Break-Down" and "Mr. Bob Sawyer's Mode of Travelling." Neither has anything to do with sport. Only "Mr. Pickwick Slides" [fig. 14] is remotely sporting in its subject, and even that focuses upon Mr. Pickwick's tame diversion – before his accident – rather than on Mr. Winkle's failure as a skater. All the other plates depict the freer range of English scenes and people Dickens spoke of in 1847.

However, I am not suggesting Dickens simply adhered to Seymour's plan, despite what he said. He rejected most of it, but he kept something. And what he kept was horses. In hiring Phiz, he kept open an option for illustrations featuring horses and Cockneys failing to cope with them. The text of *Pickwick Papers* is rich in horses, and the problems they can cause. It was a topic pregnant with social import. There were material advantages to affording horses, plainly, but the evolution of cavalry as the keystone of the feudal system had made horses, and whatever is connected with them, markers of social status. European languages testify to the fact, in words like *cavalier, chevalier, caballero,* and *Ritter.* Other words, like *pedestrian, peon,* and *plodding,*

Figure 13   "John Gilpin." Illustration for William Cowper's poem, with which Hablot Knight Browne won the Society of Arts Isis Medal, 1833.   (By permission of the Dickens House Museum, London.)

Figure 14   "Mr Pickwick slides."   Illustration for *Pickwick Papers* by Hablot Knight Browne. (By permission of the Dickens House Museum, London.)

assume meaning in relation to them.

In the 1830s, not exactly a cloud on the horizon, but a puff of smoke and whiff of steam were threatening the preeminence of the horse. The railway age had begun (House 23–26). But the railway boom was not to manifest itself until the next decade. Macadamization, turnpike roads, significant improvements in the design of stagecoaches and of other carriages, were all sufficiently recent to have the glamor of new technology. Urban transport, moreover, was still entirely dependent upon horses, and almost all of it was prohibitively expensive. Even the London omnibus, introduced in 1829, two years after *Pickwick* opens, was priced for the middle-classes (Inwood 547). Before the omnibus, cabs were almost the only option for those who owned neither horse nor carriage, and wished to be conveyed around the city. Mr. Pickwick's cab from St. Martin-le-Grand to Charing Cross (ch. 2) costs him a shilling (twenty to the pound), at a time when Sam Weller was happy to be paid twelve pounds a year. Most city dwellers could rarely or never afford the use of horse-drawn transport.

Everyone understood, though, that easy familiarity with such things was the mark of a gentleman. However he was conveyed about the city, a gentleman had roots in the country, knew about riding, knew about driving, knew about moving from one part of the country to another by the most dashing kind of conveyance. For city dwellers not so lucky, the horse was a sign of status, style, and affluence. New recruits to the middle classes, of which there were many, were eager to become familiar with horses and what went with them, anxious over their ignorance of such matters. Books like Surtees's Jorrocks novels record their eagerness and chart their anxieties.

One group of people, though, unable to claim even middle-class status, knew more about horses than many gentlemen, and enjoyed a kind of freemasonry with the gentry because of their knowledge. I am speaking of working men in horsey occupations: coach drivers, cabmen, stage-coach drivers, grooms, farriers and the like: the fraternity of the stable-yard in the great coaching inns. How often does one hear stories of young lords, gone to the dogs, spending their times with grooms and stable boys? How often does one hear of young gentlemen being patronized out of countenance by stagecoach drivers who really knew how to drive four in hand? Getting on with such people, not losing face to them, getting them to do what was needed, must have set trials for anxious town-bred members of the middle classes, ignorant of horse lore.

There is clear evidence that Dickens had endured such trials, and was only just beginning to conquer ignorance and anxiety about horses during the Doughty Street years. He had no wish to acknowledge this to his friends, but in *Pickwick Papers*, I submit, he converted his errors and misgivings into comedy.

He had no wish to acknowledge his ignorance and anxiety to anyone, in fact. The wording of the 1847 preface to *Pickwick*, as I have said, is disingenuous. "Although born and partly bred in the country," Dickens loftily declares, "I was no great sportsman, except in regard to all kinds of locomotion." Without positively lying, this permits readers to imagine the young master neglecting the gun and tackle room at the manor for the stables. Members of John Dickens's family, however, would have been able to enjoy none of the usual country sports before the repeal of the old Draconian game laws in 1827, by which time they were living in London. And it seems that the only form of locomotion regularly practiced in the family was walking. The one possible exception is rowing. Inviting a friend to visit him on holiday in Petersham, in 1836, Dickens lists amenities, which include "horse for your riding – boat for your rowing" (Pilgrim *Letters* 1: 168).

But it was riding that became Dickens's passion during the Doughty Street years. And the letters he wrote about rides he took with Forster, Harrison Ainsworth and others are revealing. They suggest, not someone doing what he had always done, but someone affording a new kind of pleasure for the first time, and proud of it. In December 1835, two months before the discussion with William Hall, Dickens had been sent to report on an election in Kettering. Catherine, his fiancée, had plainly been under no illusion about his equestrian skills, and had objected to his "doing anything in the Ducrow way" (Pilgrim *Letters* 1: 109). Andrew Ducrow was a celebrated equestrian performer and co-owner of Astley's circus. On that occasion, Dickens had assuaged Catherine's fears by joining other reporters in hiring a chaise and driver. But a couple of years later he was affecting an insouciant attitude towards riding. In short notes he sent to Forster about proposed rides, he cheerily allowed himself to speak of "osses" (Pilgrim *Letters* 1: 297,

312).   This ambiguously acknowledges his kinship with Jorrocks, demeaningly housed by Surtees in Doughty Street. It leaves the reader wondering whether Dickens is patronizing those who share his enthusiasm without his style, or apologizing for being one of them under the skin.

There are indications, too, that he was not the master of horses he encouraged people to believe, that he had good reason to be anxious about his riding skills. Mrs. Touchet, who kept house for Ainsworth, and was the widow of his second cousin, had been a famous horsewoman in her youth. She declared Serjeant Talfourd, Ainsworth, Forster, and Dickens to be "Cockney riders." This so demoralized them that they avoided mounting their horses outside Ainsworth's house, where she might scoff at them (Ellis passim).

Not much more than a year before launching *Pickwick*, Dickens was acknowledging limitations to his driving skills too. During the 1835 general election, he had been sent by the *Morning Chronicle* to report on the contest in Chelmsford. "Being unable to get a Saddle Horse," he wrote to Thomas Beard,

> I actually ventured on a gig, – and what is more, I actually did the four and twenty miles without upsetting it. I wish to God you could have seen me tooling in and out of the banners, drums, conservative Emblems, horsemen, and go-carts with which every little Green was filled as the processions were waiting for Sir John Tyrell and Baring. Every time the horse heard a drum he bounded into the hedge, on the left side of the road; and every time I got him out of that, he bounded into the hedge on the right side. When he *did* go however, he went along admirably. The road was clear when I returned, and with the trifling exception of breaking my Whip, I flatter myself I did the whole thing in something like style. (Pilgrim *Letters* 1: 53)

The very boasting here is posited on an assumption of incompetence. On 20 August 1838, however, less than a year after completing *Pickwick*, Dickens rented a coachhouse and stable in Doughty Mews, behind the opposite side of Doughty Street, for his new phaeton and horses (Parker, "Mr. Dickens Sets up a Carriage"). In a letter to Forster, written at about this time, he announces, "I shall drive down to Barnes"

(Pilgrim *Letters* 1: 427). Not, "I shall go down to Barnes," note, but "I shall drive down to Barnes." Dickens was not going to let Forster ignore his new toy, or doubt his competence in playing with it.

Not so many years previously, his anxiety about horsey matters had even extended to bargaining for horse-drawn conveyances. In a letter to Kolle, probably written just before Dickens's twenty-first birthday in 1833, he begs his somewhat older friend to engage a coach for an excursion: "I know that the terms I should make would be higher than those you paid" (Pilgrim *Letters* 1: 14).

And this is the Dickens who, in 1847, implied that he had been, since his youth, a great sportsman "in regard to all kinds of locomotion." He was evidently letting his pride at having mastered horses and things horsey get the better of him. It had been one of the most satisfying accomplishments of his ascent through the class system. His ticket to upward mobility had been shorthand – the shorthand that he had taught himself as a lawyer's clerk at Ellis and Blackmore's, the shorthand that had carried him out of Ellis and Blackmore's, through court reporting, into journalism. But it is hard to make stenography glamorous enough to exploit in fiction, *David Copperfield* notwithstanding, and Dickens had begun to find journalism truly congenial only when he was allowed out of the press gallery of the House of Commons, to travel around the country as a roving reporter. Then, skill in stenography and growing familiarity with equestrian transport had blended to assure him he was getting on in the world. He spoke proudly in later life of having transcribed political speeches into longhand for the printer, "writing on the palm of my hand, by the light of a dark lantern, in a post chaise and four, galloping through a wild country, all through the dead of night, at the then surprising rate of fifteen miles an hour" (*Speeches* 347).

Dickens did not simply overturn Seymour's plan, then, as he suggested in 1847. Scoffing at Cockneys was not an unattractive notion for him. No one is harder on the arriviste than the last arriviste but one. But Dickens could not forget he was a Cockney himself, in the eyes of some at any rate, however unwilling he was to admit it. A story of a Cockney's adjustment to a higher position in the class system, therefore, a story of self-fulfilment and self-enlargement, was a different matter. He spied within Seymour's plan something which engaged more nearly with his own experience, and which he could use more profitably. He made equestrian inadequacy, and the learning of equestrian adequacy, metonymic devices, representing the handicap of humble origins, and adjustment to upward social mobility.

Mr. Pickwick and his companions repeatedly tangle with horses in *Pickwick Papers*. They misjudge them, are humiliated by drivers and grooms, climb clumsily into and out of horse-drawn vehicles, and are upset in them. The novel is punctuated by the departure of coaches carrying people off somewhere. The density of horsey incident diminishes as the novel proceeds, and encounters with horses become progressively less humiliating, but horses never entirely disappear. The process of getting used to horses, coaches, and horsey people calibrates Mr. Pickwick's acquisition of skills to match his wealth, his acquisition of worldly wisdom, and the broadening of his sympathies.

A common error, in modern responses to *Pickwick Papers*, is locating the Pickwickians higher in the social scale than Dickens put them. Dramatizations, for instance, tend to depict Mr. Pickwick and his friends as eccentric gentlemen, getting into pickles out of sheer foolishness. But the Pickwickians clearly do not belong to the mercantile élite which was converging with the gentry. No captains of commerce, no Dombeys or Podsnaps, they are more like John Gilpin. None is of grand origin, none has country roots, none has old money. George Orwell called his family "lower upper-middle class." We might call the Pickwickians upper lower-middle class. For all their prosperity, they come from that section of the middle classes with which John Dickens's son was most familiar.

None of Dickens's contemporaries had a keener sense of class difference than Disraeli. He speaks of individuals "who rank under the designation of retired gentleman," and instances one "who had been a tallow-chandler on Holborn Hill" (*Sybil* bk. 2, ch. 3). It is to this class that Mr. Pickwick clearly belongs. The advertisement for *Pickwick Papers*, issued on 26 March 1836, contains an address written by Dickens, declaring the Pickwick Club to be "renowned in the annals of Huggin-lane, and . . . closely entwined with the thousand interesting associations connected with Lothbury and Cateaton-street." Huggin Lane was a humble row, mainly of warehouses, quite different from the prestigious banking quarter of Lothbury and Cateaton (later Gresham) Street (Kinsley xxn). Dickens was comically pretending to smuggle the prestige of Lothbury and Cateaton Street into Huggin Lane.

And unwarranted claims to prestige set the tone of the novel itself, to begin with. Mr. Pickwick is esteemed at the opening of the book, by members of the club earnestly, by the narrative ironically. The club is unconscious, the narrative conscious, that this esteem is made possible by the smallness of the Pickwickians' world, geographical and social. To the larger world, he is not the "immortal" Pickwick, but a retired merchant, unwise in its ways, ill-equipped to cope beyond the bounds of his narrow experience.

There is only one member of the club whose occupation we learn: Mr. Blotton is a haberdasher. This is a rare clue to the preposterous parody of learning and distinction we are offered in the deliberations of the Pickwick Club. We are not told what Mr. Pickwick's occupation had been. Dickens seems to have been as reluctant to give him a fully realised background, as he was to divulge details of his own. There are clues to be found, however. Readers discover that Mr. Pickwick is retired from business, if not from what business. Contemporary readers would have noted that he lives in lodgings in respectable but scarcely grand Goswell Street. Modern readers can see that he is comfortable being looked after by a landlady, but views the taking on of a personal manservant as a major step. We see that he is anxious to be friendly with respected members of country society, like the Wardle family, and chagrined at failure to live up to their expectations. At the end, we discover that his idea of felicitous retirement is to a villa in Dulwich, among the green fields surrounding London.

The only Pickwickian about whose background we learn anything is Mr. Winkle. His father is a Birmingham wharfinger: a canal wharf owner, that is (ch. 50). Mr. Winkle Junior is eventually to join him in the family business (ch. 1). The construction of the Birmingham and Liverpool Canal in 1835, the year before *Pickwick* started to appear, had finally realized James Brindley's vision of putting Birmingham at the heart of a nationwide canal system. The Winkles' business, that is to say, is built upon infrastructure developments still new in the 1830s. The implication is that theirs was new money, not old.

Slender though the clues might be, then, it is clear that the Pickwickians are in fact Cockneys, in the archaic sense. They are prosperous, but town-bred, not marked as gentlemen by knowledge of country pursuits. In particular, they know precious little about horses. For Mr. Pickwick, climbing onto a coach is a risky venture, a defiant confirmation of his changed position in the world – hierarchical rather than geographic. Spatial and social mobility are conflated.

Mobility, however, is fully to be understood only in contrast to its opposite, stasis.[2] If the novel is punctuated by people being driven off in coaches, it is also punctuated by people getting stuck. The impulse to go out into the world, and demonstrate change of rank within it, is repeatedly frustrated, by stoppages calling into question such change.

Both the text of the novel and the illustrations are marked by another legacy of the Cockney sportsman genre, the ignominious spectacle, betraying skills unlearned and humble origins unevaded. Prints within the genre routinely capture the moment of humiliation – the Cockney sportsman flying over the hedge his horse has baulked at, or climbing out of the ditch in which it has deposited him. Dickens's sensitivity to such images may well have been intensified by memories of the ignominious spectacle he had made as a boy, stuck, degraded, and exposed to public view, framed by the window of Warren's establishment in Chandos Street.

As an adult during the Doughty Street years, though, Dickens was plainly skilled at playing the part his improved status demanded, and at concealing embarrassing features of his past. He knew Alfred Jingle from within. In 1836, while writing *Pickwick*, he began to frequent the Countess of Blessington's salon at Gore House, and mingle there with such notables as the Duke of Wellington and Disraeli. In 1838, Lady Holland admitted him to her Whig salon at Holland House, and he was made a member of the Athenaeum Club, where leading writers, artists, scientists, and politicians met. He made friends with such figures as Alfred Count D'Orsay, the millionairess Angela Burdett Coutts, and Edward Bulwer, later Lord Lytton ("Fashionable London," *Oxford Reader's Companion to Dickens*).

But there were obstacles to be surmounted, delicate balances to be achieved – and not everyone was prepared to be impressed. Lady Holland took the precaution of inquiring "if Boz was presentable." Her sister found him dandified (MacKenzie 74). When Dickens lampooned unauthorized dramatizers of fiction in *Nicholas Nickleby* (ch. 48), W. T. Moncrieff, whose version of the novel was being staged at the time, accused him of not showing the "good breeding of a gentleman." Nor had Dickens to watch his own behavior alone. His father's improvidence was a repetitive embarrassment (Greaves 74–84). For many years John Dickens contracted debts, got himself arrested, even forged bills in his son's name (Ackroyd 324). While Dickens was at work on *Pickwick*, his father exasperated him by borrowing money from Chapman and Hall, on the strength of the novel's sales (Ackroyd 214). Dickens knew only too well how easy it was to stumble or to be pushed into exposure and humiliation.

His own anxieties, then, may be detected behind all those representations in the novel, textual and graphic, of Mr. Pickwick (or someone else), trapped, degraded, exposed to misunderstanding and ridicule, often protesting or threatening in vain. They are comic, but comedy is regularly underpinned by anxiety.

It is not only failure to master horses that sets traps for the Pickwickians. Bad luck, knavery, and folly can be responsible too, often the folly of the Pickwickians themselves. Delusions of grandeur, the misreading of sexual intentions, and the law pose particular dangers. It is a comic novel, so there has to be rescue or escape from traps, or the story would end. At first, good luck, or people from whom Mr. Pickwick needs to learn are rescuers, but gradually he learns to escape unaided.

Not that mobility is always seen as good, stasis as bad. Irony is at work. Mr. Jingle and Job Trotter are rootlessly mobile; Mr. Wardle and his family are static for the most part, their roots admired. Mr. Pickwick's earlier expeditions teach him little, and usually result in his becoming stuck, often more than once. Ironically, it is being stuck (being stuck voluntarily, if the contradiction is allowable), that finally teaches him most, and earns him most respect. I mean, of course, his imprisonment in the Fleet. And it is stasis that all the Pickwickians achieve eventually, to their relief.

The exploration of the Hampstead Ponds, alluded to at the beginning of the novel, must have been pedestrian, but the new Corresponding Society of the Pickwick Club was to face new dangers, enumerated in the minutes of the club: "Stage coaches were upsetting themselves in all directions, horses were bolting . . ." (ch. 1). And we need look no further than chapter 2, before we find Mr. Pickwick out of his depth in horsey matters. He and his portmanteau are "thrown" into a cab at St. Martin's-le-Grand by a disrespectful waterman. Confident Mr. Pickwick can be trifled with, the cabman tells tall stories about the horse: that it is forty-two, that it is kept out two or three weeks at a time, that it is kept from falling down only by the large wheels of the cab, "so ven he *does* move, they run after him, and he must go on – he can't help it." Like Dickens as a young reporter, Mr. Pickwick writes in the vehicle on the move, making notes on what the cabman tells him. But unlike Dickens, Mr. Pickwick gets everything wrong. Not only does he fail to see he is being hoodwinked: he arouses suspicion about his motives. At the Golden Cross, where he is to catch the Rochester coach, the cabman offers to fight the "immortal" Pickwick – together with his friends – mistaking him for a licensing-authority spy. This yields the first of the ignominious spectacles in the novel, textual and graphic [fig. 15].

At this stage, the Pickwickians are at a loss when what we can fairly call horse-sense is required. They have to be rescued from their ignominy by Mr. Jingle, humiliatingly enough at the time, more so retrospectively. Now they know neither Jingle's name nor his occupation. One thing is manifest, though. He has the gentlemanly authority they lack. "Here, No. 924," he orders the cabman, "take your fare, and take yourself off – respectable gentleman, – know him well – none of your nonsense!" Stagecoaches and their drivers daunt him no more than cabs and cabmen. He mischievously assists Mr. Pickwick onto the roof of the coach, "with so much precipitation as to impair the gravity of that gentleman's deportment very materially." He cheerfully usurps the prerogative of the coachman, and tells the Pickwickians to duck as they pass beneath the stable-yard arch. Whatever other advantages he contrives, Mr. Jingle's mastery of horsey matters enables him to dominate and patronize the Pickwickians.

It will soon become clear, though, that he can claim no superiority in birth, breeding, or social station. Even at this stage he is plainly much less prosperous than they are. But he is an actor, with an actor's sense of style, gentlemanly or otherwise. He relies on his telegraphic speech being understood as an idiosyncrasy, but it enacts his piecemeal improvisation of identity, gentlemanly, dashing, extravagant. Jingle is a charismatic and ambivalent figure. Dickens plainly had an affection for

Figure 15   "The Pugnacious Cabman."   Illustration for *Pickwick Papers* by
Robert Seymour. (By permission of the Dickens House Museum, London.)

the skilful deceivers and hypocrites he imagined. He too enacted the person he wanted to be. Only their motives are different from his. Mr. Jingle exasperates Mr. Pickwick, not just because he cheats and humiliates him, but also because, unaided by financial substance, unencumbered by moral substance, he effortlessly achieves what Mr. Pickwick struggles for. He is deferred to and respected – until he is next exposed, at any rate. That enrages Mr. Pickwick, and it excited ambivalent feelings in Dickens. Jingle's being an actor is a sign of his especial closeness to Dickens himself. He is the *pièce noir* to Mr. Crummles's *pièce rose*.

Chapters 5 and 9 of *Pickwick Papers* offer a distinctive and illuminating contrast. Each tells of the hiring of a carriage, an eventful journey in it, and a mishap. In chapter 5, in order to travel to Dingley Dell, the Pickwickians hire a horse and chaise, plus a saddle horse, from the Bull at Rochester. They are teased and laughed at by the inn-yard fraternity, which sees no need for respect. "Shy, sir?" the ostler replies to Mr. Pickwick's anxious question. "He wouldn't shy if he was to meet a vaggin-load of monkeys with their tails burnt off." Mr. Winkle's attempt to mount the saddle horse from the wrong side delights a post-boy and an "inexpressibly gratified" waiter. The sequel, inevitably, yields an ignominious spectacle (with corresponding illustration). On the road, Mr. Pickwick drops his whip. Mr. Winkle dismounts for it, and cannot remount. Mr. Pickwick gets down to help, both horses run off, and the chaise is wrecked. Mr. Pickwick contemplates the recaptured chaise horse "with looks of hatred and revenge; more than once he had calculated the probable amount of the expense he would incur by cutting its throat . . . ." They complete the journey on foot. A man at a public house supposes them to be horse thieves. Their incompetence is exposed to Mr. Wardle. Ignorance of horses has betrayed them.

Mr. Wardle's pursuit of Jingle and Miss Rachael, eloping together, is the subject of chapter 9. Mr. Wardle's social standing is an enigma for modern readers. It would have been ambiguous, I believe, for contemporary readers, but they would have learned to live with the ambiguity. He is introduced as a "stout old gentleman" in his own barouche (ch. 4), and he keeps a gig as well (ch. 9). Text and illustrations together make it plain that his home, Manor Farm, Dingley

Dell (ch. 5), is farm and manor both, not a farm producing food for consumption at a separate manor. The establishment is a large one, with many servants, some in uniform, and it is clear the family has been in occupation for generations: the custom of celebrating Christmas Eve in the kitchen has been "observed by old Wardle's forefathers from time immemorial" (ch. 28). The kitchen is not the sole focus of life in the house. There is also a parlor (ch. 6), and a "best sitting room" as well, "a good, long dark-panelled room with a high chimney piece, and a capacious chimney, up which you could have driven one of the new patent cabs, wheels and all." At least one titled member of the gentry – Lady Tollimglower – is among the family's acquaintance (ch. 28).

But Mr. Wardle is also a working farmer. His home is repeatedly called "the farm." Farmers among the guests in the parlor, during the Pickwickians first visit, compare the merits of Mr. Wardle's land with Mullins's Meadows (ch. 5). "All the men, boys, and hobbledehoys attached to the farm" assemble for the wedding in chapter 28. In the background of "Mr. Pickwick Slides" [fig. 14], we see an undeniable farm, with ancient farmhouse, farmyard, barn, and ricks.

There are moments when the text seems to suggest Mr. Wardle is a small squire working his own land. In chapter 28, for instance, he is called "the hearty old landlord." This could just mean head of the family, though, or host of the party. There are other moments when the text seems to suggest he is a substantial yeoman farmer. The same chapter extols the best sitting room, by remarking that "If any of the old English yeomen had turned into fairies when they died, it was just the place in which they would have held their revels." The ambiguity is deliberate. Landlords, freehold farmers, and large tenant farmers had done well during the Napoleonic Wars, and had been protected by the Corn Laws since. Small squires and rich farmers were converging, moreover. The latter were being criticized for "aping their betters," for changing their manners and patterns of consumption, for driving gigs and fox-hunting (Wood 17; Trevelyan 4: 30). Mr. Wardle, in other words, represents another class in which the upward mobility Mr. Pickwick has experienced was happening. But the rich farmers merging into the squirarchy were plainly not embarrassed by ignorance of country matters, as upwardly mobile Cockneys were. Mr. Wardle is supremely well-equipped to manage an equestrian expedition.

No one in the Blue Lion yard would dare tease or laugh at him:

> "Chaise and four directly! – out with 'em! Put up the gig afterwards."
> "Now boys!" cried the landlord – "chaise and four out – make haste – look alive there!"
> Away ran the hostlers and the boys. The lanterns glimmered, as the men ran to and fro; the horses' hoofs clattered on the uneven paving of the yard; the chaise rumbled as it was drawn out of the coach-house; and all was noise and bustle.
> "Now then! – is that chaise coming out tonight?" cried Wardle.
> "Coming down the yard now, sir," replied the hostler.
> Out came the chaise – in went the horses – on sprung the boys – in got the travellers.
> "Mind – the seven-mile stage in less than half an hour!" shouted Wardle.
> "Off with you!"
> The boys applied whip and spur, the waiters shouted, the hostlers cheered, and away they went, fast and furiously.

This episode highlights the contrast between Mr. Wardle's confident demeanour in such circumstances, and the Pickwickians' faltering one. During the pursuit, the gentleman farmer understands the horses, the people, the road, the customs, the tricks. Mr. Pickwick understands none of them. Mr. Jingle has bribed horsey functionaries on the road to delay pursuers:

> Had Mr. Pickwick been alone, these multiplied obstacles would have completely put an end to the pursuit at once, but old Wardle was not to be so easily daunted; and he laid about him with such hearty good-will, cuffing this man, and pushing that; strapping a buckle here, and taking in a link there, that the chaise was ready in a much shorter time than could reasonably have been expected, under so many difficulties.

Like the Pickwickians' excursion from the Bull, this expedition ends in an accident, and an ignominious spectacle (duly illustrated), but this time it is the result of taking risks, not of ineptitude. Mr. Wardle gets as much as can be got out of the chaise and horses. Mr. Pickwick is helpless. Later events, however, suggest he has learned from the experience. And he soon finds expert tuition in such matters. In the next chapter, in fact. The gentleman farmer, Mr. Wardle, befriends and teaches Mr. Pickwick. So does the servant, Sam Weller, introduced in chapter 10. And an important common denominator is horsiness. There is an ancient equation between the plebeian and the gentleman, both of them free in spirit and unconfined by bourgeois manners, the plebeian because he is beneath the bourgeoisie, the gentleman because he is above it. In literature the equation is often manifested in the tradition of the comic servant. Sam makes the equation richer by knowing about horses. He is a working man, expert with horses, enjoying thus a freemasonry with the gentry. He is the son of a stagecoach driver (ch. 20). He has worked for both a carrier and a waggoner (ch. 16). Even in Mr. Pickwick's livery there is a hint of horsiness about him (ch. 12). And, naturally, he is utterly competent with horses. "Can you drive?" the fat boy asks him. "I should rayther think so," he replies (ch. 28).

Critics ought to be cautious about proclaiming a pair of characters in a novel a neat division of the novelist's personality. All successful characters are arguably developed out of what the novelist finds within himself. Yet Samuel Pickwick plus Samuel Weller approximate to a recognizable Dickens. Neither does by himself. Add more and the image becomes diffuse. The same may be said of Oliver Twist plus the Artful Dodger, and Nicholas Nickleby plus Smike. This device of pairing was a compositional technique Dickens adopted during the Doughty Street years, in order to review and to exploit his personal history. In their different ways, Mr. Pickwick, Oliver Twist, and Nicholas Nickleby are all middle-class. In ways just as different, all three of them are exposed to degradation. And all three find companions who supply what is needed for a fuller representation of what Dickens brought away from his own degradation. Mr. Pickwick embodies Dickens's innocent ambition, Sam his worldly wisdom. Each critiques and learns from the other. At the end of the novel they are inseparable. It makes a good story, and is a parable of Dickens's own personal growth.

Sam's skill and confidence in horsey matters metonymically represent what he offers Mr. Pickwick to make him more successful in life, not least in social advancement. He supplies the common touch and common sense. But to begin with he is more of a loose cannon than readers tend to remember, won over by Dickens's subsequent development of the character. There is a marked tendency, in *Pickwick Papers*, for characters to wander away from the plot, of their own volition. From the start, however, Sam displays the sharpness of judgment Mr. Pickwick clearly lacks, which is promising. He handles Mr. Perker adroitly, he sees through Mr. Jingle and Miss Wardle (ch. 10). On the occasion of his hiring, Mr. Pickwick's demeanour is marked by diffidence and uncertainty, Sam's by supreme confidence (ch. 12).

Soon, Sam finds it expedient to dip into his reservoir of horsey wisdom, but it is not made clear to the reader whether he is trying to provoke his master or to educate him. During the Eatanswill election, Sam tells a story about his father, a stage-coach driver, and the kind of electoral malpractice the Great Reform Act had, if anything, aggravated (Altick 674–76). It is a story about a transaction between a gentleman and a horsey plebeian:

> "'It's a wery bad road between this and London,' says the gen'l'm'n – 'Here and there it *is* a heavy road,' says my father – 'Specially near the canal, I think,' says the gen'l'm'n – 'Nasty bit that 'ere,' says my father – 'Well, Mr. Weller,' says the gen'l'm'n, 'you're a wery good whip, and can do what you like with your horses, we know. We're all wery fond o' you, Mr. Weller, so in case you *should* have an accident when you're a bringing these here woters down, and *should* tip 'em over into the canal vithout hurtin' 'em, this is for yourself,' says he – 'Gen'l'm'n, you're wery kind,' says my father, 'and I'll drink your health in another glass of wine,' says he; vich he did, and then buttons up the money, and bows himself out. You vouldn't believe, Sir," continued Sam, with a look of inexpressible impudence at his master, "that on the wery day as he came down with them woters, his coach *was* upset on that 'ere wery spot, and ev'ry man on 'em was turned into the canal."
>
> "And got out again?" inquired Mr. Pickwick, hastily. "Why," replied Sam, very slowly, "I rather think one old gentleman was missin'; I know his hat was found, but I a'n't quite certain whether his head was in it or not. But what I look at, is the hex-tra-ordinary, and wonderful coincidence, that arter what that

gen'l'm'n said my father's coach should be upset in that wery
place, and on that wery day!" (ch. 13)

Mr. Pickwick is neither provoked nor educated by this. Mischief with
horses simply mystifies him. To him it is just "a very extraordinary
circumstance indeed."

But perhaps readers should suppose Sam is in fact testing his master,
and is impressed by his innocence and kindness of heart. Certainly,
from this point on, with Sam by his side, Mr. Pickwick begins to acquire
new wisdom and new social skills, both manifesting themselves in
horsey savoir-faire. Mobility is achieved with less fuss. When he again
encounters Jingle at Mrs. Leo Hunter's, he is able to organize Sam and
himself onto a coach in pursuit, as briskly as Mr. Wardle might. While
Mr. Tupman is still dancing and quaffing champagne, the two Samuels,
"perched on the outside of a stage coach, were every succeeding minute
placing a less and less distance between themselves and the good old
town of Bury Saint Edmunds" (ch. 15). And it is aboard this coach that
Mr. Pickwick's sentimental education begins, as he learns about Sam's
early vagabond experiences, about "Sights, sir, . . . as 'ud penetrate your
benevolent heart, and come out on the other side" (ch. 16).

After being introduced to Tony Weller, Sam's father, Mr. Pickwick
gradually becomes even more at ease on horse-drawn vehicles. Fellow-
feeling with horsey plebeians is a mark of the gentleman, so it indicates
development when Mr. Pickwick evolves from being the butt of a
cabdriver into the confidant of coachmen, and is repeatedly given the
place of honor on the box beside them. When the elder Weller takes
him to Ipswich, it is Mr. Magnus who makes a fool of himself, not Mr.
Pickwick (ch. 22). When the Pickwickians go to Dingley Dell for
Christmas (ch. 28), the clown is actually one of the horsey fraternity, the
guard who falls into the boot with the codfish, and it is Mr. Pickwick
who smiles and dispenses comfort in the shape of hot brandy and water.

By the time of his journey to Bath in chapter 35, Mr. Pickwick is no
longer the target of irony. The narrative is knowing and relaxed about
coaching. The ironic vignettes are at the expense of others:

> The outsides did as outsides always do. They were very
> cheerful and talkative at the beginning of every stage, and very
> dismal and sleepy in the middle, and very bright and wakeful

again, towards the end. There was one young gentleman in an India-rubber cloak, who smoked cigars all day; and there was another young gentleman in a parody upon a great coat, who lighted a good many, and feeling obviously unsettled after the second whiff, threw them away when he thought nobody was looking at him. There was a third young man on the box who wished to be learned in cattle, and an old one behind, who was familiar with farming. There was a constant succession of Christian names in smock frocks and white coats, who were invited to have a "lift" by the guard, and who knew every horse and hostler on the road and off it; and there was a dinner which would have been cheap at half-a-crown a mouth, if any moderate number of mouths could have eat it in the time.

On this journey, indeed, roles are exchanged, and Mr. Pickwick has to teach Sam common sense. It is Sam who looks for a fight because the coach proprietor dares claim his master's name, Mr. Pickwick who calms him down.

As Mr. Pickwick becomes more at ease with horses and on coaches, so he becomes less of a buffoon. He gets into pickles, less through naivety, more through sticking to principle (though that too is something about which he has to learn a lesson). He becomes indignant, less over trifles, more over real issues. Contrast the quarrel with Mr. Tupman over fancy dress in chapter 15, and the quarrel with Sam over the latter's resolve to stay in the Fleet with him in chapter 42. Mr. Pickwick's acceptance among coachmen confirms Mr. Wardle's judgment in accepting him into country society. The development of Mr. Pickwick's compassion is intimately linked with all this. He learns to feel for sufferers from poverty and misfortune. In the Fleet, he even learns to feel sympathy for rascals like Jingle and Job Trotter, dupes like Mrs. Bardell. He learns to use wealth, not just to finance self-indulgent jaunts, but also to relieve suffering, even of those who have humiliated him.

He has been educated not least by falling into humiliating traps, seeing his companions fall into them, learning to spot them, learning to endure them, and learning to escape from them. Many of the traps are pitfalls dug specially for the socially mobile.

The Pickwickians nourish delusions of grandeur, but peculiarly innocent delusions. They quarrel foolishly among themselves over procedure and style, but in their dealings with the larger world are substantially free of snobbery and malice. This leaves them dangerously exposed. In Rochester, society is meanly stratified and exclusive (ch. 2). In Mr. Jingle's words, "Dock-yard people of upper rank don't know Dock-yard people of lower rank – Dock-yard people of lower rank don't know small gentry – small gentry don't know tradespeople – Commissioner don't know anybody." And he puts the Pickwickians at risk in these circumstances, because he is anarchic and unscrupulous. He flatters an elderly widow at a ball, and excites the jealously of an army doctor, who is astounded by his impudence: "He, Doctor Slammer, of the 97th, to be extinguished in a moment, by a man whom nobody had ever seen before, and whom nobody knew even now!" The doctor's outrage, mistaken identity, and Mr. Winkle's unwisdom propel the latter onto the duelling field, where he is exposed to insult, and threatened by injury or death – an ignominious spectacle if ever there was one. Good luck and some quick thinking rescue him, together with the Pickwickians' reputation – until Dr. Slammer learns of their association with Jingle, that is, and of Jingle's profession. Then they are obliged to endure the officers' sneers (ch. 3).

Eatanswill (ch. 13) embodies civic self-importance. Its people, "like the people of many other small towns, considered themselves of the utmost and most mighty importance." In Rochester the Pickwickians had been unknown. Here they are known, and accepted at their own estimation. But lionization proves less than gratifying. They are distressed and humiliated by almost everything that happens to them: the newspaper editors' rivalry, the mayhem of the election, the Potts' domestic disharmony, Mrs. Leo Hunter's pretensions. They are trapped in ignominious spectacles. Mr. Pickwick is buffeted by the election mob, and jeered at. Mr. Winkle is compromised by the warmth of Mrs. Pott's interest (ch. 18). All three of Mr. Pickwick's companions are lured into preposterous costumes for the *fête champêtre*, only to suffer, with their leader, the indignity of having Mr. Jingle introduced to them as "a gentleman of fortune" (ch. 15). Mr. Pickwick's ability promptly to extricate himself from Eatanswill, however, marks a small improvement.

By the time he visits Bath, he is demonstrably better able to acquit himself, however trapped, demonstrably more assured in his judgment. Pump-Room society is gentlemanly, not to say aristocratic, but it is fixated upon the minutiae of class distinction and grotesquely materialistic. Its weekly balls are "rendered bewitching . . . above all, by the absence of tradespeople, who are quite inconsistent with Paradise." Social intercourse is regulated by income and expectations. "Good God, Jane, how can you think of such things?" a mother exclaims at her daughter's choice of dancing partner. "Haven't you repeatedly heard that his father has eight hundred a-year, which dies with him?" (ch. 35). Sam Weller's experience at the "swarry" counterpoints these revelations, lower down the social scale (ch. 37).

In Bath, once again, the Pickwickians are accepted at their own estimation, but Mr. Pickwick is impressed neither by flattery, nor by fops offered for his admiration. "Delightful young man, his lordship," the Master of the Ceremonies, remarks. "'So I should think,' rejoined Mr. Pickwick, drily." He is trapped here, but, significantly, not in an ignominious spectacle, even though a plate depicts the occasion. There is no loss of dignity. Forbearance is all that is needed for a trying evening in the assembly rooms, losing at cards to merciless dowagers. Mr. Pickwick's response is not related, when his friends, "all protested that they had scarcely ever spent a more pleasant evening" (ch. 35). Silence, we gradually discover, is a sign of learning in Mr. Pickwick.

In Bath, it is only Mr. Winkle's misadventure with Mrs. Dowler that calls for active escape (ch. 36). Trapped outside by a slammed door at three in the morning, clad only in his dressing gown, he seeks to conceal himself by clambering into the sedan chair she already occupies. Mr. Dowler is told his wife is "running away with another gentleman," and pursues Mr. Winkle with violent intentions. Traps such as this, sprung by perceptions of sexual incontinence, are frequent in both the text and the illustrations of *Pickwick Papers*.

Dickens plainly drew on his experience of farce in shaping such episodes. Early nineteenth-century theater programs usually concluded with a farce. In the early 1830s, Dickens later declared, he had gone to the theater every night for two or three years (Kaplan 90). And he had written two farces himself, before moving to Doughty Street. A recurrent feature of the genre is men trapped, hiding, and finally exposed, in sexually compromising circumstances. Pretensions are thus punctured, ambitions thwarted. But for all that the literary source is clear, such episodes in *Pickwick Papers* add something peculiar to this novel, among all of Dickens's works, to the standard template of farce.

Pickwick Papers is drily, unemphatically, and unmaliciously misogynous. Women in it are eager to receive the tribute of sexual attention, but respond perversely at the merest thought or suggestion of it. They demand it when it is unlikely to be forthcoming. They detect it when it is not being offered. They react with inappropriate tenderness or indignation, whether it is or is not. Their responses are generally contradictory, and bewildering to men.

On Christmas Eve at Dingley Dell, old Mrs. Wardle consents to be kissed by Mr. Pickwick beneath the mistletoe,

> but the younger ladies, not being so thoroughly imbued with a superstitious veneration for the custom – or imagining that the value of a salute is very much enhanced if it cost a little trouble to obtain it – screamed and struggled, and ran into corners, and threatened and remonstrated, and did everything but leave the room until some of the less adventurous gentlemen were on the point of desisting, when they all at once found it useless to resist any longer and submitted to be kissed with a good grace. (ch. 28)

This is a paradigm. Even old Mrs. Wardle routinely declares men can have no interest in "an old 'ooman like me," in order to have it denied (chs. 6 and 28). Even Arabella Allen, who will eventually marry Mr. Winkle, is "observed to scream very loudly," when he offers to help her over a stile (ch. 28). The comedy is genial and affectionate, but pronounced and consistent. Representations of female perversity are to be found throughout Dickens's novels, but only in *Pickwick* is it made a comic norm; only in *Pickwick* is virtually every female character incurably contrary, and incapable of learning better.

Dickens was of course exploiting an ancient tradition of anti-woman comedy (Slater 221–42), but why so single-mindedly? It is worth remembering that he began the novel within three years of losing the unforgotten Maria Beadnell, and during his engagement to Catherine Hogarth. He completed it securely and happily married to Catherine. In such swiftly changing and emotionally volatile circumstances, it must have been tempting to distance the suffering and confusion these events caused him, by constructing within the novel a universal principle of female perversity, to be laughed at rather than agonized over. Not only was caprice like Maria's, which had caused him such suffering, softened into comedy. Catherine's exasperating "cosness," at the way work kept him from her, also became material for comic celebration. Pinning men down, keeping them from exploits in the wider world, is one of the fates women threaten in *Pickwick Papers*. In winning Catherine, Dickens had secured a redoubt in the class in which he sought acceptance, but she had sought to restrain his sallies out of that redoubt, his way of winning further upward mobility for both of them.

Women are mantraps in *Pickwick Papers*, widows in particular. From among the cluster of male anxieties about widows, the novel highlights above all the supposition that they are not to be changed. If they are lucky, they have experience, property, families, habits, standards of comparison. A widow is no tabula rasa upon which a man may inscribe his own mark. On the contrary, she may try to change the man, to settle him upon hearth and home, nurture and growth, custom and habit. Widows are viewed as dangerous superwomen, especially likely to succeed at doing to a man what every woman wants to do: trap him, not merely for herself, but within a net of particularized requirements and expectations. They focus a static female threat to male mobility.

But all women are mantraps. Simply to be seen as libidinous endangers the male. The net closes. Expectations are aroused. Codes are violated, and reparations sought. Mobility is impaired by rules about who should be where, and when. A man trying to move freely through the world finds himself in a minefield.

Mr. Pickwick's attitude to sex is, substantially, a functional "given." Never mind character: think of the jokes. In so far as we try to read character through it, we see an unwisely assumed posture, of the sage detached from fleshly things. He is proud of his celibacy. Asked if he has ever proposed marriage, "'Never,' said Mr. Pickwick with great energy, 'never.'" He may have "formed some ideas" on the subject, but has "never submitted them to the test of experience" (ch. 24). Ironies reverberate on this occasion. Having persuaded Mrs. Bardell of nuptial intentions without meaning to, he is now advising Mr. Magnus on how to propose. The lady accepts, so the advice was good, but it rebounds upon Mr. Pickwick when the object of Mr. Magnus's affection is revealed to be the lady in yellow curl-papers, who has reason to doubt Mr. Pickwick's attachment to celibacy.

Both of Mr. Pickwick's principal teachers have more worldly attitudes to sex. Mr. Wardle clearly does not suppose Mrs. Bardell's case to be groundless and, affecting disappointment at the marriage of the "black-eyed little jilt" Arabella Allen, declares, "I had a great idea of marrying her myself, one of these odd days" (ch. 54). Sam Weller enters Mr. Pickwick's employment with only one black mark on his record, an "amiable indiscretion, in which an assistant housemaid had equally participated" (ch. 12). Once he falls for Mary (ch. 25), he is to be delayed in his pursuit of her, but not diverted.

Little wonder, then, that Mr. Pickwick's continence goes unrecognized. Few believe his protestations, and he is repeatedly supposed libidinous. The Pickwickians are less than entirely convinced by his explanation of how Mrs. Bardell came to be in his arms (ch. 12). They cough slightly, and look dubiously at each other. Politely greeting Mrs. Pott from the platform at Eatanswill, he is eagerly declared by the crowd to be a "wicked old rascal" and a "wenerable sinner" (ch. 13). When the serving of the writ in Bardell *versus* Pickwick is announced, Mr. Wardle dubs him a "sly dog" (ch. 18). And after the adventure with the lady in yellow curl-papers, when Sam has conducted him to his own room, even Sam is thoughtful:

> He paused when he got outside the door – shook his head – walked on – stopped – snuffed the candle – shook his head again – and finally proceeded slowly to his chamber, apparently buried in the profoundest meditation. (ch. 22)

But it is clearly lack of experience with the other sex that brings about Mr. Pickwick's misunderstanding with Mrs. Bardell, whom he sees as a provider of services rather than a complete woman. The Goswell Street lodgings, we are told (ch. 12), are "peculiarly adapted for the residence of a man of his genius and capacity." "Cleanliness and quiet reigned throughout the house; and in it Mr. Pickwick's word was law." He can relate to her as a domestic subordinate, not as a potential mate with elaborate claims upon him. She is "comely" and an excellent cook but, as a wife, would pin him down, the more particularly because, as a landlady of furnished lodgings and widow of a custom-house officer, she is socially his inferior. She has long "worshipped Mr. Pickwick at a distance," but his apparent wooing raises her "to a pinnacle to which her wildest and most extravagant hopes had never dared to aspire."

Clearly, much is threatened by her perception of a sexual overture. His ignorance of matters to do with sexual attraction blinds him to the potential for misunderstanding in questions like, "Do you think it a much greater expense to keep two people, than to keep one?" Unsurprisingly, her loss of consciousness in his arms, immortalized by Phiz, traps him in the most compromising of all the ignominious spectacles in the novel [fig. 16].

The irony of Mr. Pickwick's predicament is seen when we consider how the error arises. His words are designed, it is eventually disclosed, to broach his intention of hiring Sam Weller as a manservant. Sam is to be, in effect, an aide to Mr. Pickwick in his mobility, spatial and social. Mrs. Bardell supposes him to be talking of marriage to her. The threat is of a marriage rooted in Goswell Street and lower-middle-class domesticity, with horizons defined by tea parties, gossip, and trips no further than Hampstead (Mr. Pickwick's own furthest horizon before the formation of the Corresponding Society). The irony is redoubled at the trial (ch. 34), when the language of notes arising out of Mr. Pickwick's peripatetic way of life is perversely misunderstood. Sexual passion is declared to be masked in terse messages like "I shall not be at home till tomorrow. Slow coach."

The Westgate House episode, in chapter 16, snares Mr. Pickwick in a trap set by Mr. Jingle's knavery. Hiding at midnight in the grounds of a girls' school in Bury St. Edmunds and, later, locked in a cupboard indoors, Mr. Pickwick is a prisoner, not least of the sexual implications of his position. He disturbs the tranquillity of "the spinster lady of the establishment, three teachers, five female servants, and thirty boarders, all half-dressed, and in a forest of curl-papers." The novel is rich in the sexual implications of undress, night attire, and curl-papers. Persuaded that Jingle is about to elope with an heiress, Mr. Pickwick has been tricked into becoming "the man – the man – behind the door!" and the mantle of Jingle's sexual ruthlessness falls upon him. The talk is of his being a robber or a madman, but there is clue enough to the real *frisson* he causes. "Ladies – dear ladies," he remonstrates with the hysterical inmates, and is eagerly misunderstood. "'Oh, he says we're dear,' cried the oldest and ugliest teacher. 'Oh, the wretch!'" In this episode, Mr. Pickwick is tumbled over a wall, rained upon, ignominiously forced to hide behind a door, ignominiously discovered, ignominiously locked in a cupboard, and ignominiously required to exculpate himself from within. Needless to say, there is a Phiz illustration. He loses all claim to position and respectability. Sam Weller and Mr. Wardle have to rescue him.

Sheer bad luck is responsible for the episode of the lady in yellow curl papers, but it shows Mr. Pickwick at his most ineffectual. Losing himself in the Great White Horse at Ipswich, he finds a room he thinks his, and prepares for bed behind the four-poster, but is alarmed to hear someone else enter (ch. 22). Peeping between the bed curtains, he is horrified to see a "middle-aged lady in yellow curl papers" at her toilet (it is at this point that the Phiz illustration records the ignominious spectacle). Announcing himself with a nervous cough, Mr. Pickwick identifies himself as a gentleman. As well she might, the lady quickly translates this into "a strange man!"

> "Wretch," said the lady, covering her eyes with her hands, "what do you want here?"
> "Nothing, Ma'am; nothing whatever, Ma'am;" said Mr. Pickwick earnestly.
> "Nothing!" said the lady, looking up.

Very much a *Pickwick* lady, she is quick to review the erotic possibilities, and to take offence, even against the grain of her own interests. But Mr. Pickwick is merely humiliated, by having unwittingly transgressed rules, not least those of attire. "I am almost ready to sink, Ma'am," he avers, "beneath the confusion of addressing a lady in my night-cap (here the lady hastily snatched off hers)." Mr. Pickwick's attempt to extricate himself with dignity is unavailing: "Although he had hastily put on his hat over his night-cap, after the manner of the old patrol; although he carried his shoes and gaiters in his hand, and his coat and waist-coat over his arm, nothing could subdue his native

Figure 16   "Mrs Bardell faints in Mr Pickwick's arms."   Illustration for
Pickwick Papers by Hablot Knight Browne. (By permission of the Dickens
House Museum, London.)

politeness." But he still cuts a sorry figure as he departs, feebly protesting his "unblemished character," and the "devoted respect" he entertains for women.

Mr. Pickwick flounders in situations where sexual transgression is imputed, and finds no recognition of his merits. For all his benevolence, at the trial of Bardell *versus* Pickwick he is denounced as "the ruthless destroyer of this domestic oasis in the desert of Goswell Street" (ch. 34). He does manage to avoid being compromised again, however, and to learn from this misadventure.

He learns, among other things, about arrest and imprisonment, as Dickens himself had done. These are traps in the most literal sense, and emphatically represent the triumph of stasis over mobility in the novel.

Mr. Pickwick is first imprisoned, on doubtful authority, when he is shut up by Captain Boldwig in the animal pound (ch. 19). The captain, who finds Mr. Pickwick on his land, lame and asleep in a wheelbarrow after a bibulous picnic, is a self-important arriviste. His wife's sister "had married a Marquis, and the captain's house was a villa, and his land 'grounds,' and it was all very high, and mighty, and great." Where Mr. Pickwick seeks to confirm his growth in status by going out into the world and absorbing it, Captain Boldwig chooses the reverse, marks out his territory, spatial and social, and tries to stop the world from trespassing on it. In addition, then, to being shut up, laughed at, and pelted by boys (an ignominious spectacle recorded by Phiz), the open and adventurous Mr. Pickwick has to suffer the additional humiliation of being declared "a drunken plebeian," by the costive and suspicious captain. This is another predicament from which Mr. Wardle and Sam have to rescue him. Nor does he learn by it. Instead, he rages and threatens litigation. Mr. Wardle manages to dissuade him only by observing, "they might turn round on some of us, and say we had taken too much cold punch." Hope for the future, at least, is indicated by Mr. Pickwick's being able to laugh at this.

He is detained for a second time when he is arrested in Ipswich (ch. 24). To prevent the duel she fears, between her fiancé and Mr. Pickwick, Miss Witherfield, the erstwhile lady in yellow curl-papers, denounces Mr. Pickwick and Mr. Tupman to the local magistrate, Mr. Nupkins, mayor of Ipswich. He is "as grand a personage as the fastest walker would find out, between sunrise and sunset, on the twenty-first of June, which being, according to the almanacs, the longest day of the whole year, would naturally afford him the longest period for his search." Captain Boldwig had seen Mr. Pickwick as "a drunken plebeian." No less humiliatingly, Mr. Nupkins persuades himself that Mr. Pickwick and Mr. Tupman are "two cut-throats from London, who have come down here to destroy his Majesty's population, thinking that at this distance from the capital, the arm of the law is weak and paralysed."

An ignominious spectacle is provided (and illustrated) by the conveying of Mr. Pickwick and Mr. Tupman to Mr. Nupkins's house in an old sedan chair, escorted by constables. Sam Weller intercepts, and leads an assault upon the constables. The resultant mayhem has the usual ingredients. We see Mr. Pickwick trapped, humiliated and expostulating, a delighted mob observing.

Mr. Pickwick's ability to handle this kind of situation, however, has improved. During the hearing (ch. 25), Mr. Nupkins shows himself to be prejudiced, ignorant of procedure, and indifferent to justice. But Mr. Pickwick, thanks doubtless to Bardell *versus* Pickwick, is no longer ignorant of the law. He is dignified and collected, and able to make a stand on procedure: "I shall take the liberty, sir, of claiming my right to be heard, until I am removed by force." Sam's sharp eye and understanding prove useful too. Mr. Pickwick contrives to have the hearing dropped, so that he can expose Mr. Jingle, who has plotted his way into the Nupkins household, Sam reveals, and into the heart of the Nupkins daughter.

But it is from his imprisonment in the Fleet that Mr. Pickwick learns most. He is jailed over his refusal to pay damages and costs awarded against him in Mrs. Bardell's action for breach of promise. Gone are the days, however, when Mr. Pickwick feels his dignity affronted by the very suggestion of confinement. "Not one farthing of costs or damages do you ever get from me," he tells Dodson and Fogg, "if I spend the rest of my existence in a debtor's prison" (ch. 34). Imprisonment is preferable to yielding on principle. It is what he chooses this time, not something imposed by bad luck, knavery, or folly. These are conditions that enable him to learn. He learns about the plight of the dispossessed in the Fleet but, just as importantly, he also learns the unwisdom of adherence to principle at the expense of good judgment.

There is a preliminary ignominious spectacle, depicted by Phiz as well as by the text. Mr. Pickwick is shown "sitting for his portrait," a term used for the occasion during which the turnkeys memorize his features. There is no raging or expostulating now; only silence, the sign of learning:

> Mr. Pickwick winced a good deal under the operation, and appeared to sit very uneasily in his chair; but he made no remark to anybody while it was being performed, not even to Sam, who reclined upon the back of the chair, reflecting, partly on the situation of his master, and partly on the great satisfaction it would have afforded him to make a fierce assault upon all the turnkeys there assembled, one after the other, if it were lawful and peaceable so to do. (ch. 40)

The impulse towards precipitate action, once so characteristic of Mr. Pickwick, is now Sam's alone, and not acted upon.

But the ignominious spectacle is now transfigured. Mr. Pickwick's entire stay in the Fleet is an extended ignominious spectacle. And it is a learning situation. Stasis replaces mobility as the condition from which growth is possible. What he sees and hears in the prison enlarges Mr. Pickwick's understanding, refines his sympathies, and deepens his self-knowledge. He sees the "young woman, with a child in her arms, who seemed scarcely able to crawl, from emaciation and misery," and who "burst into such a passion of grief, that she was compelled to lean against the wall for support" (ch. 41). He hears the story of the Chancery prisoner (chs. 41 and 44). He looks more closely, too, at delusions of grandeur, mindful perhaps of his own – at Mr. Smangle, for instance, offended at being thought a stationer ("Not so low as that. No trade."), but happy to cadge burnt sherry, cigars and small loans (chs. 41, 42 and 44). Little wonder he eventually chooses even closer voluntary confinement, exclaiming, "I have seen enough. . . . My head aches with these scenes, and my heart too. Henceforth I will be a prisoner in my own room" (ch. 45). Withdrawal joins silence as a sign of learning. Mr. Pickwick abandons mobility altogether, for hermit-like voluntary stasis, and the regeneration it will bring.

He is transformed during this imprisonment. He ceases to be a man quick to react to insult and injury, and becomes instead a man quick to react to the suffering of others. Having discovered Mr. Jingle, and his accomplice Job Trotter, also in the Fleet and in woeful condition, Mr. Pickwick does *not* hit Job: ·

> "Come here, sir," said Mr. Pickwick, trying to look stern, with four large tears running down his waistcoat.
> "Take that, sir."
> Take what? In the ordinary acceptation of such language, it should have been a blow. As the world runs, it ought to have been a sound, hearty cuff; for Mr. Pickwick had been duped, deceived and wronged, by the destitute outcast who was now in his power.
> Must we tell the truth? It was something from Mr. Pickwick's waistcoat pocket, which chinked as it was given into Job's hand, and the giving of which, somehow or other imparted a sparkle to the eye, and a swelling to the heart, of our excellent old friend, as he hurried away. (ch. 42)

He has learned to let compassion overcome indignation, however justified.

But there is a further lesson for him to learn. He will not listen when his friends urge him to let good judgment overcome indignation with Dodson and Fogg. He heedlessly adheres to principle, and obstinately resolves to stay in prison. Once again, Sam Weller comes to the rescue. He contrives to be committed to the Fleet himself. He will not pay a debt, he declares. He will not give the creditor (secretly his father) the satisfaction:

> "I takes my determination on principle, sir," remarked Sam, "and you takes yours on the same ground; wich puts me in mind o' the man as killed his-self on principle, wich o' course you've heered on, sir." Mr. Weller paused when he arrived at this point, and cast a comical look at his master out of the corners of his eyes. (ch. 44)

There follows the story of the man who, against medical advice, ate three shillings' worth of crumpets, and blew his brains out, "in support of his great principle that crumpets wos wholesome, and to show that he wouldn't be put out of his way for nobody!"

Sam's stubborn loyalty provides one incentive for Mr. Pickwick to yield, direct exhortation from Mr. Perker another. Although payment of the damages and costs will benefit Dodson and Fogg, he points out, it will also release the hapless Mrs. Bardell from the Fleet, incarcerated there by the rascally lawyers, for failure to pay their fees. Mr. Pickwick's remaining in prison to defend a principle, Mr. Perker slyly adds, "would only be imputed, by people who didn't know you, to sheer dogged, wrongheaded, brutal obstinacy" (ch. 47). Mr. Pickwick does not indicate whether he recognizes himself in this sketch, but he is persuaded, leaves the Fleet, and becomes mobile once again.

The transition is sharply signalled. Chapter 47, in which the process of his release is described, ends with Mr. Pickwick and Sam setting out for Bristol in a post coach. "I wish them horses had been three months and better in the Fleet, Sir," Sam remarks.

> "Why, Sam?" inquired Mr. Pickwick.
> "Vy, Sir," exclaimed Mr. Weller, rubbing his hands, "how they vould go if they had been!"

But now Mr. Pickwick travels, no longer bent on self-improvement or vendetta. Now he travels to help others. He risks discomfort and humiliation as before, but this time with the intention of reconciling Ben Allen and Mr. Winkle senior to the marriage of Arabella Allen and Mr. Winkle junior. He is helping his young friend to settle down.

Mobility and stasis at this point in the novel undergo revaluation. The club is dissolved, and Mr. Pickwick retires to his villa in Dulwich (ch. 57). He does not regret his travels, "frivolous as my pursuit of knowledge may have appeared to many," but hopes they have contributed "to the enlargement of my mind, and the improvement of my understanding." Another Pickwickian, Mr. Snodgrass, marries and settles down, aided and abetted by his leader. Mr. Pickwick stoutly perseveres in his own celibacy but, when the "very old" housekeeper replacing Mrs. Bardell dies, she is replaced in turn by Sam Weller's bride, and the bachelor villa becomes fruitful: "From the circumstance of two sturdy little boys having been repeatedly seen at the gate of the back garden, there is reason to suppose that Sam has some family." Mr. Pickwick is happy, moreover, to become serial godfather to his friends' many children.

In retirement, he is famed, not for learning or distinction, but for charity: "He is known by all the poor people about, who never fail to take their hats off, as he passes. The children idolise him, and so indeed does the whole neighbourhood." Later in his career, Dickens threw himself into charitable work with tremendous zeal. Little is known of his charitable giving during the Doughty Street years but, in July 1839, his friend the actor, William Charles Macready, declared him to be "one who has made the amelioration of his fellow-men the object of all his labours – and whose characteristic [is] philanthropy" ("Charity and Dickens," *Oxford Reader's Companion to Dickens*). His early struggles had taught Dickens, not only to strive for acceptance, but also to understand want and suffering, and to relieve it. Mr. Pickwick learns the same lesson.

At the end of the novel, Tony Weller's inheritance, which Mr. Pickwick has invested for him, has turned into "a handsome independence to retire on, upon which he still lives at an excellent public-house near Shooter's Hill, where he is quite reverenced as an oracle, boasting very much of his intimacy with Mr. Pickwick, and retaining a most unconquerable aversion to widows" (ch. 57). Almost the first thing we saw in the novel was Mr. Pickwick being abused by a cabdriver. It ends neatly. Almost the last thing we see is his being made much of by a coach-driver.

Horses and ignominy, launching out and getting stuck – these are what shape *Pickwick Papers*. Unforgettable images lodge in the reader's memory, of coaches bowling along through the English countryside, of ridiculous and humiliating predicaments. It is an intricately organized novel. The way Dickens allowed his own experience to speak through it contributes not a little to this organization.

4

OLIVER TWIST: THE FUGITIVE FAMILY

One of the pleasures of reading Dickens is to be found in the difference between successive novels. Each is a new venture, a new fictional strategy. But Dickens's second novel, *Oliver Twist*, is not merely different from *Pickwick Papers* which precedes it, from *Nicholas Nickleby* which follows it, and from all the other novels. Despite its extraordinary power, there is something shrill and unappeased about it not found elsewhere. The circumstances of its composition provide an explanation.

It has been suggested that Dickens thought of the story of *Oliver Twist*, or something like it, in 1833 or even earlier (Tillotson ed., *Oliver Twist* xv–xvii). In a letter to Kolle of that year, he speaks of a plan to write "a series of papers (the materials for which I have been noting down for some time past) called *The Parish*" (Pilgrim *Letters* 1: 33–34). This is echoed, not only by "Our Parish," title of the first group of *Sketches by Boz*, but also by *The Parish Boy's Progress*, subtitle of *Oliver Twist* in *Bentley's Miscellany*. It was in 1833 that Dickens finally broke with Maria Beadnell. Like any twenty-one-year-old grieving at the end of his first serious love affair, he must have been reconsidering his hopes of marriage and his prospects of fatherhood.

Whenever he first thought of the story, we know he began writing the novel at the end of 1836 or beginning of 1837, nine months after his marriage, at just the time he first became a father. The first part was published in *Bentley's Miscellany* in February 1837. Charley, his and Catherine's first child, had been born a month earlier, and there is no evidence of Dickens's having actually written anything very much in advance of publication. He finished the novel the year he became a father for the second time. His daughter Mamie was born in March 1838. The volume edition was published in November.

Marriage and parenthood, then, are topics Dickens is likely to have been thinking about while planning and writing *Oliver Twist*. Becoming a father, when he finally did, clearly demanded much of him, emotionally. Childbirth was difficult for Catherine. She was very distressed at being unable to nurse her first child. "Poor Kate!" wrote her sister Mary, "it has been a dreadful trial for her . . . . It is really dreadful to see her suffer. I am quite sure I never suffered so much sorrow for any one or any thing before . . . . Every time she sees her Baby she has a fit of crying and keeps constantly saying she is sure he will not care for her now she is not able to nurse him" (*Dickensian* 63: 77). She suffered similar distress after the birth of Mamie (Ackroyd 270). But these trials were endured, and both parents plainly doted on their children. "A thousand loves and kisses to the darling boy, whom I see in my mind's eye crawling about the floor of this Yorkshire inn," Dickens wrote from Greta Bridge in February 1838. "Bless his heart, I would give two sovereigns for a kiss" (Pilgrim *Letters* 1: 366).

Yet, despite the novelty and intensity for him of such experiences, there is a striking lack of correspondence between the events in Dickens's life when he was writing *Oliver Twist*, and what is to be found in the novel. Or, to be more precise, there is a systematic dissonance between them. The sequence of marriage, childbirth, and the raising of children by man and wife, is not much in evidence in *Oliver Twist* and rarely has been, we can only conclude, from such background detail as the narrative yields. The novel is full of parentless children, single parents, childless couples, bachelors, widows, and widowers – not to mention characters for whom it is next to impossible to imagine any kind of family or family life whatsoever. More often than not, transgression or misfortune has damaged or destroyed the families of which the narrative tells. Characters whose family background we know to be more or less normal are exceptional.

Needless to say, Oliver's own family history is the least normal in the book. He is a dispossessed, illegitimate orphan. His father is dead. His mother dies giving birth to him, in the first chapter. Forced into an unsuitable marriage by an unsympathetic family, his father had been unable to marry her, despite their love for each other. Oliver is dispossessed, thanks to a conspiracy between his father's lawful wife and her son, Oliver's half-brother. The lawful wife, dead before the action begins, and the half-brother, still malevolently alive, hated each other, but were united in their hatred of Oliver. The family of Oliver's mother had foundered beneath the weight of her shame (ch. 51). This is discontinuity of courtship and marriage with a vengeance.

Disruption of family life and its re-establishment are, to be sure, traditional themes of narrative literature, as are illegitimacy and mysterious origins. Think only of *Tom Jones*. But rarely has the pudding been as over-egged as it is in *Oliver Twist*. Until the very end of the novel, such families as readers encounter are all deficient or unsatisfactory. From the beginning, the text accustoms readers to a vision of family dysfunction.

None of the families encountered near the beginning of the novel, comprising more than one generation, are anything like exemplary. Noah Claypole, we are for instance told, "could trace his genealogy all the way back to his parents, who lived hard by; his mother being a washerwoman, and his father a drunken soldier, discharged with a wooden leg, and a diurnal pension of twopence-halfpenny and an unstateable fraction" (ch. 5). A pauper family introduced in chapter 5 comprises three generations, but the mother has just died of starvation and fever, the children are ragged and terrified, the father half mad, the grandmother completely so, and unnatural: "Lord, Lord! Well it is strange that I who gave birth to her, and was a woman then, should be alive and merry now, and she lying there: so cold and stiff! Lord, Lord! – to think of it; it's as good as a play – as good as a play!"

Other families are of one generation only, or depleted. Dickens does obliquely promise readers a family of more than one generation for Mr. Sowerberry, who complains of the difficulty of making a living from coffins for paupers, "especially when one has a family to provide for" (ch. 4). But the promise is not kept. The Sowerberry establishment is evidently childless. Mr. Brownlow's housekeeper is declared to be a "motherly old lady" (ch. 12), and she does indeed have a family, but her "kind good husband" has been dead twenty-six years, and though her "amiable and handsome daughter" is married to "an amiable and handsome man," her son in the West Indies writes "dutiful letters home" only four times a year (ch. 14). Gentle irony leaves readers uncertain quite how to receive Mrs. Bedwin's stories of her family. Only one thing is certain: misfortune has touched it, perhaps even transgression.

One of the strangest families in the novel is one readers are clearly invited to see as exemplary. Mrs. Maylie, typically, has long been a widow. She and Rose Maylie, we are at first encouraged to suppose, are aunt and niece (ch. 29). The Reverend Harry Maylie, Mrs. Maylie's son, is in love with Rose, but both Mrs. Maylie and Rose caution him against marriage, because of a stain on Rose's name – her supposed illegitimacy, we later learn. Harry fell in love with Rose as a boy, he declares, when they were being raised together. At the time, he says, he was "ignorant of my own mind." But he claims to have been considering his feelings for "years and years": "I have considered ever since I have been capable of serious reflection" (ch. 34).

The implications are startling. Harry is about twenty-five, we are told, Rose seventeen. Assume he had been nineteen when he first came consciously to love her – if anything, a little on the late side for the onset of "serious reflection." Rose would have been eleven. Assume, more realistically, he had been sixteen. She would have been eight. Nor have we even begun to think about their having been raised as brother and sister, or about Harry's first having declared his love when he still supposed them cousins. The reader – prurient or just observant – is likely to detect a hint at least of paedophilia and of other transgressions here, and to find the exemplary status of the Maylie family impaired by it. Dickens, though, almost certainly failed to notice the implications. He simply neglected to do the arithmetic. But dismiss the hint of transgression, and we still have to explain the strength of a fantasy which stopped him doing sums he might have done, had he been imagining more constructively.

Rose and Harry learn the facts eventually, as does the reader. Rose is neither Mrs. Maylie's niece, nor illegitimate. They are unrelated.

Supposing Rose illegitimate, Mrs. Maylie had pretended kinship only to protect her. So Harry and Rose can marry without anxiety, and do. At the end of the novel the narrative alludes to "joyous little faces that clustered round her knee" (ch. 53). At last a family is created which seems both normal and exemplary – a family, moreover, in which Oliver is included, since it is discovered that Rose is his aunt. The blood family for Oliver, however, the exemplary and normal family, has been arrived at by a route thick with transgression and abnormality.

There are so many dysfunctional families in the novel. There is the disastrous marriage of Mr. Bumble and Mrs. Corney, for instance, a "jining of hearts and housekeeping," Mr. Bumble vainly gloats (ch. 27). There are the Sowerberrys, too. Mrs. Sowerberry, we are told, is given to hysterical laughter which greatly frightens Mr. Sowerberry: "a very common and much approved matrimonial course of treatment, which is often very effective," the narrator advises (ch. 5). The less conventional relationships of Sikes and Nancy, Noah and Charlotte, lead to murder in the one case, fraud in the other. One thing they do not lead to is children, let alone marriage.

We ask questions akin to "How Many Children Had Lady Macbeth?" when we wonder about the families of Fagin, the Artful Dodger, Bill Sikes, and their like. But it is scarcely irrelevant to note that Dickens invites little inquiry in this direction. Fagin articulates a doctrine irreconcilable with family life: "Some conjurers say that number three is the magic number, and some say number seven. It's neither, my friend, neither. It's number one" (ch. 43). Unsurprisingly, Bill Sikes finds it difficult to envisage a family for Fagin, too. "There never was another man with such a face as yours," he says, "unless it was your father, and I suppose *he* is singeing his grizzled red beard by this time, unless you came straight from the old 'un without any father at all betwixt you; which I shouldn't wonder at, a bit" (ch. 44). In accused prisoners and their friends, Noah Claypole can see "several women who would have done very well" for the Dodger's mother or sister, "and more than one man who might be supposed to bear a strong resemblance to his father" (ch. 43), but that is as near as we get to a family for the Dodger.

There is, then, a striking lack of correspondence between the events of Dickens's life when he was writing *Oliver Twist*, and the content of the novel. *Pickwick Papers*, I have argued, is about social mobility, and reflects Dickens's own ascent through the class system. As we shall see, *Nicholas Nickleby*, which follows *Oliver Twist*, reflects Dickens's experience of acquiring wealth, raising a family, and worrying about its future. But *Oliver Twist* is different.

At this stage in his career, Dickens was prepared to work on two novels simultaneously, not to mention less ambitious projects. Before he finished *Pickwick* he started *Oliver Twist*, and before he finished that he began *Nicholas Nickleby*. Twenty-one months elapsed between the appearance of the first instalment of *Oliver Twist* in *Bentley's Miscellany* and the publication of the three-volume edition of the novel. During that time, only five months passed – November 1837 to April 1838 – when there was no need for Dickens to be working on another novel at the same time (or indeed on *The Mudfog Papers*, another current project). Turning to the dark side of his imagination, and conveying a different kind of vision in *Oliver Twist*, enabled him to differentiate the tasks he was performing, and to offer readers something other than more of the same. Artistic and commercial reasons alone prompted him to deny what he was affirming in his behavior and elsewhere in his works: marriage, parenthood, responsibility. *Oliver Twist* dwells relentlessly on the failure of the institutions of marriage and the family, on misfortunes and transgressions that ruin them. Dickens was always fascinated by the dysfunctional family. In no other novel is the normal family more marginalized than it is in *Oliver Twist*.

It would be possible to leave this as a purely formal observation. We could agree that *Oliver Twist* is simply a different kind of novel. It was only Dickens's second. Unsurprisingly, he was experimenting. This was his essay in Grand Guignol. He wanted to make his readers' flesh creep. But I do not believe *Oliver Twist* is simply the result of a teleological choice made by Dickens, though doubtless such a choice was made, and should not be neglected. As always with Dickens, strong feelings were restimulated in the course of composition, and you can only restimulate what has gone before.

Echoes of each of the emotional crises in Dickens's life I described in chapter 2 can be detected, I believe, in *Oliver Twist*. Memories of his father's imprisonment in the Marshalsea, and of his own year in the blacking warehouse have something to do with the special character of the novel. So does his relationship with Maria Beadnell on the one hand, and his relationship with his wife on the other. So does the death of Mary Hogarth, Catherine's younger sister, three months after he had launched *Oliver Twist*. Feelings to do with these crises underpin Dickens's public indignation at the policy, encouraged by the new Poor Law, of deliberately destroying family ties.

Oliver Twist has a quite different tone and texture from *Pickwick* and *Nickleby*, because Dickens was taking a holiday from the normal and the normative in it, taking a holiday from what he sought in life for himself, to immerse himself in the marginal and the transgressive, to wallow in emotions which perhaps he could leave behind or call up at choice, but which here he saturated himself in. Throughout his career, his imagination required periodic immersion in these emotions. Arguably, all good novelists need something similar. But at this stage in his life, the pressures of the normal and the normative, among other things, seem to have prompted an unusually thorough and protracted immersion.

Warren's and the Marshalsea had separated him from his family, and damaged his sense of the family as something to be relied upon. The experience had humiliated him. But it had also exposed him to intense emotion – an education in itself – and conferred street wisdom upon him. One way he had of dealing with the episode was to enact in play an even worse condition. He is shown doing this in Dr. Danson's story of the young Dickens "heading us in Drummond-street in pretending to be poor boys, and asking the passers-by for charity – especially old ladies." *Oliver Twist* is such play writ large. Parallels have often been drawn between Oliver's solitary condition and the isolation suffered by Dickens when he was at Warren's, between the moral catastrophe which threatens Oliver, and Dickens's sense that, "but for the mercy of God, I might easily have been, for any care that was taken of me, a little robber or a little vagabond." Less has been made of the fact that Oliver's predicament is immeasurably worse than Dickens's had been. If we are to see the novel as a cathartic exercise for Dickens, we have to acknowledge that, to achieve catharsis, he evidently needed imaginatively to go way beyond Warren's, deeper into the abyss, for every shudder it was worth.

Nor should we neglect the figure, above all others, of the Artful Dodger, who inhabits the abyss and makes himself perfectly comfortable there, with the aid of roguish insouciance and anarchic wit, personal qualities Dickens apparently never managed to cultivate at Warren's, but which he did later, not least because of Warren's. In chapter 3 I spoke of the way Mr. Pickwick and Sam Weller, added together, approximate to a recognizable Dickens. The same may be said of Oliver Twist and the Dodger. Oliver embodies Dickens's sense of innocence violated and birthright denied, the Dodger his pride at having mastered gutter life, or what he saw as gutter life in 1824. By framing him for theft, of course, the Dodger betrays Oliver (ch. 11). Sam never betrays Mr. Pickwick. But Dickens was at least as anxious about his street wisdom as he was proud of it. And it is hard not to attach significance to the fact that the Dodger departs from the text in triumph. Committed at last for trial, he is carried off "grinning in the officer's face, with great glee and self-approval." Charley Bates and Noah Claypole are able to tell Fagin "the animating news that the Dodger was doing full justice to his bringing-up, and establishing for himself a glorious reputation" (ch. 43). The Dodger, that is to say, achieves recognition for his own kind of learning and distinction. In doing so, he constitutes an anarchic parody of what Dickens had sought for himself.

I have argued, with others, that Dickens loved his wife Catherine, but not in the same way that he had loved Maria Beadnell. It is impossible not to see, in the letters he wrote to Catherine during their engagement, the resolution of a man still nursing wounds of a less happy courtship, and determined this time to be in control. "With regard to your note my love," he could write,

> I will only say, that it displays all that amiable and excellent feeling which I know you possess, and for which I believe from my heart, you are unrivalled; – if you would only determine to *shew* the same affection and kindness to me, when you feel

disposed to be ill-tempered, I declare unaffectedly; I should have no one solitary fault to find with you. (Pilgrim *Letters* 1: 104)

This is a decidedly buttoned-up letter. We do not hear in it the voice of the unhappy victim who wrote to Maria Beadnell, "Our meetings of late have been little more than so many displays of heartless indifference on the one hand, while on the other they have never failed to prove a fertile source of wretchedness and misery." We do hear in it the voice of a man constructing a new relationship at a price. With the experience of one unhappy courtship behind him, and of one successful thanks to rigorous emotional discipline and repression, it must have been tempting for Dickens, writing *Oliver Twist*, to forget the frustration he had suffered in the one relationship, the elaborate control he felt he needed to exercise over the other, and to escape into a fantasy of overwhelming illicit love, of self-immolation on the altar of passion, and of its unforeseen result, illegitimate offspring. As he became a father, as responsibilities accrued, the notion of erotic self-abandon, regardless of consequences, must have seemed something worth at least imagining very thoroughly.

It is difficult not to believe that the death of Mary Hogarth released in Dickens a torrent of fantasies about what might have been, not excluding fantasies about relationships forbidden within families. Some features of the relationship of Rose and Harry Maylie may be traced to this. The similarities between Rose and Mary Hogarth have often been noted; not so often those between Harry and Dickens. Twenty-five and seventeen were precisely the ages of Dickens and Mary when she died. Harry "was of the middle height; his countenance was frank and handsome; and his demeanour easy and prepossessing" (ch. 34). This echoes many descriptions of Dickens as a young man. His height is repeatedly described as average. Forster speaks of his face's "candour and openness of expression." "The head was altogether well-formed and symmetrical," he says, "and the air and carriage of it were extremely spirited" (bk. 2, ch. 1). Harry is engaged in "high and noble pursuits," which a liaison with Rose could damage (ch. 35). There is a problem in her family background. There are suggestions of prohibited degrees of relationship. The point need not be labored.

To appreciate what we find there, however, it is important not to misunderstand how aspects of the relationship of Dickens and Mary Hogarth transfer into the novel. There is no evidence that Dickens used his relationship with Mary as a model for the relationship of Harry and Rose. On the contrary, the latter has all the marks of a fantasy compensating for disappointment in life – deviating, that is to say, from what might have been a model: fantasy as a substitute for creative imagination, which is usually marked by stronger roots in experience and more attention to detail. Dickens's unhappiness over the death of Mary Hogarth led him to fantasize an enduring attraction between Harry and Rose, careless of what is implied, for instance, by their difference in age. He put something of himself into Harry, and a lot of Mary into Rose, because of fantasies he had after her death, not of experiences and desires before it.

The failure of imagination shows in the melodrama:

"If your inclinations chime with your sense of duty – " Harry began.

"They do not," replied Rose, colouring deeply.

"Then you return my love?" said Harry. "Say but that, dear Rose; say but that, and soften the bitterness of this hard disappointment!

"If I could have done so, without doing heavy wrong to him I loved," rejoined Rose, "I could have – "

"Have received this declaration very differently?" said Harry. "Do not conceal that from me, at least, Rose."

"I could," said Rose. "Stay!" she added, disengaging her hand, "why should we prolong this painful interview? Most painful to me, and yet productive of lasting happiness, notwithstanding; for it *will* be happiness to know that I once held the high place in your regard which I now occupy, and every triumph you achieve in life will animate me with new fortitude and firmness. Farewell, Harry! As we have met today, we meet no more; but in other relations than those in which this conversation would have placed us, we may be long and happily entwined; and may every blessing that the prayers of a true and earnest heart can call down from the source of all truth and sincerity, cheer and prosper you!" (ch. 35)

The combination of strong feeling with logic-chopping and elaborate rhetoric is weirdly potent, but it is evidently an end in itself, inviting the the reader to forget about character, motivation, or relationships.

Strange families, unconvincing relationships, are two of the manifestations of Dickens's holiday from the normal and the normative in *Oliver Twist*. Much more pervasive is narrative irony against the family. The novel begins with an ironic commendation of the foundling condition, brutally emphasized in the words of the workhouse doctor: "The old story . . . : no wedding-ring, I see." The newborn Oliver fails to breathe immediately. "Now, if, during this brief period, Oliver had been surrounded by careful grandmothers, anxious aunts, experienced nurses, and doctors of profound wisdom," the reader is told, "he would most inevitably and indubitably have been killed in no time" (ch. 1). Left to nature and without a family, Oliver learns the trick himself – unlike little Charley Dickens, we can be quite sure, at just about the time his father was writing these words.[1]

Another early irony is to be detected in Oliver's triumph as a professional mute in Mr. Sowerberry's employment. He leads funeral processions, "in a hat-band reaching down to his knees, to the indescribable admiration and emotion of all the mothers of the town" (ch. 5). They are deeply moved by what they know to be simulation of grief. The child simulating, moreover, is an orphan, his own mother and father long since dead and past mourning.

Irony is often developed into parody, to evoke family in the novel. There are multiple parodies of family life and feeling, most of them repugnant, just one of them disturbingly seductive. The cruel, rapacious, and evidently solitary Mrs. Mann, mistress of the baby farm, provides one of the first. She tells Mr. Bumble she gives the children "Daffy" when they are unwell: a supposedly medicinal dose, that is to say, laced with gin, guaranteed at least to keep fretful infants quiet. Sampling the gin, Mr. Bumble declares himself impressed: "You feel as a mother, Mrs. Mann," he observes (ch. 2).

The workhouse board enacts a parody of family solicitude. More than once, members deliberate over Oliver's future. On one occasion the parody is made explicit:

In great families, when an advantageous place cannot be obtained, either in possession, reversion, remainder, or expectancy, for the young man who is growing up, it is a very general custom to send him to sea. The board, in imitation of so wise and salutary an example, took counsel together on the expediency of shipping off Oliver Twist, in some small trading vessel bound to a good unhealthy port. This suggested itself as the very best thing that could possibly be done with him: the probability being that the skipper would flog him to death, in a playful mood, some day after dinner, or would knock his brains out with an iron bar; both pastimes being, as is pretty generally known, very favourite and common recreations among gentlemen of that class. (ch. 4)

But the chief parody of family life in *Oliver Twist* – the disturbingly seductive one – is provided by Fagin and his gang. It is important not to be mistaken about this. The structure of *Oliver Twist*, and repeated indications in the narrative, make it clear that Fagin is evil, that he gladly conspires to ruin Oliver, that he cares as little for all his associates. Unlike Lionel Bart's musical *Oliver*, the novel eschews the suggestion that genuine warmth and belonging are to be found among a community of loveable working-class rogues. On the contrary, it shows such a supposition to be dangerous. But Dickens's imagination was at work on Fagin. We know he is dangerous, precisely because we can see him to be clever and subtle. He understands relationships, and takes pains with them. Oliver's meeting with the Artful Dodger, and his introduction to Fagin, are the closest he has ever come, at that stage of the story, to admission into a family. Whatever it threatens, it offers something better than the loneliness he had experienced at the workhouse (ch. 4).

The gang communicates much of the time through underworld cant: "Hullo, my covey! What's the row?"; "Now, then!" . . . . "Plummy and slam!" (ch. 8). This may be a warning to the reader, but there is also warmth in its informality, not at all to be found at the workhouse, even in discourse between Oliver and Little Dick. The cant might almost be the private language of a close family, especially since Oliver is warmly welcomed by Fagin, and unstintingly given food and drink, something that had never happened at the workhouse.

Fagin calls him "my dear," moreover (ch. 8). No one has ever called him that before, for all that others do afterwards. And Fagin's feigned affection is a sign of a real intimacy he contrives between himself and the boy, however perfidious on his part. Mrs. Mann, Mr. Bumble and the workhouse board are not only cruel: they are unrelentingly distant, patronizing and admonitory in what they say to Oliver, and of him. They submit him to arbitrary, capricious, always unsympathetic definition, exemplified by the refrain of the gentleman in the white waistcoat: "That boy will be hung" (ch. 2). Nor is this hectoring confined to characters condemned by the narrative. Initially at any rate, even Mr. Grimwig, one of a team of eccentric old bachelors who finally solve all the problems, is scarcely less dismissive of Oliver. He knows of only two categories of boy: "mealy boys, and beef-faced boys" (ch. 14), and assigns Oliver to the former. That is enough for Mr. Grimwig, to start with at any rate. Whatever his motives, Fagin seeks to know and to understand Oliver. Regardless of what he says of him, what he says to Oliver has about it, by contrast to what others say, a refreshing normality and directness, undiminished by underlying hypocrisy. He never speaks down to him. Enraged by Oliver's observation of him gloating over his booty, Fagin goes so far as to threaten him with a bread knife, but remembers himself in time. He plays "with the knife a little, . . . as if to induce the belief that he had caught it up, in mere sport." He knows the importance of encouragement and praise. "You're a brave boy," he tells Oliver (ch. 9).

Whatever the signs are for us to question Fagin's "benevolence," his behavior towards the Dodger, for instance, and Charley Bates, demonstrates warmth hitherto unknown to Oliver. "Good boys, good boys," he calls them. Whatever the sinister undertones, the gang provide Oliver with his first experience of teasing and playfulness:

> "You'd like to be able to make pocket-handkerchiefs as easy as Charley Bates, wouldn't you, my dear?" said the Jew.
> "Very much indeed, if you'll teach me sir," replied Oliver.
> Master Bates saw something so exquisitely ludicrous in this reply, that he burst into another laugh; which laugh meeting the

> coffee he was drinking, and carrying it down the wrong channel,
> very nearly terminated in his premature suffocation. (ch. 9)

Nobody laughs much in *Oliver Twist*, except members of the gang, and Charley Bates especially who, when Oliver is snatched back, has to ask, "Hold me, somebody, while I laugh it out" (ch. 16). We are told Mr. Losberne cracks jokes, and that people laugh at them (ch. 34), but no sample is vouchsafed us.

Like the workhouse board, Fagin parodies a father in the way he offers judgment and advice on conduct. We see what is wrong, when he says of the Dodger and Charley, "Make 'em your models, my dear" (ch. 9), but we feel he is more engaged in his advice than the board member who tells Oliver, "I hope you say your prayers every night, . . . and pray for the people who feed you, and take care of you – like a Christian" (ch. 2). Fagin no more eschews violence than Mrs. Mann or Mr. Bumble, but the irony conspires with him rather than against him:

> Whenever the Dodger or Charley Bates came home at night, empty-handed, he would expatiate with great vehemence on the misery of idle and lazy habits; and would enforce upon them the necessity of an active life, by sending them supperless to bed. On one occasion, indeed, he went so far as to knock them both down a flight of stairs; but this was carrying his virtuous precepts to an unusual extent. (ch. 10)

Nor are his pupils unappreciative. "Why don't you put yourself under Fagin, Oliver?" asks Charley Bates:

> "And make your fortun' out of hand?" added the Dodger, with a grin.
> "And so be able to retire on your property, and do the gen-teel: as I mean to, in the very next leap-year but four that ever comes, and the forty-second Tuesday in Trinity-week," said Charley Bates. (ch. 18)

Oliver's first experience of female warmth is provided by the gang. On first meeting them, he is charmed by Bet and Nancy: "Being remarkably free and agreeable in their manners," the narrative dryly tells us, "Oliver thought them very nice girls indeed. As there is no doubt they were" (ch. 9). Nor is it long before a parody of consanguinity is enacted. It is agreed that Nancy should go to the police court to find out what has happened to Oliver after his arrest:

> "Oh, my brother! My poor, dear, sweet, innocent little brother!" exclaimed Nancy, bursting into tears, and wringing the little basket and the street-door key in an agony of distress. "What has become of him. Where have they taken him to! Oh, do have pity, and tell me what's been done with the dear boy, gentlemen; do, gentlemen, if you please gentlemen!"

Far from being diminished by it, the reader's awareness of parody is sharpened by this being only a rehearsal, for the benefit of Fagin and Bill Sikes. It offers Sikes an opportunity for commentary. He declares Nancy "a honour to her sex" (ch. 13). One ironic effect of Nancy's play-acting is to remind us that, since the death of his mother, no such concern has been shown for Oliver, feigned or unfeigned.

A similar parody of consanguinity is enacted when Oliver is snatched back into the gang from Mr. Brownlow's care, by Sikes and Nancy:

> "What the devil's this?" said a man, bursting out of a beer-shop, with a white dog at his heels; "young Oliver! Come home to your poor mother, you young dog! Come home directly."
> (ch. 15)

There is even a kind of parody tug-of-love for possession of Oliver's heart. Contemplating the planned burglary in Chertsey, Fagin says, "Once let him feel that he is one of us; once fill his mind with the idea that he has been a thief, and he's ours. Ours for his life" (ch. 19).

The everyday texture of family life is conjured as much by parody, in the novel, as by unironic narrative. Consanguinity proper is repeatedly marginalized as something established and signalled by nature alone, regardless of nurture, something declaring itself in untaught behavior, detected in mysterious recognition. In Goldie Morgentaler's words, the novel "is a fairy tale in which the magical element is located within the domain of heredity" (37). Oliver's courage and spirit – he famously asks for more, fights Noah Claypole, runs away – cannot be explained by circumstances. "But nature or inheritance," we are told, "had implanted a good sturdy spirit in Oliver's breast" (ch. 2). He is fiercely loyal to the mother he has never known, ready to defend and indeed fight for her honor (ch. 6). He is honest without the least training in honesty (ch. 15). As the tears of his mother's sister, Rose, drop on his sleeping face, "The boy stirred, and smiled in his sleep, as though these marks of pity and compassion had awakened some pleasant dream of love and affection he had never known." And Rose instinctively sees what he lacks: "he may never have known a mother's love, or the comfort of a home" (ch. 30). Monks instinctively knows and hates Oliver. He had "seen him accidentally with two of our boys on the day we first lost him," Nancy tells Rose, "and had known him directly to be the same child that he was watching for, though I couldn't make out why" (ch. 40). "If you buried him fifty feet deep, and took me across his grave," Monks snarls, "I fancy I should know, if there wasn't a mark above it, that he lay buried there" (ch. 34).

Monks apart, a creature entirely of melodrama, the criminal characters in the novel are famously more vital than the honest ones. And they are the ones who stand free of families as, curiously, do the arbiters of decency in the novel. The center of normality it proposes is the prosperous old bachelor, preferably eccentric. Old bachelors, though given to amiable error, are ultimately the fount of wisdom, decency, and the good things in life. Old bachelors solve the problems. Mr. Brownlow, of course, is central in the rescue of Oliver. Mr. Brownlow, Mr. Grimwig and Mr. Losberne, between them, constitute a kind of Pickwick Club composed entirely of Samuel Pickwicks – advanced in years, prosperous, benevolent, wilful, reconciled to celibacy. In chapter 41, it is the old bachelors who successfully plot the resolution of the story, and at the end of the novel, the community in the village where the Maylies, Mr. Brownlow, and Oliver settle, seems half made up of contented old bachelors, one of whom has adopted Oliver.

In *Oliver Twist*, then, Dickens met a need to write something different from *Pickwick Papers*, by revisiting powerful emotions he had experienced, inimical to the family life he was privately constructing. *Oliver Twist* is an experiment in anarchy at the expense of family order. Within the world of this novel, family is too unreliable an institution to withstand the tide of anarchy. The old bachelors can withstand it because they are strong solitary bulwarks, unencumbered by family. The criminals, equally unencumbered, are the tide itself. What are the great set pieces of the novel – the murder of Nancy by Bill Sikes, the pursuit and death of Sikes, Fagin's responses at his trial, and his last night in the condemned cell – if they are not enactments of anarchy, licentious celebrations of the breakdown of order? Turn from the normal and the normative: anarchy is what offers itself first. You can see this, moreover, not only in the Grand Guignol set pieces. It is to be found at its best in the committal proceedings for the Artful Dodger.

> "Now then! Wot is this here business? I shall thank the madg'strates to dispose of this here little affair, and not to keep me while they read the paper, for I've got an appointment with a genelman in the City, and as I'm a man of my word and wery punctual in business matters, he'll go away if I ain't there to my time, and then pr'aps there won't be an action for damage against them as kep me away. Oh no, certainly not!"
>
> At this point, the Dodger, with a show of being very particular with a view to proceedings to be had thereafter, desired the jailer to communicate "the names of them two files as was on the bench." Which so tickled the spectators, that they laughed almost as heartily as Master Bates could have done if he had heard the request.
>
> "Silence there!" cried the jailer.
>
> "What is this?" inquired one of the magistrates.
>
> "A pick-pocketing case, your worship."
>
> "Has the boy ever been here before?"
>
> "He ought to have been, a many times," replied the jailer. "He has been pretty well everywhere else. *I* know him well, your worship."
>
> "Oh! you know me, do you?" cried the Artful, making a note of the statement. "Wery good. That's a case of deformation of character, anyway."
>
> Here there was another laugh, and another cry of silence.

"Now then, where are the witnesses?" said the clerk.

"Ah! that's right," added the Dodger. "Where are they? I should like to see 'em."

This wish was immediately gratified . . . .

"Have you anything to ask this witness, boy?" said the magistrate.

"I wouldn't abase myself by descending to hold no conversation with him," replied the Dodger.

"Have you anything to say at all?"

"Do you hear his worship ask if you've anything to say?" inquired the jailer, nudging the silent Dodger with his elbow.

"I beg your pardon," said the Dodger, looking up with an air of abstraction. "Did you redress yourself to me, my man?"

"I never see such an out-and-out young wagabond, your worship," observed the officer with a grin. "Do you mean to say anything, you young shaver?"

"No," replied the Dodger, "not here, for this ain't the shop for justice; besides which, my attorney is a-break-fasting this morning with the Wice President of the House of Commons; but I shall have something to say elsewhere, and so will he, and so will a wery numerous and 'spectable circle of acquaintance as'll make them beaks wish they'd never been born, or that they'd got their footmen to hang 'em up to their own hat-pegs 'afore they let 'em come out this morning to try it on upon me. I'll – "

"There! He's fully committed!" interposed the clerk. "Take him away." (ch. 43)

This is the trick, writ large, played in the Dodger's characterization of Fagin as "a 'spectable old genelman," an intoxicating parody of order.

Formally, of course, Dickens endorses order, the normal and the normative, endorses the family where they are nourished. But it is clear his imagination yearned for the dark side. It is especially clear in one detail of the production of the novel which has puzzled many, but which can in fact be explained.

Oliver Twist ends with a description of the memorial tablet to Oliver's mother, in the church over which Harry Maylie presides. The narrator expresses the belief that her shade "sometimes hovers round that solemn nook. I believe it none the less because that nook is in a Church, and she was weak and erring." Dickens chose to leave readers with an image of transgression rather than of the normal and normative. Cruikshank's original final plate for the novel [fig. 17], shows Oliver with Rose and Harry Maylie, and old Mrs. Maylie, gathered contentedly round the domestic fireside. Dickens loathed this.[2] Because of production schedules, he was unable altogether to stop it appearing, but he managed to have it suppressed before many copies were printed, and to have another substituted. He wrote to Cruikshank, regretting "its being what it is," and demanding another design (Pilgrim *Letters* 1: 450–51). The words tellingly foreshadow the denunciation of the Circumlocution Office, responsible for the public condition being "what it was" (*Little Dorrit*, ch. 20). Less restrained and less subtle, Forster called the etching "a vile and disgusting interpolation on the sense and bearing of the tale," and spoke of its being "long known as a Rowland Macassar frontispiece to a sixpenny book of forfeits" (Pilgrim *Letters* 1: 451n).

It is not hard to understand why Dickens and Forster disliked the plate, but it is hard to understand why they disliked it so much. Various explanations are proffered, few satisfactory. One has it that the domestic milieu depicted in it is too suburban for the country parsonage – the "rustic dwelling" – in which Rose and Harry finally make their home. But why so much anger at something merely inappropriate? Another has it that the peacock feathers arranged round the top of the mirror exemplify a fashion far too lower-middle-class. But that too would be merely inappropriate. Michael Slater suggests that Dickens was angry at the inclusion of Harry Maylie in the illustration, that he wanted his projection of Mary Hogarth to stand free of adult male attachments (94). This is persuasive only if you see Harry Maylie as an interloper introduced by necessities of plot, rather than as a projection of Dickens himself.

The key to the indignation, I am tempted to think, is to be found in Forster's curious charge, that the image had been "long known as a Rowland Macassar frontispiece to a sixpenny book of forfeits." I am unfamiliar with the precise advertisement, if there was one, to which Forster was alluding, but an unchanging principle of advertising provides sufficient answer. Associating use of a product with happy

Figure 17   The suppressed plate. The original illustration provided by George
Cruikshank as the last for *Oliver Twist*. (By permission of the Dickens House
Museum, London.)

Figure 18   "Rose Maylie and Oliver." Substitute illustration provided by George Cruikshank as the last for *Oliver Twist*. (By permission of the Dickens House Museum, London.)

normal life is not a discovery of the twentieth-century copywriter. Detach the image from the story, and it is possible to read it as a fine head of hair and whiskers yielding domestic bliss: Mum, Dad, and the nipper, with Gran in the corner. Readers of the novel, of course, know that is not what is depicted, but ending the novel with this image seems almost to suggest that appropriate closure is achieved by as near a simulacrum as possible of Mum, Dad, the nipper, and Gran around the fireside. Forster was not raging incoherently. He was saying something precise, if intemperate, when he called the etching "a vile and disgusting interpolation on the sense and bearing of the story."

Confirmation of the grounds of Dickens's and Forster's objection is to be found in the replacement plate they procured from a reluctant Cruikshank. At first, it seems, Cruikshank tried adapting the original, but Dickens rejected that. Then he supplied an earlier version of the etching reproduced in figure 18, showing Rose and Oliver sadly contemplating the memorial tablet, but with Rose wearing a light-colored dress. We can only suppose prompted by Dickens, he eventually etched the dress more heavily, to produce the version you see, with Rose soberly clad, perhaps indeed in mourning for a sister whose loss she only now knows of.

The final visual image readers were to be left with had evidently to dwell upon transgression. It had to reinforce the narrator's final words. Nothing was to detract from the thought that the shade of Oliver's mother might hover around the nook where she is commemorated by her loved ones, "none the less because that nook is in a Church, and she was weak and erring."[3]

This bleak final moment crystallizes what I have in mind when I say there is something shrill and unappeased about *Oliver Twist*. And yet there is also something immensely powerful, something that cannot be traced to the surface pattern of family dysfunction. Perhaps, in a way, this bleak moment points to it. To my knowledge, no left-wing critic has grumbled about the absence of a memorial, in the same solemn nook, to Nancy, scarcely less crucial in Oliver's life than Agnes or Rose. An opportunity missed there, perhaps. But the thoughtful reader, confronted by the image of Oliver's aunt mourning his mother, may well be reminded of the third woman, because of an easily missed but ultimately undeniable feature of the plot. When we stand back a little, we can see it. Very little happens in *Oliver Twist* uninfluenced by the love women bear, the love they bear especially for children.

Oliver was conceived because of his mother's unbounded love for his father, "the object of the first, true, ardent, only passion of a guileless girl" (ch. 49). He is born in the workhouse, the only place he can be cared for, because of his mother's love for him. Her last words are, "Let me see the child, and die." Given the baby, "She imprinted her cold white lips passionately on its forehead; passed her hands over her face; gazed wildly round; shuddered; fell back – and died" (ch. 1). During his fever at Mr. Brownlow's house, Oliver feels his dead mother has been sitting by him, that her portrait, unrecognized by him as such, wants to speak to him (ch. 12).

Oliver is unharmed by Fagin and his gang, thanks to Nancy's passionate protective instincts. She will not see him hurt: "You've got the boy, and what more would you have? – Let him be – let him be – or I shall put that mark on some of you, that will bring me to the gallows before my time" (ch. 16). She protects him from further danger, at great risk, by colluding with Rose Maylie (chs. 40 and 44).

Mr. Brownlow is strangely attracted to Oliver. "There is something in that boy's face," he muses. "He looked like . . . . No, . . . it must be imagination" (ch. 11). He is at a loss to explain the strength of his attachment:

> . . . I am more interested in your behalf than I can well account for, even to myself. The persons on whom I have bestowed my dearest love, lie deep in their graves; but, although the happiness and delight of my life lie buried there too, I have not made a coffin of my heart, and sealed it up, for ever, on my best affections. Deep affliction has but strengthened and refined them. (ch. 14)

The dead he sorrows over, we later learn, are Oliver's father, and the sister of Oliver's father, who would have become Mr. Brownlow's bride, had she not died on what was to have been their wedding day (ch. 49). One of the impulses moving him is the love of a woman, long dead.

Rose Maylie is in reality the sister of Oliver's mother, and was left a penniless little orphan after her father's death. She was taken in "by some wretched cottagers," but saved from penury and neglect by the widowed Mrs. Maylie, who "saw the girl by chance, pitied her, and took her home" (ch. 51). She and Rose find the wounded Oliver at their door, take him in, knowing him to have been involved in the attempted burglary of their home, but nonetheless care for him, and love him (chs. 28 and 30).

The risk women take in loving is emphasized. Oliver's mother dies because she loved his father, and because she bears him. Fagin is quite wrong to dismiss Nancy's maternal feelings. "The worst of these women is, that a very little thing serves to call up some long-forgotten feeling," he reflects; "and the best of them is, that it never lasts" (ch. 19). Nancy confounds him by forfeiting her life as a result of protecting Oliver. Often read as a fictionalized record of Dickens's grief at the death of Mary Hogarth (Slater 93–94), Rose Maylie's near fatal illness (ch. 33) has evidently to do with the other-worldliness of her loving femininity. Introducing her, the text declares her to be "so mild and gentle; so pure and beautiful; that earth seemed not her element, nor its rough creatures her fit companions" (ch. 29). Her illness first declares itself in weeping. And in the same chapter we first hear of Harry Maylie, whom Rose loves, we soon learn, but whom she has made up her mind to renounce.

Oliver Twist has its female monsters: its predatory widow, Mrs. Corney, its shrew, Mrs. Sowerberry, its crone, old Sally, its infatuated servant, Charlotte; but it is not misogynous like *Pickwick Papers*. On the contrary, it can be read as an encomium of womanly love, triumphing against all odds.

Womanly love, to be sure, is clearly not at the center of Dickens's vision in the novel. It is pushed to the margins. It is encountered much more rarely than family dysfunction. It tends to be constructed adjectivally, and is not often effectively dramatized. When it is, melodrama is usually the model. It does not lend itself to humorous treatment and is denied, therefore, the enrichment of Dickens's irony. Too often it seems to have been dragged in to fill holes in the plot. And yet it is fundamental. Dickens's imagination may not always have been working at full power when it created representations of womanly love in *Oliver Twist*, but without them the plot would collapse.

To satisfy his readership, and to satisfy irrepressible impulses from the dark side of his imagination, Dickens created an anarchic vision of family breakdown in *Oliver Twist*, diametrically at variance with his own experience while he was writing it. This vision fills our gaze to the very end, despite the restoration of order, not least of family order. Yet something else asserts itself, clumsily, infrequently, but insistently, arising directly out of Dickens's own experience. While he was working on the novel, he felt for the first time the emotional demands of parenthood, and witnessed at close quarters the even greater demands upon Catherine, who endured, not only two difficult births, but also a miscarriage brought on by the death of her sister (Kaplan 94).   In *Pickwick*, Dickens had diminished the suffering and exasperation women had caused him, by transposing them into a vision at once misogynous and comic. While he was working on *Oliver Twist* he found himself confronted emotionally by something much more elemental and intractable than he had hitherto known in his relations with the other gender. Old bachelors, untroubled by sex and prosperous, can be shown in the novel, figuring things out and solving problems, but the elemental will not go away. The love of women, undiminished by suffering, the love of women especially for children, underpins everything else.

However much we acknowledge this perception, though, there still seems to be something shrill and unappeased about *Oliver Twist*. The anarchy of the book overshadows all other elements. It is a coherent novel, but not a balanced one. It is emotionally lopsided. This doubtless has to do with the deliberate dissonance between the events of Dickens's life and the story. For the most part, the relationship between them is not the relationship we find in *Pickwick Papers* and *Nicholas Nickleby*. These echo his life, *Oliver Twist* travesties it. But perhaps that is the secret of its power. Perhaps that is why, more than any other novel by Dickens, it has embedded itself in popular consciousness, and not only in the English-speaking world. Readers, too, like to wallow in emotion. Dr. Johnson commended the "common voice of the multitude, uninstructed by precept and unprejudiced by authority" (*Rambler* no. 52). Critics should remember that, when judging *Oliver Twist*.

5

NICHOLAS NICKLEBY: LOVE AND MONEY

When they began to appear in March 1838, the monthly parts of *Nicholas Nickleby* sold in huge numbers (Patten, *Charles Dickens and his Publishers* 99). Readers were evidently delighted. Critics, though, had less to say about the novel than about either of its predecessors (Collins 30–51). Perhaps it occasioned less surprise than *Pickwick Papers* or *Oliver Twist*. Here was no new voice. Here was Boz doing what he had shown he could do, and doing it wonderfully well once again. Quite what he was doing, however, seemed curiously to resist definition.

For a hundred and fifty years, in fact, even the most appreciative critics struggled to explain *Nicholas Nickleby*. G. K. Chesterton, almost always astute and enthusiastic when writing about Dickens, was one of the first to analyze the novel in any detail. And how did he see it? As "a very rambling, old-fashioned romance," remarkable chiefly for its characterization (Chesterton 115). In this he set the tone. Paul Schlicke is among Dickens scholars who have more recently defended the Chestertonian view. He sees the novel as a work "loosely organised around the adventures of a central figure, and distinguished by diversity of scene, accuracy of observed detail, and above all by vividness of character and incident" (Schlicke xvi–xvii). It is hard to reconcile such judgments with the contemporary impact of the book, or with its lasting popularity.

There have been occasional attempts to detect a unifying principle in the novel, that might account for its power. "Almost all of the characters in *Nicholas Nickleby*," Steven Marcus suggests, "represent some form of a prudent or imprudent response to life" (Marcus 95).

This is not to be denied, but there are few novels surely, by Dickens or by anyone else, about which the same might not be said. Michael Slater argues that "Theatricality and role-playing are the living heart of *Nicholas Nickleby* . . . giving it such artistic unity and coherence as it can be said to possess" (Slater ed., *Nicholas Nickleby* 15). It is an earnest tribute from an undoubted admirer of the novel, but could there be praise much fainter?

As an exercise in plotting, to be sure, *Nicholas Nickleby* is unimpressive.   The advertisement circulated prior to publication promised readers "a rapid succession of characters and incidents." Probably speaking of the second monthly part, Dickens told Forster, "I . . . have yet 5 slips to finish, and don't know what to put in them for I have reached the point I meant to leave off with" (Pilgrim *Letters* 1: 395–96). The readiness to improvise suggested by these documents is evident in the text, which is plainly not fashioned to lead readers on by requiring them to suppose everything a consequence of what has happened before. It is constructed for the most part by the tagging of episode onto episode. As in not a few novels, the villain, Ralph, minds the plot while the hero, Nicholas, goes on his travels. It is difficult not to feel that Dickens hit upon Yorkshire schools as a good subject, played it out, thought of a travelling theater company, played that out too, and finally introduced a quite different set of characters to restore the fortunes of Nicholas and his family.

The way characters appear and disappear seems less calculated to sustain the reader's suspense, than to provide opportunities for the writer to invent.   Madeline Bray, whom Nicholas eventually marries, is mysteriously introduced in chapter 16, and promptly shelved until chapter 40. Dickens is more than halfway through the novel before he reintroduces his heroine. After he has killed Lord Frederick Verisopht (ch. 50), Sir Mulberry Hawk vanishes almost completely.   The reappearance of Mr. Squeers from time to time (chs. 34 and 56) is just about vindicated by plot development, but Mr. Crummles, the actor-manager, is reintroduced in chapter 48 only for the sake of a formal farewell.

To impose closure on this loose construction, Dickens had to extemporize. The techniques and stereotypes of melodrama, not always palatable to modern readers, are called upon more and more in the book's closing stages – the dastardly plot to marry luscious young Madeline Bray to ancient Arthur Gride, for instance. Comedy dwindles. New characters fail to dazzle. Many solutions to puzzles bear the marks of last-minute cobbling: the introduction, for instance, of Brooker who, many years before the action begins, had taken the infant Smike to Dotheboys Hall. Readers do not find their attention held by a carefully organized story. They read on to find out what happens to characters in whom they have become interested, and because of the energy with which the book abounds.

But they also sense coherence in it, and that coherence is thematic. A loosely constructed plot is not incompatible with tight thematic organization. *Nicholas Nickleby* is a demonstrably coherent work of art – not flawless, to be sure, but so plainly constructed around a dominant idea that I am surprised it was for so long overlooked. The novel has a clear unifying theme, more consciously chosen and more consciously adhered to, than any we find in either of its predecessors. *Pickwick Papers* and *Oliver Twist* are coherent too, but we cannot help feeling that Dickens shaped them more instinctively than consciously, out of what was happening to him, and what had happened to him in the past. He shaped *Nicholas Nickleby* out of the same material, but according to plan, and well aware of what he was doing. I can only suppose critics failed to recognize this because the theme, though far from uncomplicated, is almost too obvious. It is probably the most commonplace theme of all in prose fiction. But that is not to say it is negligible, or that Dickens must be blamed for choosing it.

I believe the hold of *Nicholas Nickleby* on the imagination of readers has to do with the intensity with which it contemplates precisely what it seems to contemplate: the relationship between love and money.

It is a theme openly stated in the first paragraph of the book, which tells of the marriage of Nicholas's grandfather, Godfrey Nickleby, to a portionless lady. "Thus two people who cannot afford to play cards for money," the narrative remarks, "sometimes sit down to a quiet game of love."[1] The chapter then proceeds to detail the past history of the Nickleby family, and raises question after question about money: how it may be gained, kept, passed on, or lost, and how love, or the lack of it, may affect all this. As the plot of the novel unfolds, the theme is intricately developed. All members of the Nickleby family provoke the reader to ask questions about money and love, and about key related topics: work, marriage, inheritance, and rank. Godfrey Nickleby has two sons, the hero's father, Nicholas Senior, and his uncle, Ralph. The first chooses to marry for love, and is content with gentlemanly subsistence in the country. He is ruined, and leaves his family penniless, because he he loves his wife and follows her bad advice. Ralph chooses a brief mercenary and clandestine marriage, and the pursuit of money. He makes a fortune as a moneylender in London, but greed and hatred undo him. Unloved, he dies alone by his own hand. The theme is a complex one – more complex than any in *Pickwick Papers* or *Oliver Twist* – but nonetheless palpable.[2]

Most of the characters in the novel, most of the episodes, provoke questions about money and love, and about the associated topics of work, marriage, inheritance, and rank. The care he shows for his family, and his worries for its future, make the villainy of Mr. Squeers, the Yorkshire schoolmaster, both more monstrous and more credible. He and his son both look forward to the day when young Wackford will take over the school. His daughter Fanny is at first enchanted by Nicholas's superior breeding but, rejected by him, joins her mother in scornfully questioning it. The departure for America of Mr. Crummles, the actor-manager, is motivated chiefly by a desire to provide for the family he dotes on. The chapters featuring the Kenwigs family amount to a subplot, no less, and work the way a subplot does. Features of the main plot are ironically reflected. For all their absurdity, the Kenwigses love each other, and are prepared to love Mrs. Kenwigs's uncle, Mr. Lillyvick, the water-rate collector. They are anxious about the inheritance they expect from him, about his feelings and theirs, about their position in society, about the manners appropriate to it. At a party they organize, Mr. Kenwigs asks, " . . . wouldn't it be better to begin a round game?"

> "Kenwigs, my dear," returned his wife, "I am surprised at you. Would you begin without my uncle?"
> "I forgot the collector," said Kenwigs; "oh no, that would never do."

"He's so particular," said Mrs. Kenwigs, turning to the other married lady, "that if we began without him, I should be put out of his will for ever."

"Dear!" cried the married lady.

"You've no idea what he is," replied Mrs. Kenwigs; "and yet as good a creature as ever breathed."

"The kindest-hearted man as ever was," said Mr. Kenwigs.

"It goes to his heart, I believe, to be forced to cut the water off, when people don't pay," observed the bachelor friend, intending a joke.

"George," said Mr. Kenwigs, solemnly, "none of that, if you please."

"It was only my joke," said the friend, abashed. (ch. 14)

The Mantalinis and Wititterlys provoke questions about love between husband and wife. Lord Frederick Verisopht and Sir Mulberry Hawk provoke fairly obvious questions about exalted rank and wealth, and the degraded kinds of love these can licence. Without benefit of inheritance, the Cheeryble brothers demonstrate how rank and wealth may be obtained and upheld with dignity, how loving family relations may be sustained by rank and wealth, instead of degraded. Even the interpolated stories, "The Five Sisters of York" and "The Baron of Grogzwig" (ch. 6), even the character of the gentleman in small-clothes, invite readers to ponder the links between love and money.

Doctrines fashionable among lovers of literature, and in the academy, have made it hard to be dispassionate about some of the topics the theme of *Nicholas Nickleby* encompasses. That may be another reason why its coherence has been overlooked. There are readers of nineteenth-century fiction who still choose not to be dispassionate and, in doing so, repudiate values at the heart of the novel. It is pointless to pretend, for instance, that it does not demand respect for the notion of birthright, and all that involves. Many of today's readers, though, are uneasy, to say no more, about the very survival of social class. Many, too, are unable to discern any position between indifference to money and greed. It is best plainly to state, then, that without exercise of the historical imagination, readers who subscribe to these views are unlikely to appreciate the theme upon which *Nicholas Nickleby* is centered.

Most early Victorians took the view that, while some might care too much for rank and wealth, no one was required to despise such things. Remembering that might help readers.

It would be surprising if Dickens had not been preoccupied with love and money during 1838 and 1839, when he was writing *Nicholas Nickleby*. The Doughty Street years were crowded with developments in his life, all more or less to do with love or money or both. He had married just two years before the launching of *Nickleby*, his first child had been born a little over a year before it, his third was born just as he was completing it. He was leaving hardship behind, and becoming prosperous. The book was written in Doughty Street, where he and Catherine could be comfortable, and lay claim to respectability. When it was finished he was able to move on to Devonshire Terrace, where they could enjoy luxury, and lay claim to fashion. In short, during this period of his life, Dickens was intent upon becoming a good provider, and succeeding spectacularly. A large proportion of novels, I suppose, are about good providers – young men who start with little or nothing, but achieve wealth and position for themselves and for those they love. *Nicholas Nickleby* is about a good provider, too, but about much more than that. In tackling the theme of love and money in this novel, Dickens exhibits a breadth of vision much more rarely encountered.

Dickens's success as a novelist was confirmed by elevation in social rank. He was beginning to be accepted in circles none of his family had ever dared aspire to. It was in 1838 that he began to frequent the Holland House salon. It was in June of that year, not long after the monthly parts of *Nicholas Nickleby* began to appear, that he was elected to the Athenaeum Club. He was beginning to be on familiar terms with many of the artistic, theatrical, and literary lions of London, and to be seen as literary lion himself. A portrait of him, painted by Maclise and engraved by Finden, would soon be in great demand, for binding in with the monthly parts of *Nicholas Nickleby* [fig. 19].

The state of mind that yielded the novel, though, can be understood only if we remember how new all this was to him, and see how it failed to obliterate old distress. When the first series of *Sketches by Boz* appeared in February 1836, it had been a collection of pieces by a young journalist, known to its readers, if at all, only by his pen name. His own

Figure 19   Dickens in 1839, painted by Daniel Maclise and engraved by
William Finden. (By permission of the Dickens House Museum, London.)

name had been known to scarcely anyone except other journalists. A few more readers had heard of Boz when *Pickwick Papers* was launched the following month and, when it soared to success after a few numbers, many more came to do so. Yet even when Dickens became editor of *Bentley's Miscellany* at the beginning of 1837, and began to serialize *Oliver Twist* in it, he had never seen his own name on a title page. He did so at last when the volume edition of *Pickwick* was published in November 1837, eight months after he had moved to Doughty Street. By the time the first part of *Nickleby* was on sale four months later, a vast public knew that Boz and Charles Dickens were one and the same. But it had not done so for long.

Unsurprisingly, Dickens was far from confident about the durability of his prosperity and eminence. Misled by hindsight, twenty-first-century readers are often astonished to learn that, in December 1839, only a few weeks after completing *Nickleby*, when there was no mistaking its success or his, Dickens registered as a law student at the Middle Temple (Pilgrim *Letters* 1: 621n). Like so many characters in the novel, he was evidently thinking carefully about income, position, and his family's future. He was hedging his bets. He never seriously pursued his legal studies, but the very fact of his registering indicates that, Devonshire Terrace, the Athenaeum, and Holland House notwithstanding, fame and prosperity had failed to erase memories and anxieties unsettling to someone acquiring so many responsibilities and commitments.

Not that he wanted them erased. On the contrary, he took steps to preserve them. They gave an edge to the indignation he felt at the suffering of those he championed – the ill-used and the dispossessed. More than that, in preserving old memories, he was maintaining the foundations on which his art was built – ultimately on which his prosperity was built. As he told Forster, "I know how all these things have worked together to make me what I am" (John Forster bk. 1, ch. 2).

In preparation for writing *Nicholas Nickleby*, Dickens researched a group of schools in Yorkshire, about which scandalous reports had been circulating for many years. His interest in these establishments plainly had to do with his own childhood ordeal, and plainly restimulated memories of it.

During the eighteenth century, a cluster of schools had begun to develop around Barnard Castle and Bowes, then within the North Riding of Yorkshire, not in County Durham as now.[3] The cost of living in the locality was lower than in most parts of the country, so fees could be competitive. By the early nineteenth century there was a concentration of private academies in the area, most of them offering more practical courses of instruction than the endowed grammar schools, often including tuition in such subjects as bookkeeping and navigation. Some of these schools, by teaching neglected subjects well, led the way in educational progress. But north Yorkshire's remoteness from London and other urban centers was considered an advantage by some proprietors – and by some of their clients. The phrase, "no vacations," is featured in several advertisements. There were some schools which became, in effect, places at which unwanted children could be dumped – stepchildren, the handicapped, the orphaned, the illegitimate. It was not unknown for children to be sent to such schools and abandoned. The Bowes parish burial register for 28 July 1821 records the burial of an eight-year-old pupil at one school, "supposed a native of Newcastle."

With his illustrator, Browne, Dickens travelled to north Yorkshire in early 1838 and, posing as an interested parent, visited a number of schools (Pilgrim *Letters* 1: 365–66). The Dotheboys Hall episode of *Nicholas Nickleby* is the result. Bowes Academy, near Greta Bridge, was one of the schools visited. Though Dickens prudently declared Mr. Squeers "the representative of a class, and not of an individual" (Preface to the first edition), it is clear he modelled him upon William Shaw, and Dotheboys Hall upon Bowes Academy [fig. 20], which Shaw ran from 1812 until 1840 (Butcher 32).

What Dickens saw and heard there evidently prompted him to look up reports in *The Times* of a successful prosecution of Shaw in 1823. Boys at the school were going blind. One twelve-year-old victim's testimony includes the following details:

> Gave us meat and potatoes four days in the week – bread and milk on Thursday – dumplings made of flour and water Friday – and black potatoes, with a bit of butter, on Saturday. When any

Figure 20   Bowes Academy, photographed by T. W. Tyrrell. Dickens's model for Dotheboys Hall in *Nicholas Nickleby*.   (By permission of the Dickens House Museum, London.)

gentleman used to come to see the school, Mr. Shaw used to come in and tell the usher to make all boys without jackets and trousers get under the table. When any of them got a hole in the jacket or trousers, they went without till they were mended. The boys washed in a long trough, like what horses drink out of: the biggest boys used to take advantage of the little boys, and get the dry part of the towel. There were two towels a day for the whole school. We had no supper; nothing after tea – we had dry bread,brown, and a drop of water and a drop of milk warmed. . . . Every other morning we used to flea the beds. The usher used to cut the quills, and give us them to catch the fleas; and if you did not fill the quill, you caught a good beating. The pot-skimmings were called broth, and we used to have it for tea on Sunday; one of the ushers offered a penny a piece for every maggot, and there was a pot-full gathered: he never gave it them. No soap, except on Saturday, and then the wenches used to wash us. I was there nine months, and there was nothing the matter with me. One morning I could not write my copy. Next morning he sent me into the wash-house. There were other boys there; some quite blind.[4]

Not all reports are so damning. Some former pupils in later life praised the school. Even the judge who presided over the 1823 hearing was "of the opinion that there was nothing to impeach the general conduct of Mr. Shaw in the management of the school." On the strength of the testimony, it is difficult not to feel Dickens's evaluation of the situation is more to be trusted than the judge's. Whether it is or not, there can be little doubt that firsthand accounts of childhood misery were likely to prevail with him. He lashed out instinctively at the Yorkshire schools and, in the Dotheboys Hall episode of *Nickleby*, constructed a devastating indictment of them. These are Nicholas's first impressions of the pupils he is to teach at the school:

Pale and haggard faces, lank and bony figures, children with the countenances of old men, deformities with irons upon their limbs, boys of stunted growth, and others whose long meagre legs would hardly bear their stooping bodies, all crowded on the view together; there were the bleared eye, the hare-lip, the crooked foot, and every ugliness or distortion that told of unnatural aversion conceived by parents for their offspring, or of young lives which, from the earliest dawn of infancy, had been one horrible endurance of cruelty and neglect. There were little faces which should have been handsome, darkened with the scowl of sullen, dogged suffering; there was childhood with the light of its eye quenched, its beauty gone, and its helplessness alone remaining; there were vicious-faced boys, brooding, with leaden eyes, like malefactors in a jail; and there were young creatures on whom the sins of their frail parents had descended, weeping even for the mercenary nurses they had known, and lonesome even in their loneliness. With every kindly sympathy and affection blasted in its birth, with every young and healthy feeling flogged and starved down, with every revengeful passion that can fester in swollen hearts eating its evil way to their core in silence, what an incipient Hell was breeding here! (ch. 8)

Dickens's researches on the Yorkshire schools are filled out by memories of his own suffering at Warren's, in particular of his own feeling of abandonment, to form a grotesque and poignant tableau.

Thanks to *Nicholas Nickleby*, Shaw, Bowes Academy, and all the private academies of north Yorkshire, were dealt a blow from which they never recovered. The American historian, Francis Parkman, travelling in Yorkshire in 1843, noted that "we passed the veritable Dotheboys Hall of Dickens, exactly answering to his description in appearance, in situation, in all things. It is deserted utterly – *Nicholas Nickleby* not only ruined this establishment alone, but many other schools with which the vicinity abounds, though some of the latter were in no way objectionable" (1: 225). Fine adult distinctions were immaterial to Dickens, where the suffering of defenseless children was concerned. Vengeance was called for, and was delivered – every bit as hotheaded as Nicholas's.

It is the same determination to dwell upon the intensity of childhood distress, free of adult judgment, that we see in the account of Warren's and the Marshalsea, which Dickens wrote for Forster nearly ten years later. Even in his mid-thirties, the pain and bewilderment persisted somewhere in Dickens's memory, and would return unbidden, or be revisited. Forgetting all his achievements, he would "wander desolately back to that time of my life."

Nicholas Nickleby expresses this recurrent pain. Perhaps it was deliberately restimulated to enrich the novel. But self-pity is avoided through balance. The novel also expresses Dickens's exhilaration at success, fame and domestic contentment. And, again, it expresses these things most strikingly through a pair of characters – Nicholas and Smike.

In *Pickwick Papers*, Mr. Pickwick and Sam divide between them the innocently ambitious, fantasizing component of Dickens's character, and the streetwise resourceful component. In *Oliver Twist*, Oliver encapsulates Dickens's anxieties about vulnerable innocence betrayed, while the Artful Dodger celebrates his triumph at having mastered street wisdom, at having constructed a hard shell into which he could withdraw.

In *Nicholas Nickleby*, Nicholas embodies what we might call, for lack of a better term, the go-getter in Dickens, who was going and getting in 1838 and 1839. Nothing in his past impedes Nicholas. On the contrary, his upbringing gives him confidence. Far from denying it, he yearns to recover the world of his childhood, and eventually does. He is clever, resourceful, confident, quick to resent injury, determined to secure an honored position for himself and those he loves – unstoppable. His taste for violence is perhaps the clearest sign of his unstoppability. Nicholas is involved, or all but involved, in five violent confrontations in the novel, with Mr. Squeers (ch. 13), John Browdie (ch. 13), Mr. Lenville (ch. 29), Sir Mulberry Hawk (ch. 23), and Arthur Gride (ch. 54). When Mr. Squeers begins mercilessly to cane Smike at Dotheboys Hall, Nicholas intervenes:

> "I have a long series of insults to avenge," said Nicholas, flushed with passion; "and my indignation is aggravated by the dastardly cruelties practised upon helpless infancy in this foul den. Have a care; for if you raise the devil within me, the consequences shall fall heavily upon you own head!"
> He had scarcely spoken, when Squeers, in a violent outbreak of wrath, and with a cry like the howl of a wild beast, spat upon him, and struck him a blow across the face with his instrument of torture, which raised up a bar of livid flesh as it was inflicted. Smarting with the agony of the blow, and concentrating into that

one moment all his feelings of rage, scorn, and indignation, Nicholas sprang upon him, wrested the weapon from his hand, and pinning him by the throat, beat the ruffian till he roared for mercy. (ch. 13)

It is a kind of violence featured in the works of Smollett, for instance, whom Dickens admired, and whose heroes regularly "rub down" opponents, "with an oaken towel." But literary influence notwithstanding, the raw ruthless energy of Dickens himself shows through incidents like this.

Smike, in contrast, is a victim of his past, and an unresisting victim of violence, both before the narrative begins and during its course. He has been thrashed regularly by Mr. Squeers since early boyhood, and is thrashed three more times during the course of the narrative (chs. 12, 13 and 38). This is what we find in chapter 13, just prior to Nicholas's intervention:

"Have you anything to say?" demanded Squeers again: giving his right arm two or three flourishes to try its power and suppleness. "Stand a little out of the way, Mrs. Squeers, my dear; I've hardly got room enough."

"Spare me, sir!" cried Smike.

"Oh! that's all, is it?" cried Squeers. "Yes, I'll flog you within an inch of your life, and spare you that."

"Ha, ha, ha," laughed Mrs. Squeers, "that's a good 'un!" . . .

Squeers caught the boy firmly in his grip; one desperate cut had fallen on his body – he was wincing from the lash and uttering a scream of pain – it was raised again, and again about to fall – when Nicholas Nickleby suddenly starting up, cried "Stop!" in a voice that made the rafters ring.

Smike embodies the hidden vulnerable aspect of Dickens's personality, the child damaged by what Dickens saw as ill-usage and neglect during the Warren's and Marshalsea period, the child in need of protection.

Together from near the beginning of the book, Nicholas and Smike might well cause Mr. Folair to wonder "how you two, who are so different, came to be such close companions" (ch. 30). Fielding, as well as Smollett and Dickens's revered Sir Walter Scott, had all given dashing young heroes grotesque attendants, but it was more than literary tradition that made Dickens yoke this pair. There is no better testimony to this than the emotional intensity of their agreement to join forces:

> "May I – may I go with you?" asked Smike, timidly. "I will be your faithful hard-working servant, I will, indeed. I want no clothes," added the poor creature, drawing his rags together; "these will do very well. I only want to be near you."
>
> "And you shall," cried Nicholas. "And the world shall deal by you as it does by me, till one or both of us shall quit it for a better. Come!"
>
> With these words, he strapped his burden on his shoulder, and, taking his stick in his hand, extended the other to his delighted charge; and so they passed out of the old barn, together. (ch. 13)

Echoes of the Book of Ruth (1.16) and of *Paradise Lost* (12.646–49) mark the engagement of Dickens's deepest personal feelings at this point in the text.

Nicholas's indignation at the treatment of Smike is constructed upon Dickens's indignation at his own treatment at Warren's. Dotheboys Hall projects Dickens's nightmare of children abandoned and mistreated, of "the dastardly cruelties practised upon helpless infancy" denounced by Nicholas. Smike – Nicholas's companion, his coeval, his cousin we finally learn – is a pitiable result of such abandonment and mistreatment, a creature Dickens bore within himself, a creature his more self-confident self had to protect, a creature he felt he might have become had not luck, talent, and application made him much more like Nicholas.

Like *Oliver Twist, Nicholas Nickleby* ends with sorrowful contemplation of a memorial to the dead, but this time it is not transgression the book invites readers to dwell upon. Now, sorrow is richly mingled with a sense of release. The melancholy note sounded by Smike's death (ch. 58) qualifies the triumphs of the book's closing chapters. Following tradition, the last chapter is devoted chiefly to detailing the happiness of characters readers are called upon to admire, but it concludes with this elegiac contemplation of Smike's grave:

> The grass was green above the dead boy's grave, and trodden by feet so small and light [those of Nicholas's and Kate's children], that not a daisy drooped its head beneath their pressure. Through all the spring and summer-time, garlands of fresh flowers, wreathed by infant hands, rested on the stone; and, when the children came there to change them lest they should wither and be pleasant to him no longer, their eyes filled with tears, and they spoke low and softly of their poor dead cousin. (ch. 65)

There is no more prominent position in the book, right at the end. The language is elevated, solemn, charged with emotion. This is not a passage to be explained away, by reference to the cult of sentiment for instance, though doubtless that had an effect on it. Old emotions are clearly being restimulated. It is an attempt by Dickens, I suggest, to lay to rest the damaged child within him. The unstoppable Nicholas can, like Dickens, claim the privileges of manhood – independence, marriage, children. Smike, the same age as Nicholas but noticeably described as a "boy" until the very end of the book (chs. 60, 62 and 65), must die, be remembered, and be mourned.

The central theme of love and money, in *Nicholas Nickleby*, is constructed as much by antithesis as by thesis – by difference, if you like. Nicholas goes and gets love and money. Deprived of both, Smike is pleased at what little trickles down to him, and is chiefly occupied with surviving abuse and neglect. Hatred and indifference, poverty and deprivation, are also central to the novel. The suffering children at Yorkshire schools, and Dickens's own suffering childhood self, are imaginatively blended into the figure of Smike. He is a key figure in the construction of the novel's theme – a dark and melancholy shadow reproaching the failure of love, the failure to use money as it should be used.

In the Dotheboys Hall episode, we see the direct effect of Dickens's own experience on *Nicholas Nickleby*, but it is at least as interesting to consider indirect effects: what Dickens's imagination turned to, not in revisiting his past, but in recoiling from it: not just fact grimly recalled, but fantasy gratefully indulged. The events of his life provide only a very inexact model for a story of the son of a gentleman, fallen on hard times, striving to regain his birthright, deemed to include prosperity, respect, the old family home, a secure place in society somewhere above the middle rank, and a loving wife of the same rank.

The notion of birthright cannot often have been invoked by Dickens's family when he was a child. Whatever their pretensions, his parents were lower-middle-class, his father a new recruit even to that class. John Dickens was no Mr. Kenwigs, to be sure, but for all his sense of the genteel, his clerkship in the Navy Pay Office, his ambition, he was the son of domestic servants, however grand the household they had served. If a biographical source is to be sought for Dickens's interest in birthright, first plainly evidenced in *Oliver Twist* and repeatedly featured in his fiction, it must be a negative one: it must be explained by what he was deprived of during childhood, not by what he experienced. He had understandably felt, as a child, some kind of entitlement to middle-class status, and to a way of life at least as prosperous and respectable as the one his parents had enjoyed before 1824, hence his sense of betrayal at Warren's and the Marshalsea. The shock of having found himself cast out from the class he believed himself to belong to prompted him to look for stories featuring a kind of belonging denied him in his life.

He did not have to look far. Stories about the recovery of birthright, about the "plot of hidden identity" (Morgentaler 45), are among the commonest in narrative literature. They are to be found again and again, for instance, in the works of Fielding, Smollett, and Scott, all avidly read by Dickens. More fundamentally, they are to be found in the fairy tales and folk tales we all learn as children. Again and again we come across the king's son, lost or kidnapped, brought up in humble circumstances, but still, against the odds, becoming king himself, and marrying a princess, aided, we are prompted to conclude, by a watchful and just Providence. Dickens, too, learned these stories, defended them in his writings as an adult,[5] and found in them a source of consoling fantasy.

What is fascinating about *Nicholas Nickleby*, in this respect, is the way the notion of birthright is used for more than structural purposes. Dickens stiffens fantasy with carefully observed fact. There can be few ideas, I suppose, more distinctly uniting the notions of love and money than birthright. Dickens exploits this to the full. The transmission of wealth and position from one generation to the next is at the center of the novel. It is a topic explored, quite self-consciously, through many intricacies. Readers are repeatedly required to make judgments about such matters.

Money was especially topical at the beginning of Victoria's reign, as capital. British industry and commerce achieved the growth they did in the late eighteenth and early nineteenth centuries, because the capital was available to finance it. For many years to come, growth would be paid for chiefly by individual entrepreneurs reinvesting profits, but other sources of capital were acquiring importance and attracting attention.

Joint-stock companies of one kind and another were springing up at an unprecedented rate, encouraging the kind of speculation we see ruining Nicholas's father in chapter 1, generating the kind of feverish excitement we see in chapter 2, at the launching of the United Metropolitan Improved Hot Muffin and Crumpet Baking and Punctual Delivery Company. Dickens was closer to contemporary truth than it might be supposed, in his hugely comic account of this. Over six hundred new companies were floated during the year or two preceding the credit crisis of 1825, which caused the failure of six major London financial houses and sixty country banks. The crisis was finally averted only by the Rothschilds' purchase of massive quantities of bullion at almost any price.

But joint-stock companies were not to dominate the economy until later in the century. Limited liability for shareholders was introduced only in 1855. Not until 1862 did an act of parliament lay the foundations of modern British company law.

Probably because of this, the Muffin Company is a one-shot joke in *Nicholas Nickleby*. After chapter 2, company and joke are abandoned together. The comedy is founded on the absurdity of treating a small-scale craft in the same way as large-scale capital-intensive enterprises like railways, gasworks, and steel foundries. There is a sublime silliness in conflating solitary itinerant muffin sellers and factory workers. The portentous style of blue books and other official reports is mimicked in Sir Matthew Pupker's declaration that "among muffin-sellers there existed drunkenness, debauchery, and profligacy, which he attributed to the debasing nature of their employment as at present exercised." Establishment paranoia about trades unions is mimicked in his undertaking

> to prove before a committee of the House of Commons, that there existed a combination to keep up the price of muffins, and to give the bellmen a monopoly; he would prove it by bellmen at the bar of that house; and he would also prove, that these men corresponded with each other by secret words and signs, as "Snooks," "Walker," "Ferguson," "Is Murphy right?" and many others.

These are all names, in fact, with comic rather than conspiratorial associations. "Snooks" was slang for a practical joker, "Walker" an expression of incredulity. "You can't lodge here, Ferguson," was a catch-phrase used to express denial or derision. "Murphy" was slang for the stereotypical comic Irishman.

In poking fun at the hysteria aroused by joint-stock companies, Dickens was remembering excitements of his childhood days, and anticipating developments in the future. But joint-stock companies are marginal to the theme of money in *Nicholas Nickleby*. Until at least the 1850s, the chief source of capital, other than reinvested profit, was credit. And it was credit rather than speculation that interested the public in the 1830s. It was credit, moreover, that aroused in Dickens, not only painful memories, but also present anxieties. The mood of the time, in the years preceding the credit crisis of 1825, may well have contributed to his father's misfortunes then. An unwise readiness to borrow, and a feeling that the growth of prosperity is unstoppable, credit limitless, invite trouble. But John Dickens's misfortunes were no distant memory during the Doughty Street years. He had been sued for debt again more than once since 1831. On one occasion, in November 1834, having backed some of his father's bills, Dickens himself had half expected to be arrested (Pilgrim *Letters* 1: 45). The success of the Doughty Street novels, moreover, seems to have encouraged John Dickens's improvident ways. The father acquired the habit of asking for loans on the strength of the son's reputation. This so exasperated

Dickens that, between April 1839 and October 1842, he exiled his parents to a cottage near Exeter.

The years of boom and recession that followed the Napoleonic Wars, not to mention the financing of the wars themselves, brought into prominence the figure of the money-dealer, be he international banker or street-corner pawnbroker. Dickens had no objection to capitalism. He eventually became something of a capitalist himself – shareholder, mortgagee, and sole proprietor of *All the Year Round*. But perhaps because of childhood experience, he never reconciled himself to the notion of wealth created solely by moving paper around. Moneylenders and financiers are always despised figures in his fiction.

Ralph Nickleby is one such. Today's readers are often tempted to see in him not much more than the classic villain of melodrama or the wicked uncle of fairy tale. Dickens's presentation of him, certainly, assimilates Ralph to such figures. Balancing almost too schematically the novel's theme of money and love, the two passions that motivate him, we read, are "avarice, the first and predominant appetite of his nature, and hatred, the second" (ch. 44). Devices used to indicate the conflict between him and Nicholas tend to be not so much theatrical as positively stagey. In chapter 20 he is blackguarding his nephew:

> " . . . Do innocent men steal away from the sight of honest folks, and skulk in hiding-places, like outlaws? Do innocent men inveigle nameless vagabonds, and prowl with them about the country as idle robbers do? Assault, riot, theft, what do you call these?"
>
> "A lie!" cried a voice, as the door was dashed open, and Nicholas came into the room.

More acceptable features of melodrama are to be found in Ralph's baffled affection for Kate, for instance (chs. 26 and 31), or his despair at the revelation of Smike's identity:

> His own child, his own child! He never doubted the tale; he felt it was true; knew it as well, now, as if he had been privy to it all along. His own child! And dead too. Dying beside

Nicholas, loving him, and looking upon him as something like
an angel! That was the worst. (ch. 62)

But even if we allow melodrama merits of its own, it is necessary to
insist that Ralph is no mere ogre from the pattern-book of fiction. The
moneylender was an undeniable presence in early nineteenth-century
London, known only too well to Dickens. Though he often employs the
old-fashioned term "usurer" for Ralph, it is with meticulous accuracy
that he details the procedure Ralph follows for discounting bills of
exchange, then the favorite mechanism for credit transactions.

Customers often paid for goods or services with bills of exchange
instead of cash. Bills authorized the supplier to demand payment at an
agreed later date. The person named to pay could be either the customer
himself, or a third party who owed money to the customer, or someone
else willing to stand surety, such as Dickens had been for his father in
1834. Bills were negotiable, and moneylenders were willing to buy
them at a discount before their due date, taking the risk of their being
dishonored, but hoping to make a profit by receiving full value at full
term. The text of *Nicholas Nickleby* is peppered with the special
terminology of bill discounting. Readers' attention is drawn, for
instance, to interest-tables, which detailed amounts of interest
accumulating at various rates upon various sums over various periods
(ch. 33); to post-obits, which were bonds promising payment after the
decease of persons from whom debtors had expectations (ch. 51); and to
renewed bills, which were bills, payment of which had been postponed,
for a consideration (ch. 57).

When Mr. Mantalini asks Ralph for discount in chapter 34, we are
taken through the whole process. "How many bills?", Ralph asks.
"What is the gross amount?" "And the dates?" "Let me see the names."
Ralph makes it his business to discover that Mr. Mantalini wishes to sell
two bills of exchange, totalling £75 in value, one with two months to
run, one with four. He buys them for £50, making his likely profit £25,
or fifty percent. Before doing so, to calculate the risk, he checks who is
named to honor them. There is nothing melodramatic about this. On
the contrary, it is tenaciously naturalistic.

Bills of exchange had taught Dickens much about profit and loss and hard-headed calculation, but he had learned about that, too, from transactions in which he was more intimately involved. The Doughty Street years saw him repeatedly negotiating and renegotiating contracts with publishers, in particular with Richard Bentley (Patten 75–87). Between 22 August 1836 and 2 July 1840, Dickens and Bentley signed nine different agreements. The contemporary practice of offering authors fixed payments for their books, agreed in advance, discriminated against an author like Dickens, whose popularity was rapidly growing. By the time they were received, payments which had seemed adequate when the contract was signed now seemed meager. In September 1838, while he was writing *Nickleby*, Dickens formally agreed to publish *Barnaby Rudge* in *Bentley's Miscellany*, to follow *Oliver Twist*. But pressure of work stopped him complying, and he complained to Forster about "the slavery and drudgery of another work on the same journeyman-terms" (Pilgrim *Letters* 1: 493) In February 1839, Bentley accepted Dickens's resignation from the *Miscellany*, and signed a much more generous contract with him, for *Barnaby Rudge*. That too came to nothing. Bentley and Dickens eventually freed themselves from mutual obligations in July 1840, with Dickens rejoicing at having escaped from the "Burlington Street brigand" (Pilgrim *Letters* 1: 619).

It is not surprising, then, that *Nicholas Nickleby* displays an interest in money, not just as capital, but as something earned. Work is at the heart of the novel, and plays an important part in constructing the theme of love and money. Any novel not set in the world of the leisure classes, is likely to feature work, but *Nicholas Nickleby* highlights it. It is populated with working people, whom we constantly see making a living for themselves, providing for their families, providing for the future – or trying to.

The novel eagerly explores the facts of work. We learn what people in different occupations do, and how they talk about it. Mr. Crummles, for instance, enthuses about Smike's potential as an actor:

> Only let him be tolerably well up in the Apothecary in Romeo and Juliet with the slightest possible dab of red on the tip of his nose, and he'd be certain of three rounds the moment he puts his head out of the practicable door in the front grooves O. P. (ch. 22)

He is speaking of a door in stage scenery which actually opens and shuts, of grooves in the stage for sliding wings and flats, and of the right-hand side of the stage, "opposite prompt." Dickens is plainly drawing on his own experience of the theater here, but the novel abounds in professional disclosures, by no means exclusively theatrical.

One of the recurrent jokes is the imparting of trade secrets. At Dotheboys Hall, boys are set to cleaning windows and rubbing down horses, as part of the "practical mode of teaching." "That's the way we do it, Nickleby," Mr. Squeers advises Nicholas (ch. 8). This is a comic allusion to the curricula of private academies, but part of a pattern too. Mr. Crummles urges Nicholas to write a play introducing "a real pump and two washing-tubs."

> I bought 'em cheap at a sale the other day, and they'll come in admirably. That's the London play. They look up some dresses and properties, and have a piece written to fit 'em. Most of the theatres keep an author on purpose. (ch. 22)

We even find Miss La Creevy disclosing secrets of miniature painting:

> . . . there are only two styles of portrait painting; the serious and the smirk; and we always use the serious for professional people (except actors sometimes), and the smirk for private ladies and gentlemen who don't care so much about looking clever. (ch. 10)

Comedy and pathos notwithstanding, much of the narrative is taken up with supplying severely factual details of Nicholas's jobs. We learn what his duties are, the conditions under which he works, and what he is paid, when he is an usher at Dotheboys Hall (chs. 3–8), when he is a part-time tutor for the Kenwigs family (ch. 16), and when he is a member of Mr. Crummles's theatre company (ch. 22). Newman Noggs procures Nicholas his engagement with the Kenwigs family. He reports how he told Mrs. Kenwigs

> that Nicholas was a tutor of great accomplishments, involved in some misfortunes which he was not at liberty to explain, and

bearing the name of Johnson. That Mrs. Kenwigs, impelled by
gratitude, or ambition, or maternal pride, or maternal love, or all
four powerful motives conjointly, had taken secret conference
with Mr. Kenwigs, and had finally returned to propose that Mr.
Johnson should instruct the four Miss Kenwigses in the French
language as spoken by natives, at the weekly stipend of five
shillings, current coin of the realm; being at the rate of one
shilling per week, per each Miss Kenwigs, and one shilling over,
until such time as the baby might be able to take it out in
grammar. (ch. 16)

We know what Nicholas's duties would have been, and what he would
have been paid, had he accepted a position with the Member of
Parliament, Mr. Gregsbury (ch. 16).   Though details of duties are
vaguer, we certainly know what he is paid by the Cheeryble brothers,
and that his working conditions are good (ch. 35).   We learn what his
sister Kate earns, too, and what she is called upon to do, when she is
working for Madame Mantalini (ch. 10), and for Mrs. Wititterly (ch 21).

A cameo scene at a general agency or register office (the equivalent
of a modern employment agency) indicates an important emphasis of
Dickens's interest in the subject. A cook is seeking a place, and asks for
details of "very light ones":

"'Mrs. Marker,'" said Tom, reading, "'Russell Place, Russell
Square; offers eighteen guineas; tea and sugar found. Two in
family, and see very little company. Five servants kept. No
man. No followers.'"
"Oh Lor!" tittered the client. "*That* won't do. Read another,
young man, will you?"
"'Mrs. Wrymug,'" said Tom.   "'Pleasant Place, Finsbury.
Wages, twelve guineas. No tea, no sugar. Serious family – '"
"Ah! you needn't mind reading that," interrupted the client.
"'Three serious footmen,'" said Tom, impressively.
"Three? did you say?" asked the client in an altered tone.
"'Three serious footmen,'" replied Tom, "'Cook, housemaid,
and nursemaid; each female servant required to join the Little
Bethel Congregation three times every Sunday – with a serious
footman. If the cook is more serious than the footman, she will

be expected to improve the footman; if the footman is more
serious than the cook, he will be expected to improve the cook.'"
   "I'll take the address of that place," said the client; "I don't
know but what it mightn't suit me pretty well." (ch. 16)

The comedy can conceal the centrality of this from us. All the work we
see in *Nicholas Nickleby* is performed in small establishments, presided
over by families, where personal relations are paramount.
   This prompts the question whether the picture Dickens draws of
work was representative of the era. We tend to suppose the nineteenth
century was marked by the impersonalization of work, the alienation of
the worker. Arnold Toynbee declared that the capitalist employers of
the Industrial Revolution were unknown to their innumerable workers,
that "the old relations between masters and men disappeared, and a 'cash
nexus' was substituted for the human tie" (Toynbee ch. 8). The changes
Toynbee perceived, however, happened neither everywhere nor all at
once. Small employers survived, of course, especially in London, which
was the milieu Dickens knew best, and which was largely untouched by
the factory system, so much a part of the industrial revolution in the
midlands and the north. As late as 1851, only seventeen industrial
employers in the city employed more than 250 workers. Eighty-six
percent employed fewer than ten. Throughout Dickens's lifetime,
London remained a city of small workshops and counting-houses
("London: Topography," *Oxford Reader's Companion to Dickens*).
   Dickens was aware of the changes Toynbee identified. In chapter
50, the narrator rejoices that Gypsy children at the race meeting spend
their days "among the waving trees, and not in the midst of dreadful
engines which make young children old before they know what
childhood is." *Hard Times* alone (1854) shows that he eventually saw
how fundamental the changes were. But the chances of his seeing that
when he was writing *Nicholas Nickleby* were diminished by an accident
of history. It was Chartism that created a national awareness of the
gravity of the situation, and the publication of *Nicholas Nickleby* was
very slightly out of phase with the birth of Chartism. The first number
of the novel was issued a few weeks before the People's Charter was
published in May 1838. The Charter was presented to Parliament in

June 1839, three months after Dickens had introduced the benevolent Cheeryble brothers, to solve Nicholas's problems. Parliament rejected the Charter in July. There was a riot in Birmingham within a week, but no serious bloodshed until troops fired on demonstrators in Newport in November, a month after the last number of *Nickleby* had been issued.

There is, then, no reason why, in 1838 and 1839, Dickens should have dwelled especially on the "cash nexus" Toynbee was to identify in 1884. He confidently modelled work in *Nicholas Nickleby* on his own experience, and in doing so reflected the experience of millions. When not working entirely for himself, Dickens had always worked with or for small organizations, often cultivating family or personal connections. At Warren's he had worked for his aunt's stepson. At the *Mirror of Parliament* he had worked for his uncle. At the *Evening Chronicle* he had married the boss's daughter. And he had felt close enough to his first publisher, Macrone, to organize fund-raising for his widow.

In *Nicholas Nickleby*, Nicholas earns his living, without exception, by working for families, as indeed does Kate. Only Nicholas's interview with the Member of Parliament, Mr. Gregsbury, promises something different, but Nicholas declines the job offered. This pattern provides obvious opportunities for exploring the theme of love and money. Nicholas works for families to benefit his own – at first to save his mother from supporting him, later to support her, finally to support his own wife and children. His family's interests have to be negotiated with his employer's family's interests. Employers are tested to see how they reconcile care for their loved ones with responsibility for their employees. Nor can we help noticing that amorous opportunities are offered Nicholas by each of the three principal jobs we see him performing. Fanny Squeers is infatuated with him at Dotheboys Hall (ch. 9). Miss Snevellicci flirts with him when he is working for the Crummles theater company (ch. 30). His job with the Cheeryble brothers gives him access to Madeline Bray (ch. 40).

There are striking parallels between all the families Nicholas works for, as well as important contrasts. Perhaps the most startling parallels are between the Squeers and Crummles families. Readers find themselves making different moral judgments about the two. Mr.

Squeers's shifts to maximize profit and justify himself, though funny, are cruel and squalid. Mr. Crummles's shifts, equally funny, without impeding judgment, invite indulgence. We forgive the real pump and tubs, but not the window and horse. This has not a little to do with Mr. Squeers's blindness to all interests except his own family's, Mr. Crummles's fairness and generosity towards his employees, only a little diminished by family piety.   Yet both Dotheboys Hall and the Crummles touring company are unequivocally family concerns.

Both Mr. Squeers and Mr. Crummles employ other members of their families. Mr. Crummles even employs his domestic animals (ch. 22). Wives are central to both operations, and revered by their husbands.[6] "Oh Lor!" Mr. Squeers exclaims at the thought of his partner, "what a member of society that woman is!" (ch. 34). Speaking of his own wife, Mr. Crummles all but echoes him: "Ah! Johnson, what a woman that is!" (ch. 48).   In both families, the next generation is at once over-indulged and exploited, in peculiarly direct and physical ways, as it is groomed to succeed its parents. Mr. Squeers looks forward to "such time as little Wackford is able to take charge of the school" (ch. 9), and declares him to be "next door but one to a cherubim" (ch. 45), but he fattens little Wackford up mercilessly, and pinches and pokes the resultant flesh to advertise the Dotheboys Hall diet (ch. 34). Regardless of talent, all the younger members of the Crummles family are given top billing (ch. 23), and their parents look to them for skills the company needs to carry on (ch. 48), but the Infant Phenomenon's growth is deliberately stunted by late nights and gin-and-water (ch. 23).

Oliver Twist clearly worked something out of Dickens's system, and enabled him to get his fascination with the dysfunctional family more into proportion.   If not always stable, families are emphatically functional in *Nicholas Nickleby*.   Now Dickens is especially interested in marriage as an economic partnership, successful or not.   Nicholas's parents had loved each other, but had not managed their affairs well. Mrs. Nickleby lamented "that the dear departed had never deigned to profit by her advice, save on one occasion: which was a strictly veracious statement, inasmuch as he had only acted upon it once, and had ruined himself in consequence . . . " (ch. 3).   Mr. Mantalini elaborately professes love for Mrs. Mantalini, his "essential juice of pine-apple" (ch. 34), in order to extract money from her. In contrast, Mr. and Mrs. Kenwigs, Mr. and Mrs. Squeers, Mr. and Mrs. Crummles, all cooperate smoothly to secure their joint economic interests.

The Cheeryble brothers, with their nephew Frank, constitute a family in a somewhat different sense from most others, and are less impressive creations than either the Squeers or Crummles families. During the Doughty Street years, and for many afterwards, Dickens plainly found it difficult to conceive married life among the middle-aged and elderly, except as comic or grotesque. His focus was upon what he knew, the experience of the lover, the young husband, the young wife. It is doubtful whether he could have taken a Mr. and Mrs. Cheeryble seriously as doers of good. A couple was needed, however, so that the doing of it could be dramatized. Nicholas witnesses deliberations, for instance, between Charles Cheeryble and a business colleague, over relief for the widow of a docker killed by an accident:

> "How many children are there, and what has my brother Ned given, Trimmers?"
> "There are six children," replied the gentleman, "and your brother has given us twenty pounds."
> "My brother Ned is a good fellow, and you're a good fellow too, Trimmers," said the old man, shaking him by both hands with trembling eagerness. "Put me down for another twenty or – stop a minute, stop a minute! We mustn't look ostentatious; put me down ten pound, and Tim Linkinwater ten pound. A cheque for twenty pound for Mr. Trimmers, Tim. God bless you, Trimmers – and come and dine with us some day this week; you'll always find a knife and fork, and we shall be delighted. Now, my dear sir – cheque from Mr. Linkinwater, Tim. Smashed by a cask of sugar, and six poor children – oh dear, dear, dear!" (ch. 35)

Dickens hit upon this awkward device of identical twins competing in good works, inspired by a pair of philanthropic Manchester businessmen, William and David Grant, whom he may have met during a visit to the city in October 1838.

What the Cheerybles lack, as literary creations, is complexity and particularity of specification. Mr. Squeers lives for the reader because, despite his grotesque cruelty, we learn in bizarrely contingent detail how he makes a living, what his hopes for the future are, where his love and loyalties lie. He is self-contained and stylish in his evil. Vincent Crummles lives for the reader because his expansiveness and geniality are underpinned by innumerable comic details of compromise and contrivance in the running of a theater company, by innumerable comic instances of husbandly and fatherly indulgence. The affections of the Cheeryble brothers are too orderly and just, the fuss made at their establishment about entries in ledgers and day-books (ch. 37) is not enough. We miss the Cheeryble equivalents of windows, horses, tubs, and pumps.

But for all their lack of impact, structurally the Cheerybles function admirably. They restore harmony and contentment, not only by being generous, but by reasserting the possibility of good behavior on all issues central to the theme. They love each other, their nephew, and the memory of their mother. They demonstrate that brothers and uncles do not always behave as Ralph does. Nor is their benevolence confined to their own kin. They intervene in Nicholas's family too, taking an interest in the welfare of Mrs. Nickleby, Kate, and even Smike. They preserve continuity, that is to say, between the values of their personal lives, and the values they subscribe to as employers and men of business. They prove that employers can be magnanimous, that the rich are not necessarily grasping or snobbish. Having risen from poverty through hard work, they value wealth, but for the good it enables them to do. They do not disparage inheritance, and prevent Madeline being cheated of hers. They respect rank, and rejoice that Kate and Nicholas, who are to marry their nephew and their protegée, are "the children of a worthy gentleman." But they value virtue above rank, and find lack of wealth no serious obstacle when there is abundance of love. The contrasts they provide may be crude, but they are not out of place.

Dickens contrives moments, moreover, when the goodness of the Cheerybles is neither cloying nor unbelievable. Forget, if you can, the egregious acts of charity he has them perform. Consciousness of their humble origin and early difficulties makes the Cheeryble brothers sensitive to the misfortunes and difficulties of others. We can see this in the sensitivity Charles Cheeryble shows towards Nicholas when they first meet, not least because, with hindsight, we realize he sees in Nicholas's predicament a reflection of his own as a young man:

> "What's the matter? What is it? How did it all come about?" said the old man, laying his hand on the shoulder of Nicholas, and walking him up the street. "You're – Eh?" laying his finger on the sleeve of his black coat. "Who's it for, eh?"
> "My father," replied Nicholas.
> "Ah!" said the old gentleman quickly. "Bad thing for a young man to lose his father. Widowed mother, perhaps?"
> Nicholas sighed.
> "Brothers and sisters too? Eh?"
> "One sister," rejoined Nicholas.
> "Poor thing, poor thing! . . . ." (ch. 35)

Love, it goes without saying, is a perennial concern of fiction. It is often linked thematically with money in novels, because love plays an essential part in the transmission of wealth and rank between families and between generations. Marriage, child-bearing, inheritance, family piety, all enforce the connection between love and money. In no novel are they more intensively linked than in *Nicholas Nickleby*.

The story of Nicholas, and of his sister Kate, is essentially the story of a test: of what might be asked of, and found in, the children of a gentleman. In particular, how can they reconcile their rank, their quest for money, and their quest for love? Some of the tensest moments in the novel are when Nicholas's claim to the rank of gentleman is challenged. "You are a villain," Nicholas tells Sir Mulberry Hawk, before thrashing him.

> "You are an errand-boy for aught I know," said Sir Mulberry Hawk.
> "I am the son of a country gentleman," returned Nicholas, "your equal in birth and education, and your superior I trust in everything besides." (ch. 32)

Nicholas seeks both love and money. He finds himself pitted against Ralph because Ralph seeks only money. Towards the end of the novel Nicholas renounces love because of lack of money, but gains both because he is loved.

Dickens's intense focus upon a central theme, in *Nicholas Nickleby*, restricted his freedom in plotting in a way new to him, and it shows. He sometimes seems unable to meet the constraints imposed upon him, except with awkward devices. All is not awkwardness, however. Despite the episodic nature of the story, despite the constant need to substantiate the theme, Dickens does contrive an organic development sustained from episode to episode. Without it, *Nicholas Nickleby* would scarcely qualify as a novel. The book is more than a chronicle of Nicholas's progress from poverty and isolation to prosperity and love. Nicholas changes. As he moves from job to job, we can trace the stages of a sentimental education, albeit lightly sketched. The novel is not as accomplished a bildungsroman, certainly, as *Great Expectations* (1860–61), but it lays the ground for such accomplishment. Nicholas's energy and dashing style qualify him as a romantic hero but, for all that, he matures during the course of the narrative, and his maturing has to do, not least, with changing attitudes towards love and money.

He departs for Dotheboys Hall, a nineteen-year-old innocent, beguiled by fantasies of making his fortune:

> " . . . suppose some young nobleman who is being educated at the Hall, were to take a fancy to me, and get his father to appoint me his travelling tutor when he left, and when we come back from the continent, procured me some handsome appointment. Eh! uncle?"
> "Ah, to be sure!" sneered Ralph. (ch. 3)

He rebels against the evidence of his senses, and does not allow himself to be deterred by Mr. Squeers's behavior or appearance: "'He is an odd-looking man,' thought Nicholas. 'What of that? Porson [the Greek scholar] was an odd-looking man, and so was Doctor Johnson; all these bookworms are'" (ch 4).

In Yorkshire, he thoughtlessly provokes the jealousy of Fanny

Squeers, who is infatuated with him, and of John Browdie, with whose fiancée he flirts. They are playing cards together:

> "I never had such luck, really," exclaimed coquettish Miss Price, after another hand or two. "It's along of you Mr. Nickleby, I think. I should like to have you for a partner always."
> "I wish you had."
> "You'll have a bad wife, though, if you always win at cards," said Miss Price.
> "Not if your wish is gratified," replied Nicholas. "I am sure I shall have a good one in that case." (ch. 9)

But, setting out again for London, he makes a frank apology to John Browdie: " . . . we parted on no very good terms the last time we met; it was my fault, I believe; but I had no intention of offending you, and no idea that I was doing so. I was very sorry for it, afterwards. Will you shake hands?" (ch. 13). Above all, on departing from Yorkshire, Nicholas accepts responsibility for Smike.

When he leaves London for Portsmouth, in order no longer to be an embarrassment to Kate and his mother, Nicholas may be supposed to have matured still more, but perhaps not in judgment. Running away to sea may be an option for him, but is scarcely one for Smike (ch. 22). However, the good fortune of falling in with Mr. Crummles enables Nicholas to acquire the stature that comes with doing a job well, and with this he develops sounder judgment. Though he meets Miss Snevellicci's advances with gallantry (ch. 23), Nicholas, "with the precedent of Miss Squeers still fresh in his memory, steadily resisted every fascination, and placed so strict a guard upon his behaviour that when he had taken his leave the ladies were unanimous in pronouncing him quite a monster of insensibility" (ch. 30).

Nicholas returns to London to take on heavy responsibilities. He is able to do so successfully, thanks to the not very convincing good fortune of his encounter with Charles Cheeryble. But it is in his emotional life we see the clearest growth. In Yorkshire he had irresponsibly toyed with Fanny Squeers's feelings. In Portsmouth he

had resisted involvement with Miss Snevellicci, without much difficulty
since he was unattracted to her. Now he finds in Madeline Bray a
young woman of his own rank to whom he is profoundly attracted. And
he finds it his duty to subdue his feelings.

Nicholas tells Kate he loves Madeline, but continues,

> "Nobody must know this but you. She, last of all."
> "Dear Nicholas!"
> "Last of all; never, though never is a long day . . . ." (ch. 61)

He cannot betray his benefactors, the Cheeryble brothers, Nicholas
explains, by seeking the hand of their protegée, so much wealthier than
he is. Kate's love for Frank Cheeryble is prohibited by similar
considerations.

To many modern readers, their renunciation of love seems stagey,
expressed as it is with the help of exclamations like, "That's my own
brave Kate!" (ch. 61). However, we should not allow this to conceal
from us the fact that Nicholas and Kate are confronted with a genuine
dilemma. They love Madeline and Frank, but they earnestly desire not
to offend benefactors who may have other plans for their protegée and
their nephew. If we assume love between two young people should
override all considerations of prudence and the wishes of elders, we fly
in the face, not only of history, but also of social practice in most parts
of the world today. Nicholas and Kate exercise self-control and
discretion. In doing so they pass the test, behave as the children of a
gentleman should, and are rewarded for it by elders who value prudence,
but not over honesty or love. This may not be especially believable.
Closure is contrived more by Nicholas and Kate being, than by their
doing. But nor is it especially unbelievable. More to the point,
thematically, it brings the novel to an appropriate close, and brings into
sharp focus the complex relationship between money and love.

Nicholas Nickleby displays a mastery of thematic organization new
to Dickens. His ability to shape a consistently convincing plot to such
organization had not kept pace. Readers are entitled to grumble about
that, but not too much. The Chestertonians are right to insist on the
novel's "diversity of scene, accuracy of observed detail, and . . .

vividness of character and incident." Add to that the greater degree of coherence, the new intensity of focus, and it is not difficult to understand why *Nicholas Nickleby* is such a powerful novel.

6

BARNABY RUDGE: NARRATIVE GAMES

From its conception, *Barnaby Rudge* was a work in which Dickens sought a direction for his art quite different from the one he predominantly followed at Doughty Street. The earliest indication to survive, of the project which eventually became *Barnaby Rudge*, is to be found in a letter he wrote to Macrone in May 1836.[1] The title Dickens gave it at that stage was "Gabriel Vardon, the Locksmith of London" (Pilgrim *Letters* 1: 150). Only later did he change the spelling of the name to "Varden." He wrote the letter after two monthly parts of *Pickwick Papers* had been published, but before the book had made Boz a famous name. "Gabriel Vardon" was to be another kind of book entirely.

Surprising as it may seem in hindsight, even as late as July 1837, when *Pickwick* was nearing completion and *Oliver Twist* well under way, Dickens saw this project as his "first Novel" (Pilgrim *Letters* 1: 283). The "low, cheap form of publication" chanced upon for *Pickwick* was to be abandoned (Preface to the Cheap Edition of *Pickwick*). "Gabriel Vardon" was to be issued in all the costly finery of the traditional three volumes. In August 1836 Dickens signed a contract with Bentley to that end (Pilgrim *Letters* 1: 648–49).

His resolve to move out of serialization was not to last, of course. Far from abandoning it, he soon reconciled himself to it. *Oliver Twist* and *Nicholas Nickleby* were serialized. So was *Barnaby Rudge* eventually. Even so, the original intention, plainly, was to target well-educated and prosperous readers who could afford a novel in three volumes. The book would establish Dickens's credentials as a serious novelist, and be something "on which I might build my fame." He would devote to it "the time, the labour, the casting about, in every direction," needed for an ambitious, carefully planned and researched work of literature (Pilgrim *Letters* 1: 165).

But during the Doughty Street years Dickens found himself able neither to complete the project, nor to forsake it. Three months after he moved to Doughty Street, the title *Barnaby Rudge* appeared in his correspondence for the first time, in itself an indication that more of the story was taking shape in his mind (Pilgrim *Letters* 1: 283). And in February 1838, while privately describing his commitment to it as "something hanging over him like a hideous nightmare" (John Forster bk. 2, ch. 2), he told Bentley he had "recently been thinking a great deal about Barnaby Rudge" (Pilgrim *Letters* 1: 369). On 3 January 1839, he began actually to write, only to give up three weeks later, in despair over his contractual obligations to Bentley (see p. 181 above). On 18 September he told Forster, "I have a good notion for Barnaby" (Pilgrim *Letters* 1: 581). In early October he told Cruikshank he was working "tooth and nail at Barnaby" (Pilgrim *Letters* 1: 589). But, before long, he was calling in lawyers to help resolve differences with Bentley, and giving up again (Pilgrim *Letters* 1: 616–18).

It was not until 1841 that he finally settled down to steady writing. He revised what he had already written on 21 January, and by 27 January was "very busy" with his work on the book (Pilgrim *Letters* 2: 191 and 195). The novel eventually appeared in weekly instalments of *Master Humphrey's Clock*, between February and November 1841.

Barnaby Rudge has never been a favorite among readers of Dickens, and critics for the most part have found it wanting (Hawes ed., *Barnaby Rudge* 668–88). Soon after Dickens's death, Forster identified defects not easily explained away. In his view, the novel lacks "singleness of purpose, unity of idea," and "harmony of treatment" (bk. 2, ch. 9). In recent decades, to be sure, the novel has been praised. Critics have applauded its poetic and visionary qualities. But these notwithstanding, *Barnaby Rudge* is less coherent and less successful than any of the other Doughty Street novels. Some of its recent apologists have been observant and astute (Marcus ch. 5, Kincaid ch. 5, Hollington 100–110), but to my mind they over-promote redeeming features.

It is tempting, therefore, simply to ignore *Barnaby Rudge* in this account of the Doughty Street novels. Most of it was written more than a year after Dickens had left Doughty Street, and after he had written *The Old Curiosity Shop* in the meantime. At Doughty Street, Dickens thought about *Barnaby*, agonized over it, negotiated about its publication, and sketched three chapters, but wrote no more than that. Yet a book relating Dickens's art to his life during a discrete period would plainly be deficient if a novel demonstrably much on his mind during that period were simply forgotten.

It is impossible precisely to distinguish what *Barnaby Rudge* owes to the Doughty Street years, what it owes to the few months preceding them, and what it owes to Dickens's work on it in 1841. Educated conjectures can be made about what he got down on paper at Doughty Street, even about some of the matters that passed through his mind, but not about the extent to which the novel was planned and imagined there. Yet this scarcely matters. The vicissitudes of his career prevented the novel's completion while he was living there but, because it is so different from the other Doughty Street novels, its publication at a later date has a kind of appropriateness about it. It is enough to recognize that he was contemplating it throughout his stay in Doughty Street, and probably during all of the time he was working on *Pickwick Papers, Oliver Twist* and *Nicholas Nickleby. Barnaby Rudge* stands apart from them, but counterpoints them. I do not believe Dickens found the new direction he sought in it, or at least a new direction worth sticking to, but the novel was nevertheless a valuable experiment for him, and is a key text for anyone who wishes to understand how his art developed.

It stands out against the others because, in it, Dickens strove to construct fiction out of material remote from his own private life and private concerns. *Pickwick Papers, Oliver Twist,* and *Nicholas Nickleby* are novels carefully crafted and organized – whether consciously or unconsciously – but they sprang out of the life Dickens was living during the Doughty Street years, and out of ineradicable memories of his past. *Barnaby Rudge* had initially to do with a soberer kind of reflection, with Dickens responding less to what he was and had been, more to what he wanted to be – the kind of novelist he wanted to be. Its inception marked it permanently. For all that the novel was eventually absorbed into Dickens's routine of production, his original ambitions for it had been different. They account both for what is lacking in the novel, and for what is successful in it.

There can be little doubt that Dickens was wise in seeking to free himself from too slavish a dependence on his own most intimate experience as source material for his fiction. For all their faults, *Pickwick Papers, Oliver Twist,* and *Nicholas Nickleby* are wonderful novels but, having completed them, Dickens was running out of exploitable material at home. The subsequent course of his career vindicated his instinct to change. The events of his life and highly charged memories continued to be potent sources for him, but they were not enough. Readers demanded variety, and Dickens was too open to what was happening in the larger world about him, too interested in too many things, perpetually to restrict his subject matter. *Barnaby Rudge* is the result of a fitful search at Doughty Street, for an exit from the Doughty Street mind-set. It was an enormously fruitful mind-set, but one which Dickens saw to be incapable of indefinite prolongation. In *Barnaby*, however, he attempted too clean a break. He cut himself off too abruptly from the energy personal experience and memory supplied. Arguably, that is why *The Old Curiosity Shop* is more successful than *Barnaby Rudge.* In it, Dickens explored regions well beyond his intimate personal experience, but sustained his energy as a writer by exploiting his memories of Mary Hogarth, and his grief at her death.

In *Barnaby Rudge*, Dickens sought to emulate his literary hero, Sir Walter Scott. He would write, not about himself, but about history. In the novels he set in Scotland's recent past, however, Scott was writing about himself, albeit obliquely, and that is what makes them powerful. At his best, Scott used history metonymically. In novels like *Waverley* (1814), *Rob Roy* (1817), and *Redgauntlet* (1824), Scott studied what he saw as epiphanies in the formation of the national character, moments of crisis which both strikingly reveal that character, and endorse the reflection of his own sensibility he found in it. In all such novels, something equivalent to Romantic impulse and something equivalent to Enlightenment shrewdness are held in delicate balance, as they were in Scott's personality. Except on specific issues, Dickens lacked Scott's energizing personal engagement with history. His *Child's History of England* (1851–53), with its denunciation of monarchs and bloodletting, is substantially a repudiation of history, or at any rate what was thought of as history before the twentieth century.

In a more modest and limited way than Scott, Dickens could in fact write about history powerfully, but only when he used it metaphorically, rather than metonymically. *A Tale of Two Cities* (1859) succeeds because, throughout it, the French Revolution is made a metaphor, prefiguring the crisis Dickens saw coming in Britain unless actively averted. There are metaphorical aspects of *Barnaby Rudge*, to be sure, but they plainly evolved late in its gestation. Dickens's presentation of the Gordon Riots embodies, among other things, his anxieties about Chartism (Butt and Tillotson 82), but Chartism was not born until 1838, two years after Dickens had decided on the novel's historical setting.

Despite his insistence on finding material in history, it is tempting to ascribe some elements of *Barnaby Rudge* to Dickens's deepest personal concerns, but it is a temptation best resisted, I believe. There is a preoccupation in the novel with unsatisfactory fathers, and the harm they do to their sons (Marcus ch. 5). I am thinking of John and Joe Willet, of Mr. Chester, Edward and Hugh, and above all of Mr. Rudge and Barnaby. During his ordeal at Warren's, and in retrospect, Dickens had plainly been deeply disappointed in his father, and John Dickens had proved an embarrassment later, too. In March 1839, during the troubled gestation of *Barnaby*, Dickens took the drastic step of procuring a cottage at Alphington, near Exeter, and sending off his parents to exile there, in the hope that it might curb his father's fecklessness (Pilgrim *Letters* 1: 517–25). His parents were still spending most of their time in Devon while the novel was being published.

But there are very pronounced differences between the relationship of Dickens to his father, and the relationships of sons to fathers in *Barnaby Rudge*. Indeed, every father-and-son relationship in the novel has features contrary to Dickens's personal experience, or vastly out of proportion to it.

John Willet is dogmatic, conservative, and slow-witted (ch. 1). John Dickens was mercurial, adventurous, and sprightly. John Willet makes his son unhappy by refusing him the dignity of an adult (ch. 1). John Dickens made his unhappy by imposing an adult role upon him before he was ready for it. Joe Willet rebels against his father's authority, and is injured physically as a result of doing so (chs. 30 and 67). Much younger at the time of his ordeal, Dickens accepted his father's authority and, as he saw it, was injured mentally as a result of doing so.

Mr. Chester, later Sir John, is ambitious and improvident, as John

Dickens was, a master of the manners of his social milieu, as John Dickens strove to be. But he is cold-hearted, restrained, and calculating (ch. 24), where John Dickens was warm-hearted, impulsive, and extravagant. Edward Chester resents his father's not allowing him to train for an occupation (ch. 15). Dickens resented his father's finding him an occupation – at Warren's. Mr. Chester looks to his son to repair his fortunes through an advantageous marriage (ch. 15). Though John Dickens was happy to exploit his son's prosperity, there is no evidence he foresaw it, and it is scarcely likely he hoped it might be achieved through marriage.

Hugh is Mr. Chester's illegitimate son. *Mutatis mutandis*, he can be seen as a reworking of the material out of which Dickens made Sam Weller, the Artful Dodger and Smike. He is a savage and rebellious creature, thrown upon his own resources as a small boy, who has tenaciously survived on the margins of society (ch. 11), "a little robber or a little vagabond" grown into a big one. It is the motif of the abandoned child once again, but darkened, and developed to extremes. Hugh is violent and treacherous beyond measure, sinned against beyond measure. Abandoned by Mr. Chester, his mother had been hanged (ch. 75). Abandoned by Sir John, Hugh, too, is finally hanged (ch. 77).

Unsatisfactory fathers and rebellious sons are among the commonest elements out of which narrative is made. Freud saw that, odd though his understanding of the subject may be. It would have taken a peculiar effort of self-denial for Dickens to avoid the subject, so it is not surprising we should find it in *Barnaby Rudge*. But, as it happens, it is hard to see what may be gained by tracing it to his personal experience. There may be a connection, there may not. If there is, the subject has been so evolved and transmuted, it is scarcely worth saying so. An interesting conjecture suggests itself, though. In a conscious bid to rid himself of dependence upon personal experience, did Dickens start with it, but deliberately change what could be changed, reverse detail, alter proportion and emphasis, to a significantly greater extent than he did in the first three novels he published?

Nowhere does this seem more likely than in his presentation of Barnaby and Mr. Rudge. Barnaby is a son even more damaged by his father than Hugh, Mr. Rudge a father even more wanting in fatherly qualities than Mr. Chester. Mr. Rudge is a murderer twice over, a thief, and a blackmailer (chs. 45 and 62). His confession to Mrs. Rudge of his initial crime, the murders of Reuben Haredale and a gardener, had damaged Barnaby in the womb (ch. 62). It was "that one horror, in which, before his birth, his darkened intellect began" (ch. 25). Barnaby out-smikes Smike, Mr. Rudge out-ralphs Ralph Nickleby. Whatever grounding in personal experience we may detect for Dickens's interest in unsatisfactory fathers and harmed sons, however much we may be prepared to see this fictively elaborated, it is clear that Barnaby and Mr. Rudge are so far evolved away from Dickens and his father that it makes little sense to dwell on the connection.

We can conclude as much the more readily because it is apparent that Dickens's first notions for the novel centered around a good father, Gabriel Varden. He has no son to harm, to be sure, but he has a daughter, Dolly, to raise, and to protect from the unreliable judgment of her mother, and he is unfailing in his support for other men's sons, Edward Chester and Joe Willet (ch. 3). Mr. Varden is "the source of light, heat, life and frank enjoyment in the bright household world" (ch. 80). He combines the good heart of Mr. Pickwick, the practicality of Mr. Wardle, and the civic responsibility of the Cheeryble brothers. The older man, prosperous and established, offering a moral center in a work, was a device Dickens used repeatedly. His sources seem to have been more literary than personal: the duke in *Measure for Measure*, perhaps, or Matthew Bramble in *Humphry Clinker*. And into such figures he poured his own values. Mr. Varden is a more than usually substantial version of the figure: married, a parent, a craftsman, and tradesman, prosperous, but not capable of solving problems simply by distributing money, dependent instead upon his goodness, wisdom, and influence. The bad father and the damaged son were elements Dickens thought of later in the process of composition.

We can deduce this from studying Dickens's letters, but the text of *Barnaby Rudge* itself scarcely encourages an intense focus upon such figures. Its preoccupation with fathers and sons scarcely amounts to a theme. The coverage of the topic is too thin, too scattered. There is so much else. *Barnaby Rudge*, it is difficult not to conclude, is a novel without a theme. It is no more, no less, than what its subtitle declares it to be, *A Tale of the Riots of 'Eighty*. Dickens freed his imagination from the momentum of personal experience and memory, and allowed it to construct at leisure an elaborate tale in historical fancy dress. He produced a workmanlike story, with some resonance beyond itself, to be sure, but one that is thematically void.

Yet he was far too resourceful a novelist simply to mark time. *Barnaby Rudge* evolved in his mind over a long period. It seems reasonable to look in it for some kind of progress in the development of his art. Reassuringly, it can be found. What Dickens failed to achieve in the tale, he achieved in the telling. Perhaps for the very reason that he was scarcely distracted by personal feeling, Dickens was able to concentrate on technique.

Narrative technique especially. *Pickwick Papers, Oliver Twist,* and *Nicholas Nickleby* are all artful narratives. Irony fundamentally shaped Dickens's sensibility. The stories he told derive their power and authority not least from the way each is mediated by a narrative consciousness, often complex and contradictory. The mock-encomium of the "immortal Pickwick," with which *Pickwick Papers* opens, comically establishes the narrator as a dupe, accepting Mr. Pickwick and the Pickwickians at their own estimation. Readers of *Oliver Twist* are prepared for the mordant satire which punctuates that novel by, for instance, the narrator's refusal in the first chapter, "to maintain that the being born in a workhouse, is in itself the most fortunate and enviable circumstance that can possibly befall a human being." And a recurrent tone is established in the first chapter of *Nicholas Nickleby* by the narrator's praise, for example, of Ralph's playground usury. "Two-pence for every half-penny," his interest rate, "cannot be too strongly recommended to the notice of capitalists, both large and small."

But in Dickens's first three novels, the narrative irony is intermittent. Though not constant in *Barnaby Rudge*, it is much more intense. Dickens was experimenting with the narrative indirectness he was to refine and perfect later in his career, an indirectness calling on readers systematically to look for crucial information not only in the narrator's words, but elsewhere too, not least in the unspoken.

For most of *Barnaby Rudge*, the main narrative is persistently self-conscious and playful, and there are what can fairly be called competing centers of narrative authority, which redouble irony. Narrative scope is extended, and narrative complexity increased. Though much of it is dark, comedy is intensified. Above all, the novel quickly establishes a persona for its narrator. He is a merciless tease.

We know a story cannot all be told at once. If it is a mystery – and most stories are, more or less – how much is told and when are critical. Readers want the solution of a mystery, but they also want the experience of it, and it stops being a mystery once the solution is supplied. Postponement of revelation, therefore, is a prerequisite of most fiction. Readers read on, because they find out some things, but still want to know more. Only towards the end of the book can curiosity be finally satisfied.

There are various methods for a novelist to manage such matters. One is to use a narrator who, explicitly or implicitly, lays claim to knowing everything worth knowing from the start, but imparts it nevertheless in an artful sequence. This is the principal model for the narrator of *Barnaby Rudge*, but not the only one. An alternative is to use a narrator who claims less than complete knowledge, who is still apparently piecing the story together from raw data while narrating. Such a narrator can withhold information which might solve the mystery, spoil the story, or just diminish drama, on the grounds of ignorance or doubt. The narrator of *Barnaby Rudge* repeatedly shifts temporarily into this mode.   He usually speaks as if he knows everything, but sometimes admits limitations to his knowledge. Each mode subverts the other, and both are subverted by irony. Omniscience is allowed to become overbearing and preposterous.   The feint of ignorance and doubt is made to seem silly. The plain intention is that readers should infer a shadowy meta-narrator responsible for both modes, and they do.   Nevertheless, perceiving deficiencies in each mode, and needing to arbitrate between them, readers find themselves constantly called upon to judge the narrator's words, to relegate many to the status of comic embroidery, and to attend more closely to the drama of character and action.

Sometimes the narrator speaks to us as a sage, no less. Not only does he know everything; he also indicates how we should respond to it. "Worldly men," we are solemnly told, "are like some wise men, who, learning to know each planet by its Latin name, have quite forgotten such small heavenly constellations as Charity, Forbearance, Universal Love, and Mercy, although they shine by night and day so brightly that the blind may see them" (ch. 29). It is a relief sometimes to hear quite another voice: that of the guileless dupe, for instance, who misjudges what is happening, and can speak brightly of Miggs's "maidenly affection" (ch. 51).

Sometimes the narrator positively boasts of his unimpeded access to everything worth knowing – but always ironically or mischievously. The more hyperbolic the claim, the more the reader looks for impudence or bathos. "Chroniclers are privileged to enter where they list," the narrator brags, "to come and go through keyholes, to ride upon the wind, to overcome, in their soarings up and down, all obstacles of distance, time, and place" (ch. 9). And the reward of such privilege? Entry into Miggs's bedroom. The effect is to devalue omniscience, to mark the narrator as a kind of clownish chorus, capering irresponsibly on the margin of things. At another point, he impudently flaunts his privilege to enter where he lists. Out walking in London, John Willet "did not walk near the Golden Key," we are told. "But the Golden Key lies in our way, though it was out of his; so to the Golden Key this chapter goes" (ch. 79). This is bravura narrative. Narrative performance is sharply distinguished from narrative content. Henry James it most certainly is not. At the end of chapter 32, by way of contrast, the narrator relishes his privilege, not to enter where he lists, but to stay out, ignore, say nothing. "And the world went on turning round as usual for five years," he says, "concerning which this Narrative is silent." It is an impudently stylish way of fast-forwarding.

Naturally, as the narrator switches his attention from character to character, setting to setting, point in time to point in time, we are reminded that the story cannot all be told at once, that some kind of sequence has to be imposed – and occasionally excused. We are told, for instance, of a circumstance occurring "which once more altered the position of two persons from whom this history has long been separated, and to whom it must now return" (ch. 45). Sequencing such as this implies no limits to the narrator's knowledge.

Limits are clearly implied elsewhere, however, and openly declared. At times the narrator, however mischievously, claims only to be evaluating testimony received. John Willet is astonished to find Mr. Chester his guest at the Maypole: "It has been reported that when he got down-stairs, he looked steadily at the boiler for ten minutes by the clock, and all that time never once left off shaking his head; for which statement there would seem to be some ground of truth and feasibility, inasmuch as that interval of time did certainly elapse, before he returned with Barnaby to the guest's apartment" (ch. 10). When Joe Willet and Dolly Varden declare their love, readers are offered only an hypothesis about the effect of this on them: "if ever two people were happy in this world – which is not an utterly miserable one, with all its faults – we may, with some appearance of certainty, conclude that they were" (ch. 78).

Sometimes testimony is indicated, only for doubt to be cast upon it. When Joe Willet rescues Dolly after her ordeal at Hugh's hands, he "tried to console her, bent over her, whispered to her – some say kissed her, but that's a fable." Or judgment may be reserved. On horseback, Joe accompanies the Vardens' chaise back towards London, after Dolly's ordeal, and trots beside it, we are told, "on Dolly's side, no doubt, and pretty close to the wheel too" (ch. 21). The narrator, we are to suppose, does not really know. Except that he does. In the next chapter, we learn that Dolly "held the side of the chaise with one little hand, all the way," and that Joe puts his own upon it. Now it is only Dolly's state of mind that is in doubt: "The most curious circumstance about this little incident was, that Dolly didn't seem to know of it. She looked so innocent and unconscious when she turned her eyes on Joe, that it was quite provoking." "What she thought about, going home," we are further advised, "and whether the coachmaker [a rival suitor] held as favourable a place in her meditations as he had occupied in the morning, is unknown" (ch. 22). The narrator is telling us he lacks reliable testimony.

Here and there, however absurdly or impudently, readers are asked to concede the status of legal deposition to testimony – the narrator's own or that of informants. He can be the deponent himself, preposterously dressing up evaluation, for instance, by swearing to the effect of Dolly Varden's costume: "this deponent hath been informed and verily believes, that you might have seen many less pleasant objects than the cherry-coloured mantle and ribbons as they went fluttering along the green meadows in the bright light of the day, like giddy things as they were" (ch. 19). Or he can hint caution about the depositions of others – of the Maypole's cook and housemaid, for instance, concerning John Willet's response to the sacking of the inn by the rioters:

These two females did afterwards depone that Mr. Willet in his
consternation uttered but one word, and called that up the stairs
in a stentorian voice, six distinct times. But as this word was a
monosyllable, which, however inoffensive when applied to the
quadruped it denotes, is highly reprehensible when used in
connection with females of unimpeachable character, many
persons were inclined to believe that the young women laboured
under some hallucination caused by excessive fear; and that their
ears deceived them. (ch. 54)

Again, various reasons are suggested why Joe Willet's sympathies are
with the lovers, Emma Haredale and Edward Chester. Which particular
reason, we are nevertheless told, "it is needless to inquire – especially as
Joe was out of the way, and had no opportunity on that particular
occasion of testifying to his sentiments either on one side or the other"
(ch. 13).

Unsurprisingly, Dickens is happy to use standard rhetorical devices
to erode the reader's sense of the narrator's omniscience. He is perfectly
ready to slip out of the indicative into the interrogative mood:

What was the Dolly of five years ago, to the Dolly of that day!
How many coachmakers, saddlers, cabinet-makers, and
professors of other useful arts, had deserted their fathers,
mothers, sisters, brothers, and, most of all, their cousins, for the
love of her! How many unknown gentlemen – supposed to be of
mighty fortunes, if not titles – had waited round the corner after
dark, and tempted Miggs the incorruptible, with golden guineas,
to deliver offers of marriage folded up in love-letters! How
many disconsolate fathers and substantial tradesmen had waited
on the locksmith for the same purpose, with dismal tales of how
their sons had lost their appetites, and taken to shut themselves
up in dark bedrooms, and wandering in desolate suburbs with
pale faces, and all because of Dolly Varden's loveliness and
cruelty! (ch. 41)

Such rhetorical questions, of course, suggest a coy unreadiness to
impart information, rather than ignorance. Another rhetorical device
suggests lordly indifference to it, and has the narrator writing himself
out of a job:

How the accomplished gentleman spent the evening in the midst
of a dazzling and brilliant circle; how he enchanted all those
with whom he mingled by the grace of his deportment, the
politeness of his manner, the vivacity of his conversation, and
the sweetness of his voice; how it was observed in every corner,
that Chester was a man of that happy disposition that nothing
ruffled him, that he was one on whom the world's cares and
errors sat lightly as his dress, and in whose smiling face a calm
and tranquil mind was constantly reflected; how honest men,
who by instinct knew him better, bowed down before him
nevertheless, deferred to his every word, and courted his
favourable notice; how people, who really had good in them,
went with the stream, and fawned and flattered, and approved,
and despised themselves while they did so, and yet had not the
courage to resist; how, in short, he was one of those who are
received and cherished in society (as the phrase is) by scores
who individually would shrink from and be repelled by the
object of their lavish regard; are things of course, which will
suggest themselves. Matter so commonplace needs but a passing
glance, and there an end. (ch. 24)

"Let me start you off," the narrator is in effect saying, "and then you
figure out the rest yourself." It is an impudent resignation of narrative
authority.

Dickens was certainly not unique in letting his narrator play games
with the claim to omniscience, nor is there is a lack of critical apparatus
to describe his procedures. There is a consensus on such matters. A
third-person narrator's words, whatever claim he makes, should always
be scrutinized as critically as a first-person narrator's, and as closely as
words uttered by characters whose story he relates. They are not
privileged words, and have to be judged.

Epistemological playfulness such as we find in the narration of
Barnaby Rudge, moreover, was fashionable among novelists of
Dickens's generation. The cavalier inconsistency of the narrative voice
is almost a trademark of Thackeray's novels. In the first chapter of
Catherine, which he wrote between 1839 and 1840 when Dickens was
tinkering with *Barnaby Rudge*, the narrator, omniscient for the most
part, only speculates that Corporal Brock fought on the losing side at the
Battle of the Boyne. He alludes to a laborer "whose name we have not

been able to learn." And he "presumes" that John Hayes gives some information to Mrs. Score, "for, on leaving the kitchen, he was seen to linger for a moment in the bar." But a denunciation of the glamorization of crime in fiction, at the end of the chapter, exposes the artifice of the narrative. On one page of *The Adventures of Philip* (1861–62), the narrative voice is that of the novelist, reproving himself for having favorite characters. On the next it is that of Pendennis, "biographer" of Philip, painstakingly disclosing conversations on which his narrative is based (ch. 12). The liberties Thackeray took with his narrative voice seem to have been based on his perception that the writing of fiction was scarcely a gentlemanly occupation, best treated with graceful negligence by a gentleman who chose it. Readers, of course, can see that as another layer of artifice to be enjoyed.

Throughout his career, Trollope played fast and loose with his narrators' claims to knowledge. He characteristically wrote as an undisguised novelist early in a book, openly explaining why he was imagining a particular kind of character, and as a baffled historian later, complaining he was unable to understand the character's behavior. This bewildering blend of sheer philistinism and narrative cunning, if it does nothing else, keeps the reader's judgment active.

Mischievous inconsistency of this kind can generate intimacy between narrator and reader. The narrator makes a game of showing his cards. It also allows him to get out of the way of developments established principally by dramatic means, developments that scarcely need a commentary, that can be rendered if anything more striking by a bumbling narrator, evidently failing to understand, or positively misunderstanding.

With Thackeray and Trollope, however, narrative inconsistency was an ingrained habit, a running joke, attitudinizing readers learn to look for, and are rarely confounded by. Their narrators may change masks, but they do not disqualify themselves as reliable sources of information and sound judgment. Or, if they do, they supply another supplementary source. In *The Adventures of Philip*, for instance, Pendennis scoffs at the love of Philip and Charlotte. But he also narrates his wife's remonstrances at his doing so (ch. 17). Dickens's narrative inconsistencies are a greater challenge to the reader, and are more intensely dramatized. The effect is much less relaxing, much more bracing. In *Barnaby Rudge* the inconsistencies are complex, frequent and systematic. The narrator plays narrative games deliberately to provoke consternation and questioning. Readers are rarely spared an intrusive narrator in Dickens's texts, apostrophizing, judging, joking. The narrator of *Barnaby Rudge*, however, is more than intrusive. He is anarchic and enigmatic. His is a more indeterminate voice than we hear in any of the previous or subsequent novels.

How can we be sure, though, that Dickens was not simply nodding? Despite the fun, may not the inconsistency be a fault of inattention? There are faults of inattention in *Barnaby Rudge*, devices that fail to work. Is there not a breach of the implicit contract between writer and reader, for instance, in chapter 17? It tells of a stormy interview between Mrs. Rudge and Mr. Rudge. The identity of the latter, however, is not revealed until much later in the novel, so readers are mystified and troubled by all the passion. It is an effect cheaply obtained, by readers being kept ignorant of what both characters in the scene know. There is no third character present, whose puzzlement readers may be invited to share. When attentive readers later discover the facts, they are entitled to be indignant – at the narrator's meanness, and at his stagey laboring after effect.

But the playfulness of the narrative is too consistent. We may complain justifiably about isolated examples, but we can scarcely ascribe all of it to inattention. The first chapter of *Barnaby Rudge* makes it clear the playfulness was calculated. It is a chapter of exposition, which welcomes readers into a veritable arena of narrative games, both played by the narrator himself, and embedded within the story.

The opening sentence, no less, pokes fun at the notion of precision in historical narrative. This is a remarkably cool way of opening an historical novel which, by virtue of the genre, compounds the epistemological problems of historical discourse with those of fiction, neither of them negligible. The Maypole, we are told, was "at a distance of about twelve miles from London – measuring from the Standard in Cornhill, or rather from the spot on or near to which the Standard used to be in days of yore." What is gained, it is hard not to ask, by invoking the spot on Cornhill from which distances were measured, or by reminding readers that the edifice which once stood there no longer did?

And how do we accommodate "about twelve miles" with "the spot on or near to which the Standard used to be"? How is the margin of error to be measured? In inches? The offer of quite unnecessary precision subverts the narrative process itself. The voice we hear mocks the kind of discourse it is uttering, something not looked for in naturalistic fiction.

It is mockery of a kind Dickens had permitted himself before. "The Great Winglebury Duel" (1836) opens with this sentence: "The little town of Great Winglebury is exactly forty-two miles and three-quarters from Hyde Park corner" (*Sketches by Boz*). But in *Barnaby Rudge* the games continue.

There is another in the second paragraph. The history of the Maypole is hard to know, it is suggested, but there is praise for the standard of evidence brought to bear on the story of Queen Elizabeth having slept there, and having boxed the ears of a delinquent page from the mounting block before the door:

> The matter-of-fact and doubtful folks, of whom there were a few among the Maypole customers, as unluckily there always are in every little community, were inclined to look upon this tradition as rather apocryphal; but, whenever the landlord of that ancient hostelry appealed to the mounting block itself as evidence, and triumphantly pointed out that there it stood in the same place to that very day, the doubters never failed to be put down by a large majority, and all true believers exulted as in a victory.

We recognize this as a joke, but it is an unsettling one – more mockery of the kind of discourse we are being offered. "Distrust me," the narrator in effect urges. "I cannot be relied upon to talk sense." We cannot help wondering how this is supposed to make us feel about the rest of the narrative.

Soon, crazy notions are being aired about who may utter narrative, and in what circumstances. Great indignation is aroused by Joe Willet's attempt to tell a stranger the story of the occupants of the Warren. His father, and the Maypole regulars following his example, evidently object to any utterance at all from Joe in their presence – observations, questions, opinions, whatever – but it is a narrative which annoys them on this occasion. Ironically, too, because Joe is better equipped than anyone else to undertake it, being alone in understanding the need for tact in Edward Chester's presence. "Silence, sir!" his father nevertheless commands; "what do you mean by talking, when you see people that are more than two or three times your age, sitting still and silent and not dreaming of saying a word?"

Nor is it just a matter of age and status conferring the right to narrate, it seems. Where a narrative belongs, and to whom it belongs can be important as well: the story of Reuben Haredale, for instance. "That," declares John Willet, "is a Maypole story, and has been any time these four-and-twenty years. That story is Solomon Daisy's story. It belongs to the house; and nobody but Solomon Daisy has ever told it under this roof, or ever shall – that's more." In the face of such nonsense, it is hard to resist questioning the ontological status of the narrative of *Barnaby Rudge* itself.

The alert reader, then, is likely to reach the end of the first chapter of the novel, his mind abuzz with preposterous notions about narrative. It is impossible to contemplate the narrative games clustered there, and to suppose Dickens was unconscious of them. The chapter establishes an attitude to narrative, more intensively playful than we find in anything Dickens had written before, and prefigures systematic subversion of the narrative process itself. The reader is prevented from determining quite how much the narrator knows, quite how much he can be relied upon. For all the continuity in style, no persistent narratorial identity is established beyond that of the tease. Dickens deliberately undermines preconceptions about narrative authority, and mischievously seems to demand acceptance of the story, despite rather than because of its narrator.

Nor do narrative games stop at tricks with the narrative voice. These are part of a greater project, to widen the boundaries of narrative.

What more distinct way can there be of doing that, than by requiring readers, some of the time at any rate, to see through the eyes of a central character declared to be an "idiot"? It was not until thirty years later that Dostoevsky tried something similar. "The king died and then the queen died," E. M. Forster famously suggests, is a story; "The king died, and then the queen died of grief" a plot (82). Transparency of cause and effect, in other words, is what makes a novel more than a chronicle. For Barnaby, cause and effect are opaque, and readers are invited to share his vision. Barnaby sees causes others do not:

> "Look down there," he said softly; "do you mark how they
> whisper in each other's ears; then dance and leap, to make
> believe they are in sport? Do you see how they stop for a
> moment, when they think there is no one looking, and mutter
> among themselves again; and then how they roll and gambol,
> delighted with the mischief they've been plotting?"

He is looking at clothes on a line, in a good drying wind. "Why, how
much better to be silly," he says, than to be wise:

> "You don't see shadowy people there, like those that live in sleep
> – not you. Nor eyes in the knotted panes of glass, nor swift
> ghosts when it blows hard, nor do you hear voices in the air, nor
> see men stalking in the sky – not you! I lead a merrier life than
> you, with all your cleverness. You're the dull men. We're the
> bright ones. Ha! ha! I'll not change with you, clever as you are,
> – not I!" (ch. 10)

This owes less to clinical observation than to Shakespeare, but that is
only another way of saying Dickens is doing unusual things in prose
narrative. One thing he is doing, here and elsewhere in the novel, and
systematically too, is promoting the association we look for in poetry
and dreams, at the expense of the inference we look for in prose and
ratiocination. He is tampering with established narrative norms.

The testing of the boundaries of narrative, through Barnaby, is
highlighted rather than overshadowed by doubts the reader must have
about Barnaby's own comprehension of it. His mother tells him stories:

> He had no recollection of these little narratives; the tale of
> yesterday was new to him upon the morrow; but he liked them at
> the moment; and when the humour held him, would remain
> patiently within doors, hearing her stories like a little child, and
> working cheerfully from sunrise until it was too dark to see. (ch.
> 45)

From the start, questions are provoked about his understanding of
narrative. We first encounter him after the assault on Edward Chester,

which he has witnessed. We are made to feel at this point that inferential narrative is beyond him. He scarcely has the syntax for it, but relies heavily on nouns and gestures, standing free in pre-syntactical association:

> "There's blood upon him," said Barnaby with a shudder. "It makes me sick!"
> "How came it there?" demanded Varden.
> "Steel, steel, steel!" he replied fiercely, imitating with his hand the thrust of a sword.
> "Is he robbed?" said the locksmith.
> Barnaby caught him by the arm, and nodded "Yes;" then pointed towards the city.
> "Oh!" said the old man, bending over the body and looking round as he spoke into Barnaby's pale face, strangely lighted up by something that was *not* intellect. "The robber made off that way, did he?"

In this distressing situation, indeed, even the nouns trouble Barnaby. The associations of the word "blood" are too strong for him. "Don't let me see it – smell it – hear the word, " he begs. "Don't speak the word – don't!" (ch. 3)

But Gabriel Varden is far from sure that understanding of narrative is beyond Barnaby. "Speak low, if you please," he urges Edward Chester, when he is inquiring about the assault. "Barnaby means no harm, but I have watched him oftener than you, and I know, little as you would think it, that he's listening now" (ch. 6). Nor is the precaution unjustified. Barnaby does construct narratives, we learn. He dreams of how pleased his mother would be if he could acquire large sums of money (ch. 45), of how proud she will be when she learns of the part he plays in the riots (ch. 49). These, however, are delusions, dangerous to himself and to others.

He is not alone in being deluded. Several characters in the novel demand its rewriting, so to speak. It is not just that they do not see themselves as readers are persuaded to see them. They are constantly engaged in composing their own versions of the events related, in setting themselves up as centers of narrative authority. One of the narrative games, that is to say, is competition between narratives. Such a device is scarcely abnormal in fiction, but in *Barnaby Rudge* the competing narratives are encapsulated in modes of behavior and utterance, distinctive as only Dickens at his most imaginative can make them.

We can see this more clearly if we compare them with what we find in the other Doughty Street novels. Each of Mr. Pickwick's companions constructs his own story. Mr. Winkle imagines himself a sportsman, Mr. Snodgrass a poet, Mr. Tupman a lover. But these are fantasies, only skin deep. Mr. Winkle, for instance, scarcely deludes himself about his ability to shoot or skate. He is simply anxious to conceal his deficiencies and delude others (chs. 7 and 30). Nor do we carry in our memories a sense of the difference between his language and, say, Mr. Tupman's. In *Oliver Twist*, the Artful Dodger, up before the magistrates, lies and fakes brilliantly, but this is defiant play-acting, not self-delusion, and it is nonce language, not an ideolect. Mr. Squeers, in *Nicholas Nickleby*, is wonderfully taken up with his own hypocrisy. "Here's richness!", he can exclaim over a glass of thin, blue milk and water (ch. 5). But readers are never allowed to forget it is hypocrisy.

The fantasists in *Barnaby Rudge* are different. All, to some extent at any rate, deceive themselves with their narratives. John Willet tells himself, as well as others, that he is an outstanding polemicist. He is "one of the most dogged and positive fellows in existence – always sure that what he thought or said or did was right, and holding it as a thing quite settled and ordained by the laws of nature and Providence, that anybody who said or did or thought otherwise must be inevitably and of necessity wrong" (ch. 1). He is always chuckling to himself about his own wisdom and the folly of others. In fact he gets things repeatedly wrong. When his assessment of the Gordon Riots is proved wrong by the sacking of the Maypole, he experiences what today we should probably call a nervous breakdown (chs. 54 and 55).

It is the Golden Key, though, rather than the Maypole, which houses the most resolute and most clearly marked composers of rival narratives: Sim Tappertit, for instance, who is short but convinced he is tall, lean but convinced he is well-built, little of leg but convinced he is admirably proportioned in that respect. "In the small body of Mr. Tappertit," we are told, "there was locked up an ambitious and aspiring soul." He grotesquely misjudges the significance of the 'Prentice Knights, of whom he is a leader, and considers what a glorious engine the 'prentices might yet become if they had but a master spirit at their head; and then he would darkly, and to the terror of his hearers, hint at certain reckless fellows that he knew of, and at a certain Lion Heart ready to become their captain, who, once afoot, would make the Lord Mayor tremble on his throne. (ch. 4)

Stagg, the blind man, is undeluded, but Sim's private narrative can withstand his systematic subversion:

"Sound, captain, sound!" cried the blind man, "what does my noble captain drink – is it brandy, rum, usquebaugh? Is it soaked gunpowder, or blazing oil? Give it a name, heart of oak, and we'd get it for you, if it was wine from a bishop's cellar, or melted gold from King George's mint."

"See," said Mr. Tappertit haughtily, "that it's something strong, and comes quick; and so long as you take care of that, you may bring it from the devil's cellar, if you like."

"Boldly said, noble captain!" rejoined the blind man. "Spoken like the 'Prentices' Glory. Ha, ha! From the devil's cellar! A brave joke! The captain joketh. Ha, ha, ha!"

"I'll tell you what, my fine feller," said Mr. Tappertit, eyeing the host over as he walked to a closet, and took out a bottle and glass as carelessly as if he had been in full possession of his sight, "if you make that row, you'll find that the captain's very far from joking, and so I tell you."

"He's got his eyes on me!" cried Stagg, stopping short on his way back, and affecting to screen his face with the bottle. "I feel 'em though I can't see 'em. Take 'em off, noble captain. Remove 'em, for they pierce like gimlets." (ch. 8)

Miggs is perhaps the least deluded – and most deluding – constructor of a private narrative in *Barnaby Rudge*, but she cannot quite bring herself, consistently at any rate, to see Sim, and his attitude to her, as they are. She lets her talent for self-dramatization run away with her. Take, for instance, the occasion when an anxious Sim pleads with her from the street, to be let in after a nocturnal excursion:

" . . . Miggs," cried Mr. Tappertit, getting under the lamp, that she might see his eyes. "My darling Miggs – "

Miggs screamed slightly.

" – That I love so much, and never can help thinking of," and it is impossible to describe the use he made of his eyes when he said this – "do – for my sake, do."

"Oh Simmun," cried Miggs, "this is worse than all. I know if I come down, you'll go, and – "

"And what, my precious?" said Mr. Tappertit.

"And try," said Miggs, hysterically, "to kiss me, or some such dreadfulness; I know you will!"

"I swear I won't," said Mr. Tappertit, with remarkable earnestness. "Upon my soul I won't. It's getting broad day, and the watchman's waking up. Angelic Miggs! If you'll only come and let me in, I promise you faithfully and truly I won't."

Miss Miggs, whose gentle heart was touched, did not wait for the oath (knowing how strong the temptation was, and fearing he might forswear himself), but tripped lightly down the stairs, and with her own fair hands drew back the rough fastenings of the workshop window. (ch. 9)

Like the great Dickens hypocrites and deceivers to come – Mr. Pecksniff springs to mind – Miggs never drops her guard, never abandons her own narrative, dazzlingly if desperately sustaining it, even during the forlorn attempt she makes to reingratiate herself with Mrs. Varden at the end of the novel:

"And did my missis think – ho goodness, did she think – as her own Miggs, which supported her under so many trials, and understood her natur' when them as intended well but acted rough, went so deep into her feelings – did she think as her own Miggs would ever leave her? Did she think as Miggs, though she was but a servant, and knowed that servitudes was no inheritances, would forgit that she was the humble instruments as always made it comfortable between them twos when they fell out, and always told master of the meekness and forgiveness of her blessed dispositions! Did she think as Miggs had no attachments! Did she think that wages was her only object!" (ch. 80)

Until she not entirely convincingly learns better, Mrs. Varden herself is another constructor of fanciful private narrative, in competition with

her husband's steadier and more prosaic one. "I might say a great deal,"
she characteristically tells Gabriel on one occasion. "But I would rather
not. Pray don't say any more."

> "I don't want to say any more," rejoined the goaded
> locksmith.
> "Well then, don't," said Mrs. Varden.
> "Nor did I begin it, Martha," added the locksmith,
> good-humouredly, "I must say that."
> "You did not begin it, Varden!" exclaimed his wife, opening
> her eyes very wide and looking round upon the company, as
> though she would say, You hear this man! "You did not begin it,
> Varden! But you shall not say I was out of temper. No, you did
> not begin it, oh dear no, not you, my dear!"
> "Well, well," said the locksmith. "That's settled then."
> "Oh yes," rejoined his wife, "quite. If you like to say Dolly
> began it, my dear, I shall not contradict you. I know my duty. I
> need know it, I am sure. I am often obliged to bear it in mind,
> when my inclination perhaps would be for the moment to forget
> it. Thank you, Varden."   And so, with a mighty show of
> humility and forgiveness, she folded her hands, and looked
> round again, with a smile which plainly said, "If you desire to
> see the first and foremost among female martyrs, here she is, on
> view!" (ch. 19)

Mr. Chester, later Sir John, offers an intriguing variation in the
pattern of private narratives. He constructs his own by deconstructing
others'. Or, to put it another way, he disputes the value – perhaps even
the very possibility – of differentiated narrative. For him there are no
individual stories, only universal templates. For him, style alone
differentiates one man's story from another's. "My dear fellow," he
remonstrates when his son tells him he loves Emma Haredale, "you do
nothing of the kind. You don't know anything about it. There's no such
thing, I assure you. Now, do take my word for it. You have good
sense, Ned, – great good sense. I wonder you should be guilty of such
amazing absurdities. You really surprise me." Nor may Edward object
to being seen as a fortune-hunter. Distinguishing such from other men
is a narrative nicety not worth the trouble:

"All men are fortune-hunters, are they not? The law, the church, the court, the camp – see how they are all crowded with fortune-hunters, jostling each other in the pursuit. The stock-exchange, the pulpit, the counting-house, the royal drawing-room, the senate, – what but fortune-hunters are they filled with? A fortune-hunter! Yes. You *are* one; and you would be nothing else, my dear Ned, if you were the greatest courtier, lawyer, legislator, prelate, or merchant, in existence." (ch. 15)

Mr. Chester's universal formulae reflect Dickens's mistrust of the Augustan sensibility, against which *Barnaby Rudge* surely protests. It is easy to oversimplify that sensibility – Dickens probably did – but it can scarcely be disputed that the Augustans prized the rational. The narrative of *Barnaby Rudge* repeatedly confronts readers with experience anterior to reason – anterior much of the time, indeed, to normal waking consciousness. Dickens had Phiz prepare a startling illustration for the novel showing Barnaby dreaming, which graphically represents such experience [fig. 21]. This is a much more radical breach with naturalism than we find in any previous illustrations for the novels. Compared with it, the goblin and ghosts of *Pickwick* and the angels carrying Little Nell to heaven are tame.[2] The boundaries of narrative itself had been pushed out thus far previously, to be sure, by writers of Gothic fiction – and by Dickens himself. Think of Oliver Twist's half-sleeping, half-waking vision of Fagin in the Maylies' garden, of Bill Sikes's delusions after the murder of Nancy. Think, best of all, of Fagin's stupor in the dock and the condemned cell (*Oliver Twist* chs. 34, 48, and 52).

But the evocation of dream experience, and of comparable states of mind, in *Barnaby Rudge*, is more impressive than anything of the kind we find in Gothic fiction, as impressive as Fagin's stupor in *Oliver Twist* – and more so, because the affective range is expanded. It is used for comic as well as for melodramatic ends. Readers are confronted with an example as early as chapter 3. Driving home to Clerkenwell from the Maypole, Gabriel Varden falls into a condition in which he feels "a strong tendency to mingle up present circumstances with others which have no manner of connection with them; to confound all consideration of persons, things, times, and places; and to jumble his disjointed

Figure 21   "Phantom-haunted dreams."   Illustration for *Barnaby Rudge*, originally untitled, by Hablot Knight Browne. (By permission of the Dickens House Museum, London.)

thoughts together in a kind of mental kaleidoscope, producing combinations as unexpected as they are transitory." Whatever else this is, it is an important structural device. *Barnaby Rudge* in its entirety mysteriously mingles past and present, confounds identities, and jumbles disjointed thoughts together. The episode formally announces the principle. And it works in context, too. Though first-time readers do not know it, Varden has just been threatened by a man he failed to recognize, supposing him dead more than twenty years. Little wonder he dreams of a perilous and intricate undertaking, of "picking a lock in the stomach of the Great Mogul." Such a lock will have to be picked before past and present can be reconciled and identities unscrambled. Little wonder Varden conflates persons, "mixing up the turnpike man with his mother-in-law who had been dead twenty years." One thing above all is clear: the episode promotes association at the expense of inference.

Barnaby's conscious grasp of narrative evidently comes and goes but, paradoxically, his dreams divulge important information, if disguised. "I dreamed just now," he tells Gabriel Varden, "that something – it was in the shape of a man – followed me – came softly after me – wouldn't let me be – but was always hiding and crouching, like a cat in dark corners, waiting till I should pass; when it crept out and came softly after me" (ch. 6). It is a fair representation of his father's conduct.

Even the sceptical Mr. Chester, after a late night interview with Hugh, has his composure and indifference to narrative contingencies broken by a dream:

> he started up and thought that Hugh was at the outer door, calling in a strange voice, very different from his own, to be admitted. The delusion was so strong upon him, and was so full of that vague terror of the night in which such visions have their being, that he rose, and taking his sheathed sword in his hand, opened the door, and looked out upon the staircase, and towards the spot where Hugh had lain asleep; and even spoke to him by name. But all was dark and quiet, and creeping back to bed again, he fell, after an hour's uneasy watching, into a second sleep, and woke no more till morning. (ch. 28)

Hugh has a claim on Mr. Chester, of which both are unconscious. That night Mr. Chester had seen something familiar in Hugh, but not until later does he realize it is his own features, and those of his dead Gypsy lover, replicated in their son. It is association, characteristic of dream narrative, not waking inference, that can represent this claim by having Hugh call for admission in a different voice, though still recognizably his own. The dream constructs a metaphor for Mr. Chester to interpret or to wonder at.

The sacking of the Maypole reduces John Willet to a dreamlike state in which all his dogmatism is forgotten, in which he makes associations instead of the inferences of waking narrative, to which he was so much given. Still tied up after the intrusion, he scarcely recognizes Solomon Daisy:

> "You know us, don't you, Johnny?" said the little clerk, rapping himself on the breast. "Daisy, you know – Chigwell Church – bell ringer – little desk on Sundays – eh, Johnny?"
> Mr. Willet reflected for a few moments, and then muttered, as it were mechanically: "Let us sing to the praise and glory of – "

And he breaks off. Sound of instinct, Solemn Daisy has appealed to him by inviting association. He has responded in kind.

Dumb things now speak to him, as they had never done before:

> "Look'ee here, sir!" cried John, turning his rueful eyes on Mr. Haredale, who had dropped on one knee, and was hastily beginning to untie his bonds. "Look'ee here, sir! The very Maypole – the old dumb Maypole – stares in at the winder, as if it said, 'John Willet, John Willet, let's go and pitch ourselves in the nighest pool of water as is deep enough to hold us; for our day is over!'"

Past and present, life and death are confounded for him:

> "You didn't," said John, looking about, as though he had lost his pocket-handkerchief, or some such slight article – "either of you gentlemen – see a – a coffin anywheres, did you?"
> "Willet!" cried Mr. Haredale. Solomon dropped the knife, and instantly becoming limp from head to foot, exclaimed

"Good gracious!"
" – Because," said John, not at all regarding them, "a dead
man called a little time ago, on his way yonder. I could have
told you what name was on the plate, if he had brought his coffin
with him, and left it behind. If he didn't, it don't signify." (ch.
56)

His ordeal in fact has an ultimately beneficial effect on Mr. Willet,
opening a mind, previously closed, to the liberating mysteries of
association. It makes possible his dying words – moving, comic and
(wonderfully for him) symbolic: "'I'm a-going, Joseph,' said Mr. Willet,
turning round upon the instant, 'to the Salwanners' – and immediately
gave up the ghost" (ch. 82). The self-satisfied polemicist has learned to
put a name, by association, to a mysterious, perilous and unvisited place.

The extension of the boundaries of narrative in *Barnaby Rudge* of
which Dickens was most proud is to be found in the chapters describing
the Gordon Riots. "I was always sure I could make a good thing of
Barnaby," he said of these to Forster, "and I think you'll find it comes
out strong to the last word" (Pilgrim *Letters* 2: 356). They do enlarge
his narrative range, to be sure. They expose readers to a bombardment
of suasive images, in a way rare in fiction, and unprecedented in
Dickens's own work.   They disclose corners of his imagination
previously only partly revealed. But it is hard to dismiss entirely Edgar
Allan Poe's observation that the riots seem an afterthought, forcibly
introduced into the novel (461).

I am not thinking of plot alone. These chapters introduce a different
and more weakly conceived narrative voice. Dickens appears to have
modelled his account of the Gordon Riots on Scott's account of the
Porteous riot, in *The Heart of Midlothian* (1818). He does capture
something of the eager curiosity and striving for historical veracity we
find in Scott, but is more bent upon emotive intensity and unadorned
moralizing than Scott was, and this grates with the layered irony we find
elsewhere.   Scott stayed masked by his elaborate fiction of Peter
Pattieson and Jedediah Cleishbotham, but Dickens is too often
unmasked in these chapters.   In the description of the sacking of
Langdale's distillery, for instance, the narrative voice becomes positively
prim and hectoring:

The gutters of the street, and every crack and fissure in the stones, ran with scorching spirit, which being dammed up by busy hands, overflowed the road and pavement, and formed a great pool, into which the people dropped down dead by dozens. They lay in heaps all round this fearful pond, husbands and wives, fathers and sons, mothers and daughters, women with children in their arms and babies at their breasts, and drank until they died. While some stooped with their lips to the brink and never raised their heads again, others sprang up from their fiery draught, and danced, half in a mad triumph, and half in the agony of suffocation, until they fell, and steeped their corpses in the liquor that had killed them. Nor was even this the worst or most appalling kind of death that happened on this fatal night. From the burning cellars, where they drank out of hats, pails, buckets, tubs, and shoes, some men were drawn, alive, but all alight from head to foot; who, in their unendurable anguish and suffering, making for anything that had the look of water, rolled, hissing, in this hideous lake, and splashed up liquid fire which lapped in all it met with as it ran along the surface, and neither spared the living nor the dead. (ch. 68)

It is a subject for emotive intensity, a subject over which to moralize, there can be no doubt about that, but not here: not in a narrative predominantly wedded to cunning indirectness. Heavy-handed adjectival judgments stop readers judging for themselves, as they are required to do elsewhere. Readers miss, in such passages, the subtlety and drama of the dream of Mr. Chester or the stupor of John Willet.

Barnaby Rudge succeeds where the narrative voice is at its most evasive, where the narrative games are at their most anarchic. It succeeds because, at such points, the omniscient narrator either misbehaves and thus submits himself to the reader's judgment, or gets out of the way entirely. Either way, the narrated is allowed to speak for itself, in counterpoint to the narrator perhaps, but not propped up by him.

I have said that the narrative voice we hear in *Barnaby Rudge* is anarchic and enigmatic, that no persistent narratorial identity is established beyond that of the tease. But if the voice which tells the story resists definition, it is nevertheless capable of being reflected. Another we hear in the novel in fact mirrors it quite uncannily. It too is used for teasing the reader. It too is anarchic, enigmatic, unpredictable. It too provokes the reader to ask how much its owner really knows.

It belongs to a character who in some respects would seem well-qualified for the role of omniscient narrator. He listens to others conversing, "with a polite attention and a most extraordinary appearance of comprehending every word, . . . turning his head from one to the other, as if his office were to judge between them, and it were of the very last importance that he should not lose a word." The discourse this attention yields, however, is less than lucid. "Halloa, halloa, halloa!" he is wont to say. "What's the matter here! Keep up your spirits. Never say die. Bow wow wow. I'm a devil, I'm a devil, I'm a devil. Hurrah!" (ch. 6)

It is, of course, the voice of Grip, Barnaby's raven. Gabriel Varden is tempted to believe that Grip understands his every word (ch. 6), and this view is eagerly abetted by the narrator, who plays a protracted narrative game centred on Grip. In chapter 25, during Mrs. Rudge's interview with Mr. Haredale in the library, Grip appears "to be profoundly studying a great folio volume that lay open on a desk."

> It was remarkable in the raven that during the whole interview he had kept his eye on his book with exactly the air of a very sly human rascal, who, under the mask of pretending to read hard, was listening to everything.

And readers are encouraged to suppose Grip thinks about what he hears – there and then, and later too, in the churchyard:

> Here again, the raven was in a highly reflective state; walking up and down when he had dined, with an air of elderly complacency which was strongly suggestive of his having his hands under his coattails; and appearing to read the tombstones with a very critical taste. Sometimes, after a long inspection of an epitaph, he would strop his beak upon the grave to which it referred, and cry in his hoarse tones, "I'm a devil, I'm a devil, I'm a devil!" but whether he addressed his observations to any supposed person below, or merely threw them off as a general remark, is a matter of uncertainty.

As Barnaby and his mother leave the churchyard, Grip is heard "entreating society in general (as though he intended a kind of satire upon them in connection with churchyards) never to say die on any terms."

There is a difference between Grip and the narrator, of course. We suppose Grip's knowledge and understanding to be limited, the narrator's to be unlimited. In both cases, though, we are teased and distracted by evidence to the contrary. What both offer us is "a matter of uncertainty."

What unites them is reflection, not replication. As befits a mirror image, categories are reversed while symmetry is preserved. Provokingly, Grip within the narrative, the narrator without, both display Dickens's fascination in *Barnaby Rudge* with narrative freed from authority and responsibility, which can nevertheless still divulge truth. Grip is scarcely less capable of that than the narrator. His observation, "I'm a Protestant kettle" (ch. 57), for instance, says as much about the riots and rioters as anything more explicit.

Barnaby Rudge, then, is an arena for narrative games. Narrative can scarcely be supposed the novel's theme, though. Little is to be gained from reading it as a narrative about narrative. Dickens conducted experiments with narrative technique in the book, to be sure. In my next (and final) chapter I shall suggest how profitable they were. But he was, I submit, more interested in narrative as a means than as an end. Although the tricks he plays with it in *Barnaby Rudge* initially proclaim its opacity, ultimately they persuade readers they can see through or past narrative. When the narrator tells us some say Joe Willet kissed Dolly, "but that's a fable," we infer that Joe did. When the narrator praises John Willet's appeal to the mounting block as evidence of Queen Elizabeth's having boxed the ears of a delinquent page from it, we see the unwisdom of both John Willet and the narrative voice. When Sim Tappertit drops hints about "a certain Lion Heart" ready to lead the 'Prentice Knights, our understanding of his character is deepened. Dickens's playful indirectness shifts onto readers more of the work of fiction-making than they usually undertake. Its effect is not primarily to draw attention to itself, but to enhance the reader's sense of unmediated perception.

The problem is that, when we compare *Barnaby Rudge* with *Pickwick Papers, Oliver Twist,* and *Nicholas Nickleby,* we find there is relatively little to perceive beyond an entertaining yarn. Despite his early ambitions for the the book – and perhaps because of its complicated and protracted gestation – in the end *Barnaby Rudge* served Dickens chiefly as a laboratory. He conducted experiments in it, but constructed little of durable substance. Thematically, *Barnaby Rudge* is empty. But the experiments are fascinating, and Dickens emerged from the laboratory a decidedly more accomplished writer.

7

AFTER DOUGHTY STREET

We are often invited to suppose that the Doughty Street novels take their character from Dickens's having improvised them as he wrote. He improvised with genius, it is conceded: *Pickwick Papers, Oliver Twist,* and *Nicholas Nickleby,* at any rate, became organized after a fashion as they developed, part after monthly part. But we are asked to believe they took shape, driven less by a quest for coherence and integrity, than by the vicissitudes of Dickens's career and the imperatives of his emotional life. For *Barnaby Rudge,* to be sure, he set himself objectives, but the novel was absorbed anyway by the demands of his career. Only after the Doughty Street period, it is suggested, do we find evidence of effective organization in Dickens's novels. Only after the Doughty Street period do we find novels in which more or less every part is related more or less successfully to every other part.

I have tried to show that, on the contrary, even this early in Dickens's career, we can detect a discriminating artist at work. He did not always see where he was going or eschew improvisation, and the imperatives of his emotional life were vital to him, but three out of the four novels, at any rate, are shaped from the start, consciously or unconsciously, into stories both powerful and coherent.

At Doughty Street, Dickens was in control of his art, just as he was of his life. That is not to say that he got everything right (witness *Barnaby Rudge*) nor, certainly, that he was incapable of developing his skills during that time. Wide and intelligent reading, and the practice of journalism had equipped him plentifully with both stylistic and narrative skills, but he refined those he possessed, acquired new ones, and gradually learned discipline in applying both (DeVries passim).

After Doughty Street, Dickens continued to refine his art, but we can fully appreciate his achievement there only when we understand how the Doughty Street years laid foundations for much that was to follow. It should not be forgotten that it is to those years we must turn for the first signs of conscious artistry in his works.

Needless to say, my revaluation of the Doughty Street novels calls into question the status of landmark in the development of Dickens's art sometimes granted to *Martin Chuzzlewit* (1843–44). "My main object in this story," he says in the preface to the Cheap Edition, "was, to exhibit in a variety of aspects the commonest of all the vices; to show how Selfishness propagates itself; and to what a grim giant it may grow, from small beginnings." Critics have seen this as the first sign of artistic self-consciousness in Dickens, and Steven Marcus declares *Martin Chuzzlewit* to be "the first novel of Dickens's maturity" (213). Kathleen Tillotson, however, questions "whether a reader lacking preface and biography, would recognise that Selfishness . . . was its theme" (*Novels of the Eighteen-Forties* 161). She is right to do so. *Nicholas Nickleby* is manifestly more organized than *Martin Chuzzlewit*. The latter builds upon the Doughty Street experience in quite another respect: characterization. In the characters of Mr. Pecksniff and Mrs. Gamp in particular, Dickens applies the lessons he taught himself in *Barnaby Rudge* about competing centers of narrative authority – and improves his performance.

The true landmark after *Nicholas Nickleby* is *Dombey and Son* (1846–48). In the Doughty Street novels, Dickens had contemplated society from the perspective of someone ascending through it, from class to class. He had contemplated marriage and the family from the perspective of a young man finding out about these things. In *Dombey and Son*, he contemplates society, marriage, and the family as a passionate commentator on his times, certainly, but not as one struggling with all the issues in his personal life. Perhaps this more disinterested perspective permitted the extraordinary advance in discernment and technique found in *Dombey and Son*. The novel exhibits an intensity of vision to be found in none of the novels that precede it, but unmistakably in the three short Christmas books that do: *A Christmas Carol* (1843), *The Chimes* (1844), and *A Cricket on the Hearth* (1845). In *Dombey and Son* we see, not only part related to part, but part implicit in part. Links are forged with a new obliqueness, a new delicacy.

Like *Oliver Twist*, it begins with the birth of a child, the death of his mother, and the consequences that follow. Like *Nicholas Nickleby*, it begins with family disharmony. But it quickly becomes apparent how much more work even the opening chapters of *Dombey and Son* are made to do. They perform simultaneously tasks which, in the Doughty Street novels, are performed serially. Exposition is exploited for other purposes as well.

We mark in chapter 1 how the dying Mrs. Dombey seems principally aware neither of her newborn son nor of her husband, but of her daughter Florence, how Florence clings to her mother "with a desperate affection very much at variance with her years," and how Mr. Dombey expresses testy consternation at this: "A very ill-advised and feverish proceeding this, I am sure." We mark how it is Florence who elicits the last sign of life from Mrs. Dombey:

> "Mama!" said the child.
> The little voice, familiar and dearly loved, awakened some show of consciousness, even at that ebb. For a moment, the closed eye-lids trembled, and the nostril quivered, and the faintest shadow of a smile was seen.
> "Mama!" cried the child sobbing aloud. "Oh dear Mama! oh dear Mama!"
> The Doctor gently brushed the scattered ringlets of the child aside from the face and mouth of the mother. Alas how calm they lay there; how little breath there was to stir them!
> Thus clinging fast to that slight spar within her arms, the mother drifted out upon the dark and unknown sea that rolls round all the world. (ch. 1)

This is vastly more controlled and powerful than the language used to describe the death of Oliver Twist's mother (see p. 143 above).

And this passage is no mere "given." It is an event in the causally linked chain of events that constitute the story of *Dombey and Son*. This highly charged moment changes the relationship between father and daughter, making worse what is already bad enough. In chapter 3, set some weeks later, Mr. Dombey sees Florence again, in response to

Polly Toodle's suggestion that the new baby and his sister should be together in his presence.   He remembers and resents "that closing scene":

> He could not forget that he had had no part in it. That, at the bottom of its clear depths of tenderness and truth, lay those two figures clasped in each other's arms, while he stood on the bank above them, looking down a mere spectator – not a sharer with them – quite shut out.

The coldness this engenders in him constrains Florence's behavior, and this alienates them even further.   Neither father nor daughter can respond to the other successfully.   "Have you nothing to say to me?", he asks.

> The tears that stood in her eyes as she raised them quickly to his face, were frozen by the expression it wore.   She looked down again, and put out her trembling hand.
> Mr. Dombey took it loosely in his own, and stood looking down upon her for a moment, as if he knew as little as the child, what to say or do.
> "There! Be a good girl," he said, patting her on the head, and regarding her as if it were by stealth with a disturbed and doubtful look. "Go to Richards! Go!"
> His little daughter hesitated for another instant as though she would have clung about him still, or had some lingering hope that he might raise her in his arms and kiss her. She looked up in his face once more. He thought how like her expression was then, to what it had been when she looked round at the Doctor – that night – and instinctively dropped her hand and turned away.

At once a demonstration and an explanation of tension within a family, this is vastly more effective and moving than Ralph Nickleby's commonplace grumble in chapter 3 of *Nicholas Nickleby*, about being looked to for help by "a great hearty woman, and a grown boy and girl."

From the first three chapters of *Dombey and Son*, we learn about the principal characters, and how they relate to one another but, in the case of Mr. Dombey and Florence at least, we see a relationship developing dynamically, in response both to a family catastrophe and to everyday accidents of behavior. This brings the novel to instant life. There is no sense of the story being cranked up. The motor is running from the very start. The advance in technique is unmistakable.

Dickens left Doughty Street, then, plainly capable of further development, and went on to achieve it. The development we find in *Dombey and Son* is chiefly attributable to technical innovations he devised after he left Doughty Street. But it is hard not to notice how they are applied to motifs first seized on for the Doughty Street novels: the birth of a central character immediately followed by the death of his mother, the origins and development of family discord. By no means everything in Dickens's subsequent career is referrable to the Doughty Street years, of course, but we repeatedly find him exploiting growing technical accomplishment and deepening moral understanding, to rework material first tackled there. Later books are often sustained by the Doughty Street experience, even while effectively critiquing the novels it yielded. This is particularly evident in two of the great landmarks of his career.

In *David Copperfield* (1849–50), Dickens revisits the Marshalsea and Warren's episode of his childhood (see chapter 2 above), responsible for so much that we find in the Doughty Street novels. Technically, though, it is best understood as a reworking of material he had first used in *Nicholas Nickleby*. In *Copperfield*, he re-examines the notion of birthright. Inevitably this has consequences. In a fashion at once oblique and strangely powerful, Dickens bids farewell to the traditional romantic hero and, more distinctly than hitherto, attempts a bildungsroman, centered upon the moral growth of an unglamorous protagonist.

Steerforth, in *David Copperfield*, can be seen as a morbid version of Nicholas Nickleby. If we attended only to David's first-person narrative, we should be tempted to suppose Steerforth the novel's hero. Though the narrative eventually expresses pain at his failings and hope that he might be forgiven, it is full of admiration for him, and never positively condemns his ruthlessly egotistical behavior – the behavior of a go-getter like Nicholas, but untested by adversity. Nor is David alone in his admiration. There are exceptions, but almost every other character in the novel is captivated by Steerforth. David warms even to their sadistic headmaster, Mr. Creakle, "for not resisting one so irresistible as Steerforth" (ch. 20). Like Nicholas, Steerforth has a position in society above the middle rank, and is proud of his birthright. His sense of self-worth is applauded – too much, we feel, but we are not told so. His mother commends the way that, at his and David's school, Salem House, "he found himself the monarch of the place, and he haughtily determined to be worthy of his station. It was like himself" (ch. 20).

The drama of the novel, though, condemns Steerforth, even if David's narrative does not. One episode eerily echoes Nicholas's confrontation with Mr. Squeers at Dotheboys Hall (see pp. 000–000 above). In front of all the boys, Steerforth exercises his preeminence at Salem House to humiliate Mr. Mell, the under-master:

> "Young Copperfield," said Steerforth, coming forward up the room, "stop a bit. I tell you what, Mr. Mell, once for all. When you take the liberty of calling me mean or base, or anything of that sort, you are an impudent beggar. You are always a beggar, you know; but when you do that, you are an impudent beggar."
> (ch. 7)

Tommy Traddles forthrightly denounces his behavior: "Shame, J. Steerforth! Too bad!" But no explicit condemnation is to be found in David's narrative. What we see here is the dark side of Nicholas's insistence on his status as the son of a gentleman, and his determination to live up to it.

Steerforth is egotistical, but glamorous too, a natural candidate for the position of romantic hero. His behavior exhibits a kind of careless *noblesse oblige*. He befriends and encourages David, even while exploiting him. He knows what goodness is, moreover, and is partially redeemed by his troubled soul, the troubled soul of a Byronic hero, attractive to nineteenth-century readers, attractive to many modern ones.[1] Agnes Wickfield warns David against him (ch. 25), but so does Steerforth himself, if vainly:

> "Daisy, if anything should ever separate us, you must think of me at my best, old boy. Come! Let us make that bargain. Think of me at my best, if circumstances should ever part us!"

"You have no best to me, Steerforth," said I, "and no worst.
You are always equally loved, and cherished in my heart." (ch.
29)

Steerforth's troubled self-knowledge helps us to share David's grief at
his fall from grace and his death, so memorably encapsulated in David's
finding him lying dead upon the beach at Yarmouth, "with his head
upon his arm, as I had often seen him lie at school" (ch. 55).

In the character of Steerforth, Dickens probes the myth of the hero
and the myth of gentlemanly birthright he had entertained and consoled
himself with at Doughty Street. We are made to see and deplore
Steerforth's ruthless egotism. But unless we are devoid of imagination,
we respond to his glamor too, as David does. It is a lingering and
reluctant farewell to the romantic hero.

While bidding thus farewell, Dickens tentatively shapes a different
kind of hero in David Copperfield himself, a bildungsroman hero,
whose growth is more thoroughly documented than either Mr.
Pickwick's or Nicholas Nickleby's. David is without glamor. He is
passive rather than active, a sufferer rather than a doer for most of the
novel, more akin in this respect to Oliver Twist. David's tribulations,
for instance, at Murdstone and Grinby's wine warehouse (chs. 9–12) – a
redaction of Dickens's suffering at Warren's – display him above all as a
victim, albeit a resourceful one, again like Oliver. On the rare occasions
that he does perform a decisive act, we are told as much about his
agonizing over it as about his doing it. When Mr. Murdstone beats him,
David bites his hand, but there is little feeling of triumph:

My stripes were sore and stiff, and made me cry afresh, when I
moved, but they were nothing to the guilt I felt. It lay heavier on
my breast than if I had been a most atrocious criminal, I dare
say. (ch. 4)

David's moment of rebellion plainly echoes Oliver's asking for more
(*Oliver Twist* ch. 2), but Oliver is never as introspective as David. It is
only the loss of his aunt's fortune that makes David as much an active
doer as a passive sufferer (ch. 34 et seq.).

His heroism is substantially the heroism of inner struggle. The text
of the novel, during one episode, incorporates striking echoes of a

seminal work in the evolution of the bildungsroman, John Bunyan's *Pilgrim's Progress*, a copy of which Dickens possessed (Stonehouse 16), and which he knew well.[2] In chapter 58, after the deaths of his first wife Dora and of Steerforth, David goes abroad, to make what he calls a "pilgrimage." Like Christian, he carries a "burden," which is eventually lightened. Like Christian he falls into despondency: "When this despondency was at its worst, I believed that I should die." Like Christian he is eventually relieved of his burden. One evening, he finds himself amid spectacular scenery, descending from the mountains into a Swiss village:

> In the quiet air, there was a sound of distant singing – shepherd voices; but, as one bright evening cloud floated midway along the mountain's side, I could almost have believed it came from there, and was not earthly music. All at once, in this serenity, great nature spoke to me; and soothed me to lay down my weary head upon the grass, and weep as I had not wept yet, since Dora died!

David, to be sure, does not achieve full self-knowledge. He cannot bring himself explicitly to condemn Steerforth. Nor does he acknowledge what a disaster it was for her, that he should have married Dora. But even if it is not exactly a classic of the genre, in *David Copperfield* Dickens achieved a peculiarly compelling bildungsroman, tailored for the mid-century, precisely adjusted to values taking shape in the zeitgeist, eagerly being discussed.

David becomes at ease with himself through discovering the work he can do, and doing it well. As it is in *Nicholas Nickleby*, work is foregrounded, but with greater sobriety and authenticity. David's chief complaint against Murdstone and Grinby's is that, while employed there, he was "put to work not fit for me" (ch. 13). But after his aunt loses her fortune, he finds he can do what Dickens did: he learns shorthand and becomes a parliamentary reporter, "working pretty hard, and busily keeping red-hot all the irons I now had in the fire" (ch. 37).

After his enlightenment in Switzerland, he is able to build upon this:

> I worked early and late, patiently and hard. I wrote a Story, with a purpose growing, not remotely, out of my experience, and

sent it to Traddles, and he arranged its publication very advantageously for me; and the tidings of my growing reputation began to reach me from travellers whom I encountered by chance. After some rest and change, I fell to work, in my old ardent way, on a new fancy, which took strong possession of me. As I advanced in the execution of this task, I felt it more and more, and roused my utmost energies to do it well. (ch. 58)

Nicholas Nickleby works in order to have to do so no more. Readers are never made to feel he positively enjoys any of the jobs he does. In *David Copperfield*, however, Steerforth's life of idle pleasure is implicitly condemned. And for David, work is both redemption and fulfilment. Dickens could have taken Carlyle as his text, and probably did. In *Past and Present* (1843), every man is declared to be "a potential hero," because of his capacity to find himself through work:

The latest Gospel in this world is, Know thy work and do it. "Know thyself": long enough has that poor "self" of thine tormented thee; thou wilt never get to "know" it, I believe! Think it not thy business, this of knowing thyself; thou art an unknowable individual: know what thou canst work at; and work at it, like a Hercules! That will be thy better plan. (177)[3]

Dickens's masterpiece is *Great Expectations* (1860–61). In it he creates a superb bildungsroman by inverting the values of the Doughty Street novels, and by abandoning entirely myths with which he had consoled himself at Doughty Street. Yet it is impossible not to detect in it lessons learned at Doughty Street. Dickens could not have documented Pip's childhood so brilliantly without having created its prototype in *Oliver Twist* (not to mention *David Copperfield*). One of the most effective features of the novel, moreover, can be traced back to *Barnaby Rudge*.

Pickwick Papers, *Oliver Twist*, and *Nicholas Nickleby* are all, in one way or another, about the securing of higher status for their central figures. So is *Great Expectations*, but there is a difference. Pip, the central figure, wants to be a gentleman, but has no entitlement to that status, no birthright to claim. Luck makes him one, however, but he is disappointed by the experience, and finds himself forgetting values he has painfully to relearn. His story is made irresistible, not least by Dickens's mastery of narrative indirectness, explored so eagerly in *Barnaby Rudge*. The narrative of *Great Expectations* is not playful, but again and again we have to see through it or past it.

Like *David Copperfield*, a first-person narrative, *Great Expectations* is a masterpiece of reticence. Pip's narrative is a brilliantly convincing mixture of keen observation, painful recollection, self-reproach, and thankfulness – for perils avoided, for lessons learned, for people known and loved. But as often as not it is the unsaid that moves and troubles the reader.

The said is powerful enough. The adult Pip openly confronts the effect upon him, as a small boy brought up in a country smithy, of the rich and embittered Miss Havisham, her capricious adoptive daughter Estella, and their big crumbling home, Satis House:

> How could my character fail to be influenced by them? Is it to
> be wondered at if my thoughts were dazed, as my eyes were,
> when I came out into the natural light from the misty yellow
> rooms? (ch. 12)

After he is told he has expectations of a fortune, and while he is being educated as a gentleman in London, Pip is visited there by Joe Gargery the blacksmith, his older sister's husband, and sole provider of unfailing love during his childhood. The young Pip is embarrassed by Joe's efforts to behave appropriately in genteel company, but the adult Pip judges more soundly. "I had neither the good sense, nor the good feeling to know this was all my fault," he confesses, "and that if I had been easier with Joe, Joe would have been easier with me" (ch. 27).

Explicit self-reproach such as this, however, is mingled with much more powerful implicit self-reproach. It is not understated. It is not stated at all. It is underdramatised, and all the more emphatic for it. Readers can easily miss some of the niceties during a first reading but, once they become attuned to it, the effect is profound. In the narrator, it suggests a loss of words, morally triggered, a shameful amazement, which open self-reproach or apology are not equal to, and would only contaminate.

In chapter 17, oppressed by his infatuation with Estella, and by his yearning to become a gentleman, Pip confesses all to Biddy, who is helping to care for his brain-damaged sister. Pip has noticed Biddy's "curiously thoughtful and attentive eyes; eyes that were very pretty and very good" and has begun to think her "rather an extraordinary girl." Congratulating her on her many accomplishments, he has been astonished to glimpse a tear in response. Now, watching the Thames with her, from the marshes near the forge, he tells Biddy:

> "if I could have settled down and been but half as fond of the forge as I was when I was little, I know it would have been much better for me. You and I and Joe would have wanted nothing then, and Joe and I would perhaps have gone partners when I was out of my time, and I might even have grown up to keep company with you, and we might have sat on this very bank on a fine Sunday, quite different people. I should have been good enough for you; shouldn't I, Biddy?"
>
> Biddy sighed as she looked at the ships sailing on, and returned for answer, "Yes; I am not over-particular." It scarcely sounded flattering, but I knew she meant well.

Everything of importance is left unsaid. The implicit is made explicit only much later, and ironically. In the final chapter, having lost all he had hoped for, Pip makes up his mind to return to the forge and offer himself to Biddy. He will ask her forgiveness, and tell her, "I hope I am a little worthier of you than I was – not much, but a little." When he gets there he finds it is Biddy's wedding day. She has married Joe, now a widower.

Readers struggle to interpret and to judge when, after his expectations have been announced, the young Pip supposes Miss Havisham to be "the fairy godmother who had changed me" (ch. 19). They do so again when he deduces that "Estella was set to wreak Miss Havisham's revenge on men, and that she was not to be given to me until she had gratified it for a term" (ch. 36). They are scarcely less dismayed than he is by the revelation that his benefactor is in fact the former convict Magwitch (ch. 39). For much of the narrative, the only perceptual advantage readers enjoy over the young Pip derives from confidence in the integrity of the story, easily half forgotten: confidence that Pip's early kindness to Magwitch (chs. 1–5) will have consequences; confidence in the clues that it is doing so (chs. 10 and 28).

The unsaid convincingly mediates Pip's merciless self-exposure, which makes *Great Expectations* the great bildungsroman it is. Readers are provided with the best of both worlds: the intimacy of a first-person narrative, and the remorselessness of a drama unfolding, step by inevitable step.

The process of Pip's sentimental education is made more coherent and striking by Dickens's introduction of a new formative principle, unlike anything to be found in the Doughty Street novels, if foreshadowed in the great novels of the 1850s – *Bleak House* (1852–53), *Hard Times* (1854), *Little Dorrit* (1855–57), and *A Tale of Two Cities* (1859). Perhaps it is too much to say *Great Expectations* is essentially religious in nature, but it undoubtedly follows a rhythm attributable to Judaeo-Christian tradition: the rhythm of sin or error, of scourging, of the asking and granting of forgiveness.

Pip goes back to his old home, in chapter 35, for the funeral of his sister. During his childhood, she had been unsympathetic and abusive (chs. 1–13), but head injuries sustained during an assault had profoundly disabled her (chs. 15–16), and Pip finds his mind softened towards her. There are comically elaborate funeral customs to be endured but, despite these, the text generates a powerful sense of peace and forgiveness:

> And now the range of marshes lay clear before us, with the sails of the ships on the river growing out of it; and we went into the churchyard, close to the graves of my unknown parents, Philip Pirrip, late of this parish, and Also Georgiana, Wife of the Above. And there, my sister was laid quietly in the earth while the larks sang high above it, and the light wind strewed it with beautiful shadows of clouds and trees.

Biddy tells Pip his sister had emerged from a bad episode just before she died, uttering the name "Joe." Joe had sat by her, and put her arms around his neck, and laid her head on his shoulder. "And so she presently said 'Joe' again, and once 'Pardon,' and once 'Pip.'" And then she had died. Throughout the entire episode, intensive use of the coordinating conjunction *and* sustains the power of the unsaid. Events are related chronologically, but not otherwise. Readers are left to infer any more complex relationship themselves.

This episode is the first in a deeply moving series. Remorseful at Pip's unhappiness over the loss of Estella, Miss Havisham begs him to write under her name, on a tablet she gives him, "I forgive her." Fatally burned, she continues to murmur, "Take the pencil and write under my name, 'I forgive her'" (ch. 49). Fatally injured in a bid to flee the country, after his illegal return from transportation to Australia (ch. 39), Magwitch is taken into custody and sentenced to death. But he dies in bed, "humble and contrite," and Pip prays for him: "Oh Lord, be merciful to him, a sinner!" (ch. 56). Pip is more aware than anyone of the need for forgiveness. He has betrayed those who love him. He too is scourged: by burns incurred trying to save Miss Havisham (ch. 49), by injuries at the hand of Orlick, his sister's assailant (ch. 53), and by a fever resulting from the accumulation of his troubles, which include the forfeiture of his expectations (ch. 57). All this brings him to a condition in which he can ask forgiveness of Joe and Biddy. It is granted:

> "O dear old Pip, old chap," said Joe.   "God knows as I forgive you, if I have anythink to forgive!"
> "Amen! And God knows I do!" echoed Biddy. (ch. 58)

At the end of the novel Estella acknowledges the same need. On a misty December evening, amid the ruins of Satis House, eleven year after they had last parted, Pip meets her again. She reminds him how he had said on the earlier occasion, "God forgive you!", and asks him to repeat it: "I have been bent and broken, but – I hope – into a better shape. Be as considerate and good to me as you were, and tell me we are friends."

Both of them have sinned, both have been scourged, both have asked forgiveness. They are redeemed, and can be reconciled. The final words of the novel, indirect as ever, hint that their future may be together:

> I took her hand in mine, and we went out of the ruined place; and, as the morning mists had risen long ago when I first left the forge, so, the evening mists were rising now, and in all the broad expanse of tranquil light they showed to me, I saw no shadow of another parting from her.[4]

Later in his career, Dickens surpassed his achievement at Doughty Street, there can be no doubt about that. *Great Expectations* is a perfectly astonishing book, complex, subtle, and immensely moving. With other later novels like *Bleak House*, it can overshadow and diminish the Doughty Street novels for us. But they were no fumbling prelude to a career culminating in later, greater works. *Pickwick Papers*, *Oliver Twist*, and *Nicholas Nickleby* are remarkable in themselves, intricately structured and powerful. *Barnaby Rudge* is remarkable in its way too, if less successful. And they all lay the foundations for Dickens's later achievements. He repeatedly returns to the same problems, the same themes, the same character types, the same techniques, in order to rework them, develop them further, re-explore the moral implications. His doing so is a sign of the value to him of the Doughty Street novels. But we can appreciate that value only by attentively reading the Doughty Street novels themselves.

NOTES

Chapter One (pp. 1–28)

[1]   My chief sources of published information for this chapter are the Pilgrim *Letters* 1; Johnson 1: 61–270; and Greaves passim.

[2]   "Chambers" (*The Uncommercial Traveller*) contrasts the experience of living in chambers – a building divided into more than one dwelling – with the experience of living in an undivided "dwelling-house."

[3]   The cash book is now in the Dickens House Museum.

[4]   Republished in *Sketches by Boz* as "Mr. Minns and his Cousin."

[5]   Dickens probably contributed no more to this project than the facetious introduction and notes, and a few details of the text, but it was not a task he disdained (Pilgrim *Letters* 1: 536n1).

[6]   Only rarely did his sense of irony falter.   It did when, later in life, he began to embellish his china, silver, and stationery with a "family crest" – a lion couchant grasping a Maltese cross.   He declared it was the crest his father had used, and that he himself did so out of mere filial piety (Nonesuch *Letters* 3: 717).   There is no evidence to substantiate this, and Dickens knew his father to have been the son of a butler.   The crest is in fact that of a genuinely armigerous Dickens family, any connection between which and Dickens's own has yet to be proved.   It is precisely the kind of imposition that he excoriates brilliantly in the novels.

[7]   See Pilgrim *Letters* 1: 256, 264, 267, 268, 269, 288, 302, 322, 417.

Chapter Two (pp. 29–80)

[1]   My sources are Forster bk. 1, chs 2 and 3; Ackroyd 67–99; Kaplan 38–44; and Allen 79–194.

[2]   See, for instance, Samuel Jeans, *Peeps at Great Men* (1929); and Maude Morrison Frank, *Short Plays about Famous Authors* (n.d.).

[3]   Allen draws attention to John Dickens's being a named subscriber to a book on local history, and to his sitting on a vestry committee to relieve sufferers from the disastrous Chatham fire of 1820 (Allen 60).

[4]   That at any rate is the date Forster gives, but it is possible Dickens wrote it a year or two earlier (Burgis xviii–xxi).

[5]   My chief sources of information about Maria are the Pilgrim *Letters* 1: 5–29; Slater, *Dickens and Women* 49–59; Kaplan 50–54; and Ackroyd 130–49.

[6]   My chief sources have again been the Pilgrim *Letters* 1: 60–143; Slater 103–62; Ackroyd passim; and Kaplan passim.

[7]   Catherine's younger sister. See pp. 000–000 below.

[8]   My chief sources of information about Ellen Ternan have been Slater 202–17; Ackroyd 830–1140; and Kaplan 367–555.

Chapter Three (pp. 81–120)

[1]   "Social mobility" is, of course, a twentieth-century term, and Dickens would not have been familiar with it. But the same fairly obvious metaphor was already in use, in talk of people "coming up" or going down" in the world.

[2]   I had formulated my ideas about Mr. Pickwick and horses before Steven Connor published his perceptive study of *Pickwick Papers* (Connor ch. 1). That taught me the wisdom of seeing the horsey business against elements of the novel in contrast with it, and I am happy to acknowledge my indebtedness.

Chapter Four (pp. 121–146)

[1]   An unpublished letter written by Dickens's father in February 1841, after the birth of Dickens's fourth child, indicates the kind of attention Catherine's confinements attracted. "Charles is quite well but looks jaded," John Dickens writes, "in consequence I suppose of the state of anxiety his wife has kept him in, but which must have been greatly alleviated by Mrs Dickens's [Dickens's mother's] close attendance upon her. Indeed I think my wife the most damaged of the party, which is sufficiently accounted for, by her mental as well as physical exertions in Kate[']s behalf" (quoted by permission of the Rare Books Department, The Free Library of Philadelphia).

[2]   Patten disputes this in *George Cruikshank's Life, Times, and Art*, and suggests Dickens was simply following Forster (84–86), but I take the view that Dickens's coldness is proportionate to Forster's heat.

[3]   John Bowen's persuasive reading of the substituted illustration (104–06) is conformable with mine. He sees it as a means of preserving Dickens's indignation against the 1834 Poor Law amendment and the values it embodied,

as resistance to the cosy domestic solution of social problems fiction is prone to.

Chapter Five (pp. 147–180)

1   A "game of love" was a card game for points rather than cash.

2   Since I first expounded these views, in the introduction to my 1994 edition of *Nicholas Nickleby*, they have been vigorously seconded by John Bowen, who observes that, in the novel, "almost every significant relationship (with the important exception of Kate and Nicholas) is at some point challenged, mediated, or enabled by economic demands or needs" (111).

3   I have assembled information about the Yorkshire schools from my appendix to the Everyman Paperback edition of *Nicholas Nickleby*, and from a copy of John D. Butcher's essay in the Dickens House Library.

4   Quoted in Slater 941–42.

5   See, for example, "Frauds on the Fairies," *Household Words* 1 October 1853. Reprinted in Nonesuch *Collected Papers* 1: 463–70.

6   *Nicholas Nickleby* brings women from the margins to the center of Dickens's works. In not quite the terms I should choose, John Bowen remarks that, in this novel, "the peculiarly ambivalent transformational energies of Dickens's writing undercut the domestic ideology of early Victorian capitalism through the frankness of its recognition of the economic forces beneath it" (109).

Chapter Six (pp. 181–212)

1   My account of the gestation of *Barnaby Rudge* is based on "*Barnaby Rudge*," *Oxford Reader's Companion to Dickens*; and on the Pilgrim *Letters*, vols. 1 and 2.

2   "The Goblin and the Sexton" and "The Ghostly passengers in the ghost of a mail" in *Pickwick Papers*; the final wood-engraving of *The Old Curiosity Shop*.

Chapter Seven (pp. 213–226)

1   One octogenarian visitor to the Dickens House told me she had been in love with Steerforth since first reading *David Copperfield* at the age of twelve. Hers is only the most memorable confession on the subject I have encountered.

[2]   Mrs. Gamp expresses her sense of the tribulations of life by speaking of "this Piljian's Projiss of a mortal wale" (*Martin Chuzzlewit* ch. 25).

[3]   See also Sanders xiii–xiv.

[4]   Dickens's original ending had Pip and Estella meet one last time, and then part for ever. He showed it in proof to Bulwer-Lytton, who persuaded him to change it (Gilmour ed., *Great Expectations* 445–47). Lytton's advice may have been proffered for the wrong reasons, but the published ending seems to me unquestionably superior. Its indirectness, its openness, its promise of peace and harmony, are utterly at one with the rest of the novel, and it is much more powerful.

WORKS CITED

Dickens's Works

American Notes and Pictures from Italy. Ed. F. S. Schwarzbach and Leonée Ormond. London: Everyman Paperback, 1997.
Barnaby Rudge. Ed. Donald Hawes. London: Everyman Paperback,1996.
Bleak House. Ed. Andrew Sanders. London: Everyman Paperback, 1994.
A Child's History of England. Holiday Romance and Other Writings for Children. Ed. Gillian Avery. London: Everyman Paperback, 1995.
Christmas Books. Ed. Sally Ledger. London: Everyman Paperback, 1999.
Christmas Stories. Ed. Ruth Glancy. London: Everyman Paperback, 1996.
Collected Papers. 2 vols. Bloomsbury: Nonesuch, 1937.
David Copperfield. Ed. Malcolm Andrews. London: Everyman Paperback, 1993.
Dombey and Son. Ed. Valerie Purton. London: Everyman Paperback, 1997.
Great Expectations. Ed. Robin Gilmour. London: Everyman Paperback, 1994.
Hard Times. Ed. Grahame Smith. London: Everyman Paperback, 1994.
The Letters of Charles Dickens. Ed. Walter Dexter. 3 vols. Bloomsbury: Nonesuch, 1938.
The Letters of Charles Dickens. Ed. Madeline House, Graham Storey et al. The Pilgrim/British Academy Edition. 11 vols to date. Oxford: Clarendon, 1965–.
Little Dorrit. Ed. Angus Easson. London: Everyman Paperback, 1999.
The Loving Ballad of Lord Bateman. (Wrongly attributed to Dickens and W. M. Thackeray.) London: Dent, 1969.
Martin Chuzzlewit. Ed. Michael Slater. London: Everyman Paperback, 1994.
Master Humphrey's Clock. Ed. Peter Mudford. London: Everyman Paperback, 1997.
The Memoirs of Joseph Grimaldi. Ed. Richard Findlater. London: MacGibbon & Kee, 1968.
The Mudfog Papers. In *Sketches by Boz.* The Oxford Illustrated Dickens. Oxford: Oxford Uuniversity Press, 1957. 605–67.

Nicholas Nickleby. Ed. David Parker. London: Everyman Paperback, 1994.
The Old Curiosity Shop. Ed. Paul Schlicke. London: Everyman Paperback, 1995.
Oliver Twist. Ed. Steven Connor. London: Everyman Paperback, 1994.
Our Mutual Friend. Ed. Joel B. Brattin. London: Everyman Paperback, 2000.
The Pickwick Papers. Ed. Malcolm Andrews. London: Everyman Paperback, 1998.
Sketches by Boz. In *Sketches by Boz.* The Oxford Illustrated Dickens. Oxford: Oxford University Press, 1957. 1–494.
Sketches of Young Couples. In *Sketches by Boz.* The Oxford Illustrated Dickens. Oxford: Oxford University Press, 1957. 549–603.
Sketches of Young Gentlemen. In *Sketches by Boz.* The Oxford Illustrated Dickens. Oxford: Oxford University Press, 1957. 495–548.
The Speeches of Charles Dickens. Ed. K. J. Fielding. Oxford: Clarendon, 1960.
Sunday Under Three Heads. In *The Uncommercial Traveller and Reprinted Pieces.* The Oxford Illustrated Dickens. Oxford: Oxford University Press, 1958. 635–63.
A Tale of Two Cities. Ed. Norman Page. London: Everyman Paperback, 1994.
The Uncommercial Traveller. In *The Uncommercial Traveller and Reprinted Pieces.* The Oxford Illustrated Dickens. Oxford: Oxford University Press, 1958. 1–362

Other Works

Ackroyd, Peter. *Dickens.* London: Sinclair Stevenson, 1990.
Allen, Michael. *Charles Dickens' Childhood.* Houndmills, Basingstoke: Macmillan, 1988.
Altick, Richard. D. *The Presence of the Present: Topics of the Day in the Victorian Novel.* Columbus: Ohio State University Press, 1991.
Baugh, Daniel A. "The Eighteenth-Century Navy as a National Institution, 1690–1815." *The Oxford Illustrated History of the Royal Navy.* Ed J. R. Hill. Oxford: Oxford University Press, 1995. 120–60.
Bowen, John. *Other Dickens.* Oxford: Oxford University Press, 2000.
Burgis, Nina. Introduction. *David Copperfield.* By Charles Dickens. Ed. Burgis. Oxford: Clarendon, 1981.
Butcher, John D. "'Education at the delightful village of Dotheboys': The schools and academies of Bowes, North Yorkshire, 1657–1850."

Unpublished essay submitted to University of London Institute of
Education, 1985. Dickens House Library, London.

Butt, John, and Kathleen Tillotson. *Dickens at Work*. London: Methuen,
1957.

Carey, John. *The Violent Effigy*. London: Faber, 1973.

Carlyle, Thomas. *Past and Present*. Ed. A. M. D. Hughes. Oxford: Clarendon,
1918.

Chesterton, G. K. *Charles Dickens*. London: Methuen, 1906.

Collins, Philip. *Charles Dickens: The Critical Heritage*. London: Routledge,
1971.

Connor, Steven. *Dickens*. Oxford: Blackwell, 1985.

DeVries, Duane. *Dickens's Apprentice Years: The Making of a Novelist*.
Hassocks, Sussex: Harvester Press, 1976.

Dexter, Walter, and J. W. T. Ley. *The Origins of Pickwick*. London: Cecil
Palmer, 1928.

Disraeli, Benjamin. *Sybil*. Oxford: Oxford University Press, 1981.

Eliot, T. S. *Selected Essays*. 3rd ed. London: Faber, 1951.

Ellis, S. M. "Mrs. Touchet." *The Dickensian* 28 (1932): 179–86.

Fitzgerald, F. Scott. *The Great Gatsby*. Oxford, New York: Oxford University
Press, 1998.

Forster, E. M. *Aspects of the Novel*. London: Edward Arnold, 1949.

Forster, John. *The Life of Charles Dickens*. Ed. J. W. T. Ley. London: Cecil
Palmer, 1928.

Frank, Maude Morrison. *Short Plays about Famous Authors*. London: Wells
Gardner Darton, n.d.

Greaves, John. *Dickens at Doughty Street*. London: Elm Tree Books, 1975.

Grego, Joseph. *Pictorial Pickwickiana*. 2 vols. London: Chapman and Hall,
1899.

Hatton, Thomas, and Arthur H. Cleaver. *A Bibliography of the Periodical
Works of Charles Dickens*. London: Chapman and Hall, 1933.

Hollington, Michael. *Dickens and the Grotesque*. London: Croom Helm,
1984.

House, Humphry. *The Dickens World*. London: Oxford University Press,
1942.

Inwood, Stephen. *A History of London*. London: Macmillan, 1998.

Jeans, Samuel. *Peeps at Great Men*. London: A. and C. Black, 1929.

Johnson, Edgar. *Charles Dickens: The Triumph and the Tragedy*. 2 vols.
Boston, MA, Toronto, London: Little Brown, Hamish Hamilton, 1952.

Kaplan, Fred. *Dickens: A Biography*. London: Hodder & Stoughton, 1988.

Kincaid, James. *Dickens and the Rhetoric of Laughter*. London: Oxford
University Press, 1971.

Kinsley, James, ed. *The Pickwick Papers*. By Charles Dickens. Ed. Kinsley. Oxford: Clarendon, 1986.

Kitton, F. G. *Charles Dickens by Pen and Pencil*. 3 vols. London: Sabin and Dexter, 1890–92.

Kucich, John. *Repression in Victorian Fiction*. Berkeley: University of California Press, 1987.

MacKenzie, Norman and Jeanne. *Dickens: A Life*. Oxford: Oxford University Press, 1979.

Marcus, Steven. *Dickens: from Pickwick to Dombey*. London: Chatto and Windus, 1965.

"Mary Howitt on Dickens." *The Dickensian* 17 (1921): 152.

Miller, J Hillis. *Charles Dickens: The World of His Novels*. Cambridge, MA, London: Harvard University Press, Oxford University Press,1958.

Morgentaler, Goldie. *Dickens and Heredity*. Houndmills, Basingstoke: Macmillan, 2000.

"New Letters of Mary Hogarth and her Sister Catherine." *The Dickensian* 63 (1967): 75–80.

Newsome, David. *The Victorian World Picture*. London: John Murray, 1997.

Olsen, Donald. *Town Planning in London: The Eighteenth and Nineteenth Centuries*. New Haven and London: Yale University Press, 1982.

Orwell, George. "Charles Dickens." In *Discussions of Charles Dickens*. Ed. William Ross Clark. Boston, MA: D. C. Heath, 1961. 30–46.

Oxford Reader's Companion to Dickens, ed. Paul Schlicke. Oxford: Oxford University Press, 1999.

Parker, David. "Dickens's Archness." *The Dickensian* 67 (1971): 149–58.

——. "Mr Dickens Sets up a Carriage." *The Dickensian* 75 (1979): 32–34.

——. "The Reconstruction of Dickens's Drawing-Room." *The Dickensian*, 77 (1982): 8–18.

Parkman, Francis. *Journals*. Ed. Mason Wade. 2 vols. New York and London: Harper, 1947.

Patten, Robert L. *Charles Dickens and his Publishers*. Oxford: Clarendon, 1978.

——. *George Cruikshank's Life, Times, and Art*, vol. 2, 1835–1878. Cambridge: Lutterworth, 1996.

Poe, Edgar Allan. "Charles Dickens." *The Centenary Poe*. London: Bodley Head, 1949. 453–68.

Richards, Laura E. *Samuel Gridley Howe*. Quoted by Louis B. Frewer. "From Recent Books." *The Dickensian* 31 (1935): 192.

Sanders, Andrew. ed. *David Copperfield*. By Charles Dickens. Ed. Sanders. Oxford: Oxford University Press, 1997.

Schlicke, Paul, ed. *Nicholas Nickleby*. By Charles Dickens. Ed. Schlicke.

Oxford, New York: Oxford University Press, 1990.

Schwarzbach, F. S. *Dickens and the City*. London: Athlone Press, 1979.

Scott, P. J. M. *Reality and Comic Confidence in Dickens*. London: Macmillan, 1970.

Shaw, George Bernard. Foreword. *Great Expectations*. By Charles Dickens. London: Hamish Hamilton, 1941.

Sladen, Douglas. "The Home of Dickens and Du Maurier." *The Windsor Magazine* January 1897: 271–278.

Slater, Michael. *Dickens and Women*. London: Dent, 1983.

——, ed. *Nicholas Nickleby*. By Charles Dickens. Ed. Slater. Harmondsworth, Middlesex: Penguin, 1978.

Smith, Grahame. *The Novel and Society: Defoe to George Eliot*. London: Batsford, 1984.

Staples, Leslie, C. *The Dickens Ancestry: Some New Discoveries*. London: published by the author, 1951.

Sterne, Laurence. *The Letters of Laurence Sterne*. Ed. Lewis P. Curtis. Oxford: Clarendon Press, 1935.

Stonehouse, J. H. *Reprints of the Libraries of Charles Dickens and W. M. Thackeray Etc.* London: Piccadilly Fountain Press, 1935.

Storey, Gladys. *Dickens and Daughter*. London: Muller, 1939.

Surtees, R. S. *Jorrocks's Jaunts and Jollities*. London: Methuen, 1951.

Thackeray, William Makepeace. *The Adventures of Philip*. London: Smith, Elder, 1895. Vol. 6 of *The Works of William Makepeace Thackeray*. 13 vols. 1894–97.

——. *Catherine*. London: Smith, Elder, 1896. Vol. 11 of *The Works of William Makepeace Thackeray*. 13 vols. 1894–97. 1–148.

Tillotson, Kathleen. *Novels of the Eighteen-Forties*. Oxford: Clarendon, 1954.

——, ed. *Oliver Twist*. By Charles Dickens. Ed. Tillotson. Oxford: Clarendon, 1966.

The Times London History Atlas. Ed. Hugh Clout. London: Times Books, 1991.

Toynbee, Arnold. *The Industrial Revolution*. London: Beacon Editions, 1957.

Trevelyan, G. M. *Illustrated English Social History*. 4 vols. Harmondsworth, Middlesex: Pelican, 1964.

Welcome, John. *The Sporting World of R. S. Surtees*. Oxford: Oxford University Press, 1982.

Wilson, Angus. *The World of Charles Dickens*. London: Martin Secker and Warburg, 1970.

Wilson, Edmund. "Dickens: The Two Scrooges," *The Wound and the Bow*. London: W. H. Allen, 1941.

Wood, Anthony. *Nineteenth Century Britain 1815–1914*. 2nd ed. Harlow, Essex: Longman, 1982.

INDEX

[Illustrations are indexed in **bold**. There are no entries under "Dickens, Charles," except for portraits. Entries relating to the man, to his works, and to their contents, are dispersed throughout the index.]

"Lucy" poems, the (Wordsworth), 76–77
Lytton – see Bulwer-Lytton

macadamization, 90
MacKenzie, Norman and Jeanne, 96, 234
Maclise, Daniel, 4, 61, 152, 153
Macready, William Charles, 120
Macrone, John, 5, 16, 18, 172, 181
Magnus, Peter, 82, 105, 110–11
Magwitch, Abel, 223, 225
Manchester, 174
Manette, Dr., 44, 46
Mann, Mrs., 131, 133, 134
Manor Farm, Dingley Dell, 100
Mantalini, Madame, 151, 170, 174
Mantalini, Alfred, 151, 167, 173
Marcus, Steven, 147, 182, 214, 234
marriage, 1, 5, 33, 47–69, 70, 72, 76, 110, 111, 112, 119, 121–26, 149–50, 162, 173, 176, 186, 192, 214,
Marshalsea prison, 23, 30–47, 74, 82, 127, 158, 160, 163, 217
Martin Chuzzlewit, 16, 55, 214, 231
Mary, Sam Weller's sweetheart, 111
Marylebone, 21
Master Humphrey, 77
Master Humphrey's Clock, 17–18, 182, 231
Master of the Ceremonies, the, 108
Maylie, Harry, 124, 129, 130, 138–39, 144
Maylie, Mrs., 124–25, 139, 144
Maylie, Rose, 124, 125, 129, 130, 136, 139, **141**, 142, 143–44
Maypole, the, 190–91, 195–96, 197, 200, 204, 207
Mealy Potatoes, 36, 46
Measure for Measure (Shakespeare), 187
Mecklenburgh Square, 7, 19–21
Mell, Mr., 218
melodrama, 54, 130, 136, 144, 148, 166, 167
Memoirs of Joseph Grimaldi, The, 18, 231
memory, 14, 29–30, 32, 35, 44, 46, 48, 54, 55, 56, 69, 70, 74, 75, 78, 80, 96, 127, 154, 158, 165, 183, 184
Micawber, Mr., 43
middle class, 19, 20, 32–35, 50, 64, 83, 90–91, 94, 103, 112, 139, 163
Middle Temple, 154
Miggs, 190, 201–02
Miller, J. Hillis, 23, 234
Mirror of Parliament, The, 16, 51, 172
"Misnar, the Sultan of India," 35
misogyny, 109–15, 145
Mitton, Thomas, 12
mobility, 96–106, 110, 112, 115, 117
mock-heroic, 24, 26
Moncrieff, W. T., 96
money, 11, 41, 94, 95, 97, 104, 147–80, 187, 199
Monks, 123, 136
Monthly Magazine, The, 16
Morgentaler, Goldie, 135, 163, 234
Morning Chronicle, The, 16–17, 51, 56, 92
Moses, 78
"Mr. Pickwick addresses the Club," 84, **86**
"Mr. Pickwick slides," 87, **89**, 101
"Mr. Bob Sawyer's Mode of Travelling," 87
"Mr. Minns and his Cousin," 227
"Mrs. Bardell faints in Mr. Pickwick's arms," **114**